Literary America
1903~1934

Mary Hunter Austin. *Courtesy of Henry E. Huntington Library, San Marino, California.*

Literary America
1903~1934
THE MARY AUSTIN LETTERS

Selected and Edited by T.M. PEARCE

CONTRIBUTIONS IN WOMEN'S STUDIES, NUMBER 5

GREENWOOD PRESS
WESTPORT, CONNECTICUT • LONDON, ENGLAND

Library of Congress Cataloging in Publication Data

Austin, Mary Hunter, 1868-1934.
 Literary America, 1903-1934.

 (Contributions in women's studies ; no. 5
ISSN 0147-104X)
 Includes index.
 1. Austin, Mary Hunter, 1868-1934—Correspondence.
2. Authors, American—20th century—Correspondence.
I. Pearce, Thomas Matthews, 1902-   II. Title.
III. Series.
PS3501.U8Z53   1979   813'.5'2 [B]   78-67914
ISBN 0-313-20636-8

Copyright © 1979 by T. M. Pearce.

Letter by Ezra Pound, dated April 13, 1930. Copyright 1979 by the
Trustees of the Ezra Pound Literary Property Trust. Published by
permission of New Directions Publishing Corporation, Agent.

Library of Congress Catalog Card Number: 78-67914
ISBN: 0-313-20636-8
ISSN: 0147-104X

First published in 1979.

Greenwood Press, Inc.
51 Riverside Avenue, Westport, Connecticut 06880

Printed in the United States of America

10 9 8 7 6 5 4 3 2 1

CONTENTS

INTRODUCTION

Mary Austin was a paradox in American literature. Despite the fact that she wrote thirty-four books and was acclaimed by Joseph Conrad and H. G. Wells as among the most important American writers, the general reading public scarcely knew her. Born Mary Hunter in Carlinville, Illinois, on September 9, 1868, she attended rural schools and was graduated from a small denominational college in Carlinville. When her father died, the family moved to homesteads in the arid grazing country south of Bakersfield, California. Mary had to find a position teaching school to help herself, her mother, and two brothers survive during the homesteading period. The Hunters then moved into Bakersfield. Mary became the bride of Stafford Wallace Austin and accompanied him to an irrigation project in Owens Valley. From the surroundings there, among Indians in the nearby mountains and Spanish neighbors on the high slopes, she gathered material for stories submitted to the *Overland Monthly, Out West, Munsey's Magazine, Cosmopolitan,* and the *Atlantic Monthly.* Her first book, *The Land of Little Rain,* published in 1903, was hailed by critics as an American classic.

Mary Austin's earliest published work was an account of the trip she made with her family, by horseback and wagon, to the homesteads they had signed for in Kern County northeast of Los Angeles. She told how three of the Hunters drove in a wagon and she started out on horseback toward the Tehachapi Mountains. The journey was made in the fall of 1888. She entitled her narrative "One Hundred Miles on Horseback," and sent it to *The Blackburnian,* literary magazine of Blackburn College where she had earned her baccalaureate degree four years earlier. The travel account was printed in January 1889. The pages made a booklet when they were published by Dawson's Book Shop of Los Angeles, in

1963, and have become a collector's item. In November of 1892, Mary Austin saw her first story printed by the *Overland Monthly*. The title was "The Mother of Felipe," and along with some of the other early stories, it has been reprinted in a collection produced for the Book Club of California in 1950.

Nine novels, more than fifty short stories, a book of poems, three plays, and a dozen titles of nonfiction were written by Mary Austin following *The Land of Little Rain*. She was awarded the honorary degree of Doctor of Letters by Mills College in 1928 and by the University of New Mexico in 1933. The distinguished critic Carl Van Doren called her "Master of the American Environment," and spoke of her books as "wells driven into America to bring up water for her countrymen though they may not have realized their thirst."

Mary Austin's contacts with authors and leaders in political and social fields included many of the influential figures in England and America. In her autobiography, *Earth Horizon* (1932), she had taken the opportunity to speak about them, favorably or unfavorably, as she viewed their personalities and their points of view. Her correspondence preserved in the Mary Austin Collection at the Henry E. Huntington Library, San Marino, California, offers evidence that both supports and contradicts the personal story in *Earth Horizon*.

An editor of letters becomes more than a bystander to personal or literary events and confidences exchanged in correspondence. He feels that he is entering into the lives of people who knew each other well enough to express themselves freely. Letters portray aspects of personality and character which often are hidden by a professional career. Few, if any, of the letters in this collection have subject matter too personal to be made public, and only Willa Cather ever indicated that she would object to having her letters in print. The correspondence from Jack London reveals his philosophic purpose in writing *The Sea Wolf* and *The Strength of the Strong*. Former President Herbert Hoover discloses a side of his nature not widely known: he makes suggestions for a play Austin was writing about a mining engineer. The novelist Fannie Hurst disagrees with Mary about Anne Nichols's *Abie's Irish Rose*, which Austin claimed to be authentic American folklore; Hurst found no such significance in the play.

In general, the letters reflect the interests of individuals, but some letters are related to groups, as illustrated by the Carmel, California, circle (George Sterling, James Hopper, Jack London, Upton Sinclair, Lincoln Steffens, and Robinson Jeffers); the Herbert Hoovers and their acquaintances in London, California, and Washington, D.C.; and the Santa Fe-Taos, New Mexico, group (Witter Bynner, Alice Corbin Henderson, Mabel Dodge Luhan, and such visitors as Vachel Lindsay, Willa Cather, and Sinclair Lewis).

Anyone who edits handwritten material can be grateful for the invention of the typewriter. Printing lacks the personality of a scrawl or a stroke, but typed letters help to identify the alphabet when strokes are obscure. Sherwood Anderson's pen slides along the horizon of his paper as though seeking a destination without discernible stretches of meaning. Lola Ridge edited a magazine which published poetry, but the flourishes of her pen leave the reader struggling to translate scrawls into words. Willa Cather's epistles are marvels of imprecise calligraphy. The risk of misreading may have contributed to her edict against their publication. Paraphrases of her meaning, however, are legitimate.

The happiest periods in Mary Austin's life were those during her stay at Carmel-by-the-Sea, from 1904 to 1911, and those at Santa Fe where she first visited in 1918 and where she lived from 1923 to 1934. Trips to Europe were also rewarding as interims from 1907 to 1910 and in 1922. After Wallace Austin and she had built the "brown house under the willow tree" at Independence in 1903 (now California Historical Landmark No. 229), Mary alone built the houses at Carmel and Santa Fe, where she entertained visitors and created personal kingdoms for activities that were supremely satisfying. It is doubtful that she wrote or received any more letters or was any more productive than when she was living in New York City at various times from 1912 to 1923. The letters tell the story. Despite the absence from New York, she never lost her desire to be remembered and talked about there. Her publishers were chiefly in that city and in Boston.

A number of the letters in her correspondence express concern about Mary Austin's health. In *Earth Horizon*, she tells of the nervous breakdown which occurred during the year at State Normal School in Bloomington, Illinois, and her collapse following the homesteading episode. A period of illness also occurred at Carmel in 1909, and again in 1923 when she took a long trip into the Arizona desert while preparing to write *The Land of Journeys' Ending*. A circumstance which produced recurrent depression was the knowledge that her only child was mentally retarded. This daughter, Ruth, born October 30, 1892, stayed with her mother for eight years and then, either in a private home or a private institution, lived until 1918.

My acquaintance with Mary Austin began in the fall of 1928, a year after I had joined the English Department of the University of New Mexico in Albuquerque. It took me a year to learn about her books and her way of interpreting the American scene. She belonged to the school of naturists and was a vocal conservationist, a champion of finding ways to advance both human and natural resources. In Santa Fe, the capital city of New Mexico, she found a meeting of Indian, Spanish, and Anglo-American life styles not unlike the patterns in rural Southern California. She also found the beginning of a colony similar to the one she helped to establish at Carmel. By 1925, she had planned and built a large Spanish-Indian house, to be constructed of adobe on a street named El Camino del Monte Sol, or "The Highway of the Sun Mountain." The Camino was a winding dirt road named for a mountain southeast of the city. It passed through a residential area for artists and writers, whose studios were located among piñon trees, chamisa, and sage brush. With limitless skies and long views to the west and north, the atmosphere was conducive to serenity and such freedom as the artistic temperament required. Mary Austin drew this isolation to herself, but she filled it with neighbors and visitors as her time permitted. When I called upon her, she was cordial, offering to help with literary projects planned by the University of New Mexico and agreeing to visit the campus at a later date. She named her house *La Casa Querida*, "The Beloved House." She lived there until her death on August 13, 1934.

The editor expresses his thanks to the Trustees of the Henry E. Huntington Library for permission to print letters selected from the Mary Austin Collection. In addition, he acknowledges his appreciation to heirs or executors of estates for approving particular items chosen to represent the writers. These permissions, however, have not been acknowledged unless specifically requested. Mary Hunter Wolf of New Haven, Connecticut, Mary Austin's niece, has endorsed the project and lent her support. When credit lines have been requested for individual letters, they are given either in the text or when the letter is presented.

The letters have been organized in terms of the places where Austin lived, establishing a pattern of where the letters were mailed or delivered, plus a chronology of dates for the time when they were sent. No changes have been made in any letter except for a few omissions for economy of space and some emending of spelling and standardizing of punctuation. Nothing is gained by perpetuating a slip of memory or inattention to formal details of composition. When an omission has been made, dots will indicate that material has been excluded. Names of the letter writers are printed as a Table of Contents. Letters from Mary Austin are shown with both her name and the name of her correspondent.

The problem of explanatory notes has been solved by information presented before each letter. Placing these annotations on individual pages became cumbersome and time consuming. A comprehensive index includes references throughout the book to letter writers and also references to other people mentioned in the correspondence. Mary Austin was an activist as well as a writer. She was in the thick of feminist campaigns as they led to the emancipation of women. She was a crusader for community activities in theater arts, folk crafts, weaving, song, and dance. Viewed as a literary panorama of people, places, and events, her correspondence with friends and friendly foes presents a truly innovative and creative period in the history of the United States. For this reason, the title *Literary America* is not presumptuous. The communications herein reported are both portraits and memories. They integrate, to a degree, the mental life of an extensive company of gifted people in the early decades of this century. Further details about persons mentioned in the letters or editorial introductions may be found in the Appendix.

T. M. Pearce
Albuquerque, New Mexico

Literary
America
1903~1934

EARLY CALIFORNIA DAYS

I

Independence, California, where Mary Austin wrote *The Land of Little Rain* (1903), is located in the Owens River Valley, between the Sierra Nevada Mountains and the Panamint Range. Death Valley lies behind the Panamints, and the wooded heights of the Sequoia National Park are due west of Owens Lake, which at one time delivered water to a large area of orchards and fields. Austin's husband, Stafford Wallace Austin, managed the irrigation project here in 1891 and again from 1895 to 1897, while she taught at an academy in Bishop, north of Independence. Water from the Sierras runs through the length of the state, supplying the reservoirs for both inland and coastal cities. Since the fortunes of her husband depended upon financial backers in San Francisco, Mary also found contacts there with people in literary circles, including librarians and magazine editors. Ina Coolbrith was one of those librarians. She was also a consultant for the editors of the *Overland Monthly*, a magazine made famous by publishing the early stories of Bret Harte. He was not only a contributor to the magazine, but became its editor as well. Coolbrith introduced Mary Austin to a later editor who in November of 1892 published "The Mother of Felipe," her first story as a professional writer.

Ina Donna Coolbrith (1841-1928) has the introductory letter in this book. She was known as the poet laureate of California and founder of the California Literary Society. Coolbrith came to California as a child. Her parents were Mormons who fled from Nauvoo, Illinois, to escape persecution from hostile neighbors. Nauvoo is a settlement some 100 miles northwest of Carlinville, where Mary Austin was born twenty-seven years later. Thus, when Mary visited Oakland at the time Coolbrith was librarian there, she was seeking advice about publishers from a former resident of her home state, a woman who had left the Midwest and attained fame as a writer.

In her letter, Coolbrith announces that Mary has been named an Honorary Member of the Pacific Coast Women's Press Association, a group with associates who were not primarily journalistic. A literary group in which Mary would have had greater interest were the older friends, Joaquin Miller, Henry George,

Mark Twain, Bret Harte, and others who attended Coolbrith's literary soirees. Jack London recalled that when he was a boy in Oakland, he went to the public library and borrowed a book on Peru. As Coolbrith stamped the date for returning the book, she complimented the lad for reading such a worthwhile volume. From that early acquaintance, he always regarded her as a patroness of his literary career. Her own two books, *A Perfect Day and Other Poems* (1881) and *Wings of Sunset* (1929), contain poems rich in sentiment, with exotic images of sensuous appeal. Such titles as "The Dancers," "Loneliness," and "The Mariposa Lily" explore themes of nature and beauty.

In the summer of 1907, Ina Coolbrith visited the colony of writers living at Carmel-by-the-Sea, some of whom, such as Jack London, knew her from her library days at Oakland. Coolbrith's home had been destroyed in the earthquake of the previous year, and there was much sympathy for her loss. Manuscripts and personal possessions were burned in the rubble. She had assumed a new post with the Mercantile Library of San Francisco, and then had been appointed librarian of the Bohemian Club, a position that made her an honorary member of a club exclusively for men.

In 1919, friends of Coolbrith founded the Ina Coolbrith Circle with the purpose of promoting poetry and the study of California writers. Today the organization numbers some 200 members throughout the state. Pictures of Ina Coolbrith confirm her physical beauty as her letter confirms her warmth in friendship. In this *Letter 1*, the Dorothea Moore to whom she refers was a San Francisco physician, who was married to Charles F. Lummis from 1880 to 1891. In 1904, Lummis was joint editor of *Land of Sunshine*, a magazine in Los Angeles (see *Letters 9*, *10*, and *11*). Mrs. W. C. Morrow, mentioned in the letter, was the wife of a well-known author and journalist in San Francisco. The story by Mary Austin in the *Atlantic* is "Mahala Joe." It appeared in the magazine of July 1904.

_____ 1

Bohemian Club
San Francisco
June 23/04

Dear Mary Austin:

You may scold me, call me names, punish me in any way that seems best to you, and I won't say one word. You could not say more than does your dear little Indian water-bottle which hangs by my library door, a constant reminder of you and of my delinquency. And yet I am not wholly to blame. I have been busy beyond reason or right; I have been miserable in health; and last, and *most*, worried almost beyond bearing by the illness of my half-brother, who has been, and still is, in a very precarious condition from *blood-poison*, the result of a hurt received in his mine in Death Valley, over two months ago. Every moment I can spare I give to him—and I write this now at my desk, *stealing* the time from my legitimate work.

So you will forgive me?

I was greatly disappointed at seeing so little of you during your visit. I *did* hope to have you in my own den for a brief moment, and really thought (the conceit of me!) that, except dear Dorothea Moore, I had a better right to you than any woman in San Francisco!! I did not get one word with you alone, and I resent it. . . .

Did Mrs. Morrow send you notice of your election to Honorary Membership in our P.C.W.P.A.? I hope you do not object to it. It entails no obligations whatsoever. I am looking for the story in the "Atlantic" with impatience.

I hope you are well, and as happy as anyone is permitted to be in this puzzling old world of ours.

Sincerely yours,
Ina Coolbrith

Coolbrith's expressed eagerness to read a forthcoming story in the *Atlantic* points to the success of the series of Mary Austin's story sketches, some of which were to be printed in her book *The Land of Little Rain* (1903). A second printing in the succeeding year established the book as almost unique among literary works describing and interpreting the natural history of arid regions in California, Nevada, and Arizona. The book also introduced Mary Austin to a fellow western writer, whose first book had been published by the same company in the same year with drawings by the same illustrator, E. Boyd Smith. This writer was Andy Adams (1859-1935), who was nine years older than Mary Austin and had come West in 1882, six years before Mary's mother, Savilla Hunter, had brought Mary and her two brothers to settle on the homestead near Bakersfield.

At the time Andy Adams wrote his first letter to Mary he was living in Colorado Springs. His second letter is datelined from Columbia, Nevada, a post office considerably closer to the Austin home in Independence, but the ties between Adams and Austin were not a matter of distance. They had interests in common. Both had knowledge about sheepherders and their skills. Mary was preparing her next book, *The Flock* (1906), so that Adams's report of a sheep drive from Fort Sumner, New Mexico, to Lodge Pole, Nebraska, must have stirred her imagination. Adams was one cattleman who never took part in a feud with sheepmen. *The Flock* and *The Log of a Cowboy* will rank among the finest volumes ever written about the cattle industry and sheep raising. Each is a masterpiece in its field.

Adams and Mary Austin spent their childhood in neighboring states, Indiana and Illinois. The family into which Adams was born owned a stock farm in Whitley County, Indiana. After limited schooling, he made his way to Arkansas, where he worked in a lumber camp. Late in 1881, he found a job in a stockyard at San Antonio, Texas. In the following year, he took a herd of horses by rail to Caldwell, Kansas. He made other trail drives across Texas and Oklahoma Territory, the last in 1889. Then he went into the feed and seed business at Rockport, Texas, near Corpus Christi. Word of the gold fields in Colorado drew him north and west where he spent the rest of his life. Mary Austin's father was a lawyer, and she grew up in a more bookish atmosphere, finishing high school and studying for a teaching degree at Blackburn College in Carlinville.

Andy Adams and Mary Austin admired each other as writers, for in one letter he praises her novel *Isidro*, and she sent her publisher a note favoring Adams as a consultant in preparing her material for *The Flock*. However, in a letter on August 11, 1909, he said that he found *The Flock* somewhat disappointing because she did not introduce a note of romance, but he confesses in turn that his own work lacked a knowledge of women: "having never had a wife, or even a sister, compels me to grope at times."

Twenty-three letters, written by Adams between 1904 and 1916, are preserved in the Austin Collection. In one he sends a clipping which tells of the killing of 5,000 sheep by 100 Colorado cattlemen, who invaded the ranch of a sheep man in Taylor Park, Gunnison County. In another, he reports that a woman, a neighbor, had made $11,000 in one month buying mining stocks with feminine names, which leads him to say: "If you want a tip on Goldfield stocks, the only one I can give you, ask some woman, as her intuition is safer than a man's judgment. Possibly Providence watches over them."

Two of Adams's missives, written in 1908, speak of his friendship with the novelist Emerson Hough. In the following year, answering a letter Mary Austin had written to him from England, Adams mentions a juvenile he is writing, and adds: "I would gladly take your advice and fall in love, but having been exposed so often to regular charmers, I am beginning to doubt my capability to experience the tender passion." His last letter includes the comment: "Instead of going to church, I read your late book 'The Man Jesus.' Your theme is almost beyond me." *Letter 2*, as reproduced here, is a folktale in itself, told with the skill of a master storyteller. The "pretty story" he praises is the same as that referred to by Ina Coolbrith in *Letter 1*.

———— 2

Colorado Springs
Colorado
July 8th, '04

Dear Mrs. Austin,

I enclose you the card of Mr. Albert B. Persinger of Lodge Pole, Nebraska. Since writing you last, I have met Mr. Persinger, and learned from him that in '84, he drove 20,000 sheep from Fort Sumner, New Mex. to his present home of Lodge Pole in southwest Neb. His drive was a sample of the exodus of sheep which I mentioned before, starting in the south and following up the front range of mountains until Montana was reached and occupied. Should such material be available in your book on sheep, write Mr. Persinger, mentioning my name, and I think he will give you the details of the drive.

Another item which I have picked up—and from life—strikes me as a good idea for a chapter or story. Years ago, in the southern portion of this state, a little girl walked off a train in her sleep. Evidently she was unhurt by the accident which occurred at night, and was not missed for hours afterward. When morning came, having wandered during the night, the little girl sighted a flock of sheep on the plain in charge of a Mexican shepherd. The *pastor* did not see the approach of the child until she was near at hand, and taking her for a ghost, he fled. The girl followed him waving her hands, when he deserted his flock and fled to the nearest ranch some twenty miles distant. No one at the ranch paid any attention to the superstitious Mexican, and he was ordered back to his flock. The railroad caused a search and the little girl's remains were found. It strikes me that in this incident there is material for a good story. You can set it anywhere you wish—there is very little variation in the atmosphere of the plain.

How is the book coming on? That is a very pretty story which you have in the current number of the *Atlantic Monthly*.

Very truly yours,
Andy Adams

In *Letter 3*, Andy Adams seems to be replying to a publisher who tried to edit some of his stories or, perhaps, to someone else who commented about the language in the *Log of a Cowboy*. He shows that he is a true artist in acknowledging that words are often inadequate to fully portray the subject matter with which they deal. Adams was not brought up to "speak Texian." Perhaps that is why he recognized the lingo and the tone that accompanied it. He justifies the speech recorded in *Reed Anthony, Cowman* (1907) with persuasive charm. With good humor and perhaps a slight trace of envy, he refers to Mary Austin's trip to Europe which began in December of 1907 and and lasted until the fall of 1910. He speculates about her good fortune in being able to finance the trip, as a friend well might. Of course, she was not divorced by her husband until November 19, 1915, but she never expressed thanks if support came from Wallace Austin. The report Adams gives of his own income from royalties indicates that he had not acquired wealth from his writing.

_____ 3

Columbia
Nevada
May 17th, '07

Dear Mrs. Austin,

Your kind acknowledgment of my Cowman to hand. As you read his life more fully, I hope you will believe that his pulse and heart beats true. It has been my good fortune to know thousands of such men, and, according to my light, I must draw them to life. It would be impossible for me to give them that heavy, labored form of speech, so dear to the

Eastern viewpoint. I like to hear my characters talk natural, feel their pulse, and know that the blood in them runs red. One thing, I regret to say, is almost impossible to transfer to the printed page, and that is the splendid languor of the Texan. An actor could impersonate it where the cold type conveys no impression of that true Southern charm. Marooned as I am on the desert of Nevada, it is quite a temptation to hear you mention afternoon drives on the California coast. It has a tendency to make one uncontented in their little orbit of this dreary waste of dust and wind. And on the heels of that, threaten us with a trip abroad. Fortune must be kind to you, or else your books are better sellers than mine. I did manage to reach the Goldfield mining district where I have bogged down awaiting further orders. This leads me to inquire the financial success of your books. Personally, mine have run from $750 to $1,500. After the first six months, the returns amount to very little with me, and I naturally wonder how others fare. "There's tricks to all trades but ours; roll your wool in the sand, boys" is a proverb in Mexican shepherd life, though I hope publishers are above suspicion.

So you leave us in August. I can promise myself nothing. People here are talking about Lake Tahoe. Do you know it—have you ever been there in the summer? If the mining stock market was unusually kind to me, I might go there for a week—a month is beyond my dreams. I am dabbling in stocks in a small way, have begun a book, and between these two, I have hopes of blotting out, becoming oblivious to, the heat of summer, to say nothing of the eternal dust and wind. No doubt your residence at Independence, or the remembrance of it, assists me in my weak effort to make myself understood. I enclose you a clipping. If this holds true, I will be drunken with work, and therefore consumed with forgetfulness. Always glad to hear from you.

Very truly yours,
Andy Adams

The *Atlantic Monthly* was the most prestigious magazine to publish Austin's early work, but two other periodicals, *Cosmopolitan* and *St. Nicholas*, accepted her poems and stories. A third was *The Land of Sunshine*, a magazine edited by Charles F. Lummis (1859-1928), who was its sole editor from January of 1895 until February of 1903. Before Lummis assumed his editorial post, he had written ten books about the history and folklore of the southwestern United States, including stories of travels in the region and the trip across the continent he made on foot in order to arrive there. Lummis was famous, and his relationship to Austin was that of mentor to pupil. She did not respond kindly to this attitude, as *Letter 9* from Lummis will illustrate.

Associated with Lummis on the staff of *The Land of Sunshine* was Charles Amadon Moody (1863-1910), who came from New Haven, Connecticut, to Pasadena, California, in 1899, planning to investigate California mines. The direction of his interest shifted when, in 1903, he was appointed assistant editor of the Lummis magazine. The name of the periodical was changed in 1905 to *Out West* and Moody was listed as joint editor. He was a year younger than Austin and closer than Lummis to her point of view, as his letters indicate. The first of the letters printed here establishes a contact which must have pleased her very much. The "Christmas story" mentioned in *Letter 4* was entitled "The Kiss of Niño Dios." It was printed in *Out West*, Volume XXI (December 1904).

_____ 4

Out West
A Magazine of the Old Pacific and the New
   EDITED by Chas. F. Lummis   Los Angeles
Charles Amadon Moody, ASS'T EDITOR   November 3, 1904

Dear Mrs. Austin:
        Night before last, I read the installment of "Isidro" in the current "Atlantic." Last night, I read your "Basket Woman" and this morning I have been preparing for the press the Christmas story with which you have honored us. Remembering, besides, "The Land of Little Rain," the "grey coyote with lean grey mate," and many other delightful things, I feel bound to say to you that I do not know of any woman in America who has the variety of literary power which you possess. Your publishers make a mistake in speaking of "The Basket Woman" as the Western Jungle Book. It is something very much more delicate and very far different from that. Two or three of those little tales remind me of, and will match well with, Hans Christian Andersen at his best.

I try to believe in some sort of infinite ordering which lies back of the blind trails along which we stumble. You seem to have been intended to do a certain work that no one else could; and could only achieve the power for that work under the pressure of a constant and not-to-be-remedied grief. It is surely true that the things you have done, and shall do, never would have been done if motherhood had given to you what mothers pray for, instead of what it has.

Assuredly, to believe this would be no consolation—only an explanation; but the Infinite appears to care not at all for consoling individuals—only to get its desire accomplished.

Very sincerely
C. A. Moody

Moody's *Letter 5*, August 15, 1905, invites Mary to contribute an article dealing with the Owens River Reclamation Survey, which was an irrigation project that had once been confined to the Owens Valley, but as need for water developed in the Los Angeles area, the City Water Board called upon the Reclamation Service of the United States Government to join with "The City," as the Los Angeles City Water Board came to be known, in a vast scheme to transport water from both the lake and the river all the way to the San Fernando Valley north of Los Angeles. The pattern followed was for agents of The City to purchase all the land with existing water rights adjacent to the lake. Thus by using canals and drilling wells all the water on and under the surface of the land could be conveyed 250 miles or more through aqueducts to southern California. Supporters of The City cited the big prices paid by Los Angeles for land of marginal value. Mary Austin, on the other hand, saw pleasant rural communities destroyed by grasping industrial and agricultural interests of great political and economic power. As one of the early ecologists in the twentieth century, she foretold the types of water and air pollution which would occur with population congestion. She also believed that much of the creative thinking and expression in America developed in small towns and rural environments. This is what she would have proclaimed in her article for *Out West* had she written it. Today small towns still offer recreational and commercial activities in the Owens Valley, but the full potential of the area was arrested by the capture of its water nearly seventy years ago. Austin supplies a résumé of the Owens River Project in her *Earth Horizon.*

————— 5

Out West
A Magazine of the Old Pacific and the New
   Chas. F. Lummis
   Charles Amadon Moody   EDITORS   Los Angeles
   Sharlot M. Hall, ASS'T EDITOR   Aug. 15, 1905

Dear Mrs. Austin:
       Mr. Lummis hands me your letter to him in reply to mine of a
couple of weeks ago. I met your brother on the street two or three days
ago and he told me that any article which we would get from you on the
diversion of the Owens river would probably be a "scorcher," judging
from what he had heard from you on the subject.

       I do not yet see why you could not write just the kind of article that
we want—that is, an article about the Owens river; its sources of supply,
what it is now being used for and what the expectations were for its use
in your own valley. I suppose your feeling is that if you with the other
residents of the valley are compelled to march in chains behind the
triumphant car in Los Angeles, you will do so, but you will be hanged if
you will sing during the procession. My recollection is, however, that
the Hebrews in captivity used to gather under the palms of Egypt and
sing about the glories of Jerusalem, from which they have been violently
reft.

       The reason we turned to you in this matter is just that no one else alive
combines the affectionate knowledge of that section with the master
hand. Think it over again and see if there isn't something you can give us.

       The last paragraph in your letter reminds me to say that I should have
reviewed "Isidro" two or three months ago, but for the fact that Lummis
expressed a wish to say something about it himself. It has been lying on
his pile of books ever since.

                                   Very sincerely,
                                   C. A. Moody

———————————————————————————————————

       Mary Austin must have enlisted the help of Stewart Edward
White (1873-1961) in the Owens Valley-Los Angeles confrontation, for in *Letter 6*,

September 29, 1905, he promised to forward her statement to President Theodore Roosevelt. The letter identifies both White and Austin not only with the water problem in California, but also with political figures who influenced decisions in the battle. Mary was acquainted with two presidents of the United States. In her autobiography, she recounts that President Roosevelt sent a forestry expert to interview her after he learned of the withdrawal of grazing lands from sheepherders as reported in her book *The Flock* (1906). At a later time, Roosevelt read other books she had written, and invited her to visit in his home. As he walked with her to the station, he said, "I wish you would write another Indian book, a book I could read aloud to my grandchildren" (*Earth Horizon*, pp. 289, 325). Mary's friendship with President Herbert Hoover and his family also occupies considerable space in her autobiography. The Hoover letters printed in this volume will contribute to further understanding of this friendship and the problems incurred during its course.

Stewart Edward White was born in Michigan and could be called a member of the Midwestern School of Western Fiction Writers, a group which included Emerson Hough, born in Iowa, and Eugene Manlove Rhodes, born in Nebraska. All three writers gravitated to the Far West at some period in their writing careers. After graduating from the University of Michigan in 1895, White studied law in New York City and practiced there briefly before he wrote successful novels based on lumber and mining camps in Michigan and South Dakota. He was drawn to the Southwest early, as his letter from Santa Barbara indicates. "The Rawhide," one of the finest stories in *Arizona Nights* (1907), was published in the *Saturday Evening Post* during the year 1904. In subsequent years, White traveled in Africa, wrote stories and novels about woodsmen in Kentucky, trappers and traders in the Rockies, and a trilogy about California. The breadth of his plots traces the scope of his travels.

If White forwarded Austin's letter to Theodore Roosevelt, the president received it in the last year of the administration he began as vice president under McKinley. The secretary of the interior at that time was E. A. Hitchcock, but the greatest assistance to Los Angeles was rendered by the chief of the Forest Service, Gifford Pinchot, a great reclamationist who must have believed in sending water where it would render service to the greatest number of people. Pinchot was ably assisted by J. B. Lippincott, who in 1903 directed a government survey in the Owens Valley. He left the reclamation service later to work for the City of Los Angeles. Today, with increased water storage available to Los Angeles, more of the Owens Valley is being irrigated and farmed. Recreation and tourist travel to the mountain resorts to the north have also helped the economy of towns like Lone Pine, Independence, and Bishop. Both of the Stewart Edward White letters are reprinted by permission of the Crocker National Bank, Santa Barbara, California, proprietor of the Stewart Edward White Estate.

_____ 6

The Jumping Off Place
Santa Barbara
California

My dear Mrs. Austin;

I am only too glad to send your letter on to the President. I am sure it states the case much more convincingly than I could myself, especially as I know nothing of other arguments, and so could not conscientiously make recommendations. Mr. Roosevelt is absolutely just, and absolutely honest, but the extent of his interference will depend to a large extent on his confidence in the man who makes the final decision. Vigorous representations should be accompanied by a copy of the Reclamation report, and a refutation of the reasons therein given for the contemplated step. I have observed that if a case can be forced to the highest officials, direct, and not through subordinates, it is apt to be considered from the standpoint of justice; while the under clerks are apt to be strongly swayed by the ideas of the field men.

I sincerely hope you may win out, and if there is anything more I can do, I should be very glad. I have written the President telling him what I know; and now it seems to me that he would be open to a direct appeal from yourself. Certainly it could do absolutely no harm for you to write him.

Most sincerely yours,

Sep. 29 1905   *Stewart Edward White*

Strangely enough I just received a letter from Mr. Lungren, friend of Lippincott, saying incidentally that the latter "thought himself very badly treated by the people of Owen's Valley."

Letter 7, also written by White, is dated March 30, 1933. It has a letterhead using the design of the footprint of an animal. The address is "Little Hill, Burlingame, Cal." He apologizes for failure to answer a letter from Mary written a long time before. Belatedly, he thanks her for writing and assures her that he "fled from the Sierras" only because Africa, Alaska, and other places had called to him. He confides that he and his wife have just read Austin's *Experiences Facing Death* (1931), and he feels that his mind has traveled the same path as hers. The tone of this letter confirms that the space of silence between letters has not meant a space of indifference on his part.

————— 7

Little Hill
Burlingame, Cal.

Dear Mrs. Austin:

After lo these many years, and in a very roundabout way, I am about to answer a letter you evidently wrote to me, and which I never received. Jack Gavit informs me that you did write such a letter; and that I never answered it; and that I "must have taken it seriously." It is sad that all these years I have lived in your mind as a person with so little sense of humor and with such a sense of importance that such a lack indicates. I've never taken myself so hard. I have always stoutly maintained that room to write about any subject whatever is not a matter of space but of point of view, so that the same chicken coop might be material for a dozen people. "Our territories" are within our own minds. So now, belatedly, I am glad of the chance to thank you for writing; and to assure you that I fled from the Sierra only because there was Africa and Alaska and other way ports. The whole thing reminds me rather deliciously of a charming elderly gentleman I used to know who would listen to some of my brightest efforts to be amusing, would take my remarks under due consideration, and then would say, with an air of enlightenment: "Ah! That is a jest!"

But I am more glad at the fillip this all gives a half-formed determination to tell you how deeply interesting both Mrs. White and myself have found your "Experiences Facing Death." I have long suspected we talked at least dialects of the same language, but this book convinces me. Our minds, through a variety of experiences, somewhat differing of course from yours, but nevertheless along the same general trail, have closely tracked yours. I wish sometime we could talk these things over, at leisure, and find out where each thinks he has seen through the fog.

Perhaps we may. In the meantime, low salaams; apologies for a seeming rudeness; and this very delayed "yours of recent date received."

Most sincerely

March 30 1933   *Stewart Edward White*

The first of six letters written by Bliss Perry (1860-1954) from the editorial offices of the *Atlantic Monthly* is dated February 25, 1902. In it, speaking for "The Editors," he congratulates Austin upon the "charm and faithfulness" of the sketches she has sent, concluding with the statement that "it isn't often that prose sketches of outdoor life have given us such unalloyed satisfaction." In successive letters during 1902 and 1903, he advises her that upon conclusion of the series in the *Atlantic*, the Houghton Mifflin Company has agreed to publish the series in a book, using the general title of *The Land of Little Rain*. Perry expresses his preferences for six story sketches, all of which would appear before publication of the book. In another letter, he gives critical advice about stories in her manuscript called *The Basket Woman*, two of which he has chosen for publication in the *Atlantic*. He gave his 12-year-old daughter these and others to read, and she returned a favorable report. The final letter, dated May 14, 1906, congratulates Mary Austin upon escaping "the great calamity," an event she witnessed and described in the following year in a chapter called "The Temblor," written for David Starr Jordan's book *The San Francisco Earthquake* (1907). All of the letters express a cordial relationship between editor and author.

As a matter of fact, Mary Austin did not abandon her intention to write about Death Valley. In a note dated April 21, 1933, addressed to L. J. Alber of the World Celebrities Lecture Bureau, she volunteered that she planned a visit to Death Valley in order to write about it, and would like to combine her visit with a lecture tour. The dates had been fixed for autumn of that year and the winter of 1934, but sickness in the early period was prolonged in the following year, ending with her death on August 13, 1934. She might have begun a novel as proposed in *Letter 8*, but more likely she would have used the pattern established as historical background in *The Land of Journeys' Ending* and stories like those in her book *Lost Borders*.

_____ 8

Editorial Office of
THE ATLANTIC MONTHLY   December 1, 1905

Dear Mrs. Austin,

   I find that I have somehow forgotten to thank you for your letter
of November 5th dated from Independence, California. I think myself
that when we return to a place formerly familiar to us the atmosphere
and personality of the region makes even a deeper impression than
when it was a matter of everyday experience. I am sure, therefore, that
you will sometime write your novel of Death Valley, and very likely you
may find that the place takes even a stronger hold on your imagination
after you have been living for a few months or years in a town where
you have to do things by the clock. At any rate, be sure that the Atlantic
is following with interest everything that you write, and that we hope
we may again have the pleasure, and that before very long, of printing
some more of your work.

                              Cordially yours,
                              Bliss Perry

_____

   Mary Austin called the writing corner in her house at Independence the "wickiup," an Indian word for a shelter. Both house and wickiup
were midway between San Francisco and Los Angeles. In order to find publishing
contacts in the southern metropolis, she applied to teach at the Los Angeles
Normal School. The position there in 1899 sustained her while she entered the
literary circle gathered around Charles F. Lummis, who had lived among
Pueblo Indians in New Mexico and in Spanish villages there and in other parts
of the Southwest. He was a pioneer in finding material for stories among ethnic
groups. His writings were accepted by magazines of national prominence. He
had planned and was building a very large stone and adobe house on the west
bank of the Arroyo Seco between Los Angeles and Pasadena, naming the place
El Alisal, because of the grove of alder trees in the canyon (the house is now
California State Monument No. 531). Here in the large patio and before the
fireplace in the central room, Mary Austin met Frederick Webb Hodge, who was
to build the Southwest Museum in later years; David Starr Jordan, lecturer

and president of Stanford University; John Burroughs, the naturalist; Charles Dudley Warner, editor and author; and many others of influence in the publishing world.

Lummis was a colorful figure, wearing a corduroy suit, widebrimmed Stetson hat, soft white shirt, beaded Indian belt or red silk sash, and moccasins or sandals. He walked and talked with energy. His enthusiasm showed in the vigor of both his spoken and written storytelling. After several years of undergraduate study at Harvard University, Lummis came west for his health, arriving in Los Angeles by way of a long detour in New Mexico. His career in California embraced reporting on the *Los Angeles Times*, editorial chores for the magazine *The Land of Sunshine*, establishing a society called the Sequoya League, and serving for six years as librarian for the Los Angeles Public Library. During the ten years he wrote a column called "In the Lion's Den," he espoused the climate and beauty of California; preservation of Spanish place names; statehood for New Mexico and Arizona; and opposed British and American imperialism, including the Spanish-American War.

One of the plans Lummis employed to entertain his guests was to arraign them on such trumped up charges as disloyalty to California by something they had published or failed to publish. This type of summons and trial is illustrated by the subpoena that accompanies *Letter 10*, February 18, 1913, in which he orders Mary Austin to appear under the vast sycamore in the Old Pueblo of Our Lady of the Angels, there to come before the Alcalde Mayor and acquit herself of all charges, past and present, accusing her of high misdemeanors and "Not Knowing an Old California Good Time" when she sees it.

The tone of the Lummis *Letter 9*, November 24, 1904, illustrates the relationship between Austin and Lummis as friendly adversaries. She resented his admonitory attitude, but relied upon him for advice about details of Southwestern history, flowers, Spanish gardens, and local customs. In her autobiography, she records that Lummis "did not take to her, nor she to him." He also condoned the program of the Los Angeles City Corporation to take the water from the valley where she had lived. To a considerable degree, however, she modeled her career upon his, exploring regional history and folklore as themes for essay and narrative. Three letters to Mary Austin from Lummis's wife Eve are affectionate and confidential in discussing domestic problems. Austin dedicated *The Land of Little Rain* "To Eve, The Comfortress of Unsuccess."

_____ 9

Out West
A Magazine of the Old Pacific and the New   Los Angeles, Cal.
EDITOR'S OFFICE   Nov. 24th, 1904

Dear Mrs. Austin:
 I am just starting east but must answer, even if briefly, your friendly letter. If you are "not in the least ashamed of your ignorance of Spanish derivations" then you ought to be. You are more than right in assuming that there are lots of things about which I am equally ignorant. But you have brains enough, and enough intellect, to understand the difference. I don't try to write about the things I am ignorant of. If you want to take a historic period, or a geographic setting, to make fame or money, for you—or even, let us say, in the very extreme of liberality, to fulfil your mission toward rounding out literature—you are entitled to give them a fair bargain. It is your business to treat them with the respect that you would like to have for your own work. If you ignorantly and carelessly mutilate them, then by all justice your work ought to be laughed at. Fair exchange is no robbery; but to feather your nest with stolen plumage is worse than robbery.
 I never have, and I never shall have, "scorn" for modest ignorance. My whole life long, many of my trusted friends have been ignorant people. My whole life long I have been kind to ignorant work. But that was modest ignorance. You know perfectly well that in the easily satisfied East you are assumed to know as much about California as you certainly do know about expressing yourself; and no one has a higher estimate of this your great gift. This, in itself, puts you under a moral obligation not to swindle your readers; not to fill them up with any more ignorance, which is already so predominant there and here.
 You will never, my dear child, find anything "more important to your stunt in the world's work" than knowing what you are talking about. When you use Spanish names, it is your business as a decent woman, and as a writer, to have them right. What would you think of yourself if, as a Californian, writing of California, you described seasons as they are in New England? What would you think of yourself if you made your stage-setting in Inyo county and described the landscape such as the people of the north-east of Maine are familiar with, and as

no one ever saw in California? Now you happen to know about these things, and therefore realize the iniquity it would be to misrepresent them. It is an equal iniquity—and I mean that word—to misrepresent other things just as characteristic, just as easy to learn and just as necessary to the picture.

Don't fill yourself with that Chautauqua idiocy about leaving it to the dreadful scientists to know anything. It won't hurt you any more than it hurts other people to be right. There is a great deal to learn in this world, and most of it is expensive education. Where in some case a person who happens to have learned is willing to give you your examinination paper for nothing, do not look on it with sneerness.

There is no such word as Relles; there never was; there never will be. If illiterate persons care to corrupt their own language, that is no reason why you should, with your larger gift and therefore your greater responsibility. You could call a heroine Mazen and explain that it meant "amazing grace"—for this would not add to the fund of ignorance. You can spell your own name as you like, for that is an American privilege. But you have not any business to write my name Loomis nor to write Callafunnier as the name of this state, nor to do any other high handed treason against the things which should be a comfort and a glory to you, and which you have no right to make cripples of for your own advantage.

I don't think I wrote you with any rage. God knows what I dictated— my stenographer doesn't, no more do I. I am not writing to you with any rage now. But I have softly whispered to you several times vague hints as to—not what I think but what every scholar knows about certain facts. You are not yet convinced; therefore I am going to see if I cannot make the matter plain.

Now, my dear child, your letter does not "seem unappreciative," nor do I wish mine to be. If you were not worth while, you may be sure I would not waste the time I cannot give my work, to you. I do not even wish to "make you uncomfortable"—except when it is temporarily necessary in order to set you right. For I do want you to be right. You have a right to be. We have a right to have you.

I am starting east directly to lecture to the eastern affiliated societies of the Archaeological Institute of America. I wish you would send your proofs to Mrs. Lummis, and I will instruct her to forward them to me wherever she can reach me at that time, and I will read them just as soon as they reach me.

With kindest regards and remembrances from all of us,
Always
Your Friend
Chas. F. Lummis

    In interpreting *Letter 10*, a reader should be told that Lummis was born on March 1, 1859, and that date would make him a "March hare." However, his youngest daughter, Turbese, was born on June 8, 1892. If the reference is to her, Lummis may simply be joining two birthday parties into one. Rosendo was an attendant at El Alisal, who not only performed odd jobs, but also entertained with songs and provided his own accompaniment. A guess might be hazarded that the "Long-Missing Link" was Mary's husband, Wallace Austin, from whom she was not divorced until nearly three years later.

_____ **10**

The Southwest Society

To Show the Story of Man   Los Angeles, California
Secretary, Chas. F. Lummis   February 18, 1913

Dear Mrs. Austin:
    Bully! I'm glad you are coming! This time the Alcalde Mayor befalls with the March Hares—which celebrate the important time when my little daughter and I and a few other Deserving Persons favored the world by coming into it.
    And to have you here will make a good Birthday.
    Come early and avoid the Hush! Rosendo can't stay for Feed, but will be in our Midst from 2 till 5. If you never heard him, you've a new Experience ahead; if you have, you won't need the sheriff to fetch you again.

Come early anyhow!
Always your friend,
Chas. F. Lummis

Dinner at 6.
Of course! as to your brother and the Long-Missing link.

An enclosure in this letter was the mock "Summons and Subpoena" for Mary Austin's appearance on March 2, 1931, at an "old California dinner in an old California house, with old California music and old California hearts." Lummis calls himself the constable sending the "Summons," which can benefit from some translations of the Spanish: *por acá* means "around here"; *yo soy la ley,* "I am the law"; *el alcalde mayor,* "the mayor or justice of the peace"; *alguacil,* "constable" or "peace officer"; and *escribano,* "notary public." The couplet in Spanish may be translated as:

> Whoever seeks shelter under a good tree,
> Finds a refuge and protection as a cover.

Lummis was right in saying that the old days were gone, but some old customs should still be preserved, and his fiestas at El Alisal were memorable.

Summons and Subpoena

Por Acá
    Yo Soy La Ley
    No. . . . .
Docket. . . . . Page. . . .
    Supreme Court of
    Old California
El Alcade Mayor,
    Chief Justice

_____

_____

Case of
    The Good Old Days
    Plantiff
    vs
    Mary Austin
    Defendant

_____

_____

    Subpoena

Ya
    Alcalde Mayor
Summons (cont'd)
The *Alguacil* will produce you

Summons:
    Quien a Buen Arbol se arrima,
    Buena sombra el Cobija.

The *Alcalde Mayor,* or Chief Justice, was the historic head of the Pueblo of Our Lady, Queen of Angels. And still is, if you do but know. Today, the *Alcalde Mayor* is a vast sycamore that was here when the Pueblo began in 1781. Under its four-fold spread, 100 feet each way, there gather upon occasion (and YOU are an Occasion) some of those that knew and still love the Old Days, and try to Hold them It is the only Family ever Elected—its children Picked Ripe, so as to avoid disappointment in their growing up. They stand for many things in the progressive city and state of Today; but they mean to RIDE Progress, instead of being trampled by it. Once in a while they Pause Long Enough to Live. It is about the Last Stand of the Frontier—of the old Patriarchal Days. We cannot entertain every stranger, as was done then; but before this honorable court, (where the Jury is packed in your favor), and will be responsible for your safe return to your bondsmen, hotel or other place of imprisonment. If you have Appendices—bring them. They are safe from being Cut. Come on in—the chile is fine!

In the name of the
Alcade Mayor.

NO RIOTOUS RAIMENT

In the Court of

> *El Alcalde Mayor*
> In the Pueblo of
> Our Lady of the
> Angels
> The Good Old Days
> Plaintiff
> vs
> Mary Austin
> Defendant

we ARE here to welcome unto the old hospitality, those who ARE NOT STRANGERS—and You are Not. This is on purpose for YOU. Just because we like you for what you have done.

If you think an old California dinner in an old California house, with old California music and old California hearts, would be as Californian and as pleasant as the modern city—wire to Charles F. Lummis, 200 East Avenue 43, Los Angeles, Cal., (Home Phone 31533) Escribano.

Subpoena
California Civil Procedure
Vol. 1, Sec. 1
1542 to date

Greeting: . . . .
. . . .
. . . .

You stand charged, before this court, with the High Misdemeanor of "NOT KNOWING AN OLD CALIFORNIA GOOD TIME WHEN YOU SEE IT"

Thereby robbing those that love you for what you have done, and picking your own pockets of a Good Memory. You are also accused of being an Accomplice Before the Fact that you Never Did See One.

WE COMMAND YOU, that all and singular business and excuses being laid aside, you appear and attend before the undersigned at 200 East Avenue 43, Los Angeles, Cal, on the Second day of March, 1913, at 5 o'clock p.m., then and there to defend yourself in the above entitled action. Disobedience to this Subpoena will be punished as a contempt by the said Court, and you will also forfeit to the party aggrieved the sum of One Hundred Dolors, and all damages which may be sustained by your failure to attend. You will also forfeit your own experience of Something Different.

AND YOU ARE REQUIRED, also, to bring with you the following, to wit:

Any appendages, appendixes, wives, sweethearts, cousins, babies, friends or other witnesses against you. Also your digestion and mouth. Item, your Disposition.

The prosecutor is Fierce, but the Jury of 18 has been Carefully Packed in Your Favor. If you can put up any sort of defense the verdict will be "Not Guilty, Come Again."

Grief, when shared, is a bond greater than almost any other kind of human experience. Nearly five years after the joyous celebration at El Alisal, Mary Austin wrote *Letter 11* to Charles Lummis in which she apologized for her failure to visit with him again when she made a trip to Los Angeles. Illness of relatives in Los Angeles and the death of her daughter, on October 6 in Santa Clara, had changed all plans for a trip to El Alisal. The fact that Lummis's son had played with Ruth before the girl's infirmity required confinement made her mother's gratitude doubly poignant. Her story of a mystical communion between the children doubtless affirmed Mary Austin's belief in psychic phenomena, as reported in *Letter 46* written to Sonya Levien, on September 1, 1917. Mary Austin devotes four pages of her autobiography to the Lummis family, revealing especially her devotion to Eva Douglas Lummis, the second wife of Charles Lummis. In *Earth Horizon*, Mary reports that she did not communicate readily with Lummis, who said she had talent and a certain kind of knowledge, but little gift and no genius. In turn, she believed that he deferred to the "higher ups" in political and economic circles, was uncritically romantic, borrowed his wife's translations of Spanish manuscripts, and drank too much. However, in her letter of December 28, 1918, she calls him "the pioneer" in Southwestern studies and ends with a salutation of the utmost good will.

The reference in the fifth paragraph to Amado Bandelier, Lummis calls to mind the relationship between Lummis and two friends. One was Adolph Bandelier (1840-1913), the famous archeologist and author of *The Delight Makers* (1890), who instructed Lummis in the cliffdwelling sites of Arizona and New Mexico. The other, Amado Chavez, was the owner of a ranch at San Mateo, New Mexico, where Lummis spent two months in 1886 recovering from a paralytic stroke that occurred from overwork as city editor of the *Los*

Angeles Times. Amado Bandelier Lummis did not carry his distinguished name into manhood. Born in the pueblo of Isleta, New Mexico, he lived at El Alisal for only six years, dying on Christmas Day, 1900.

_____ 11

School of American Research
Museum of New Mexico
Santa Fe, New Mexico   Dec. 28, 1918

Dear Charles:

I had not expected to come away from Los Angeles without seeing you again. But the next week after arranging to come out to tea, both my nieces came down with influenza, and then my poor little Ruth, who never grew up, fell a victim to it, and that carried me away to Santa Clara where she has been safe, and I hope happy for many years.

I meant to come and tell you about that, she was so fond of Amado, and you were of the very few of my friends who knew her. I was glad to have her go so easily and quickly as she did for my one fear has always been that she would outlive those who loved her, and the one restraining care of my life has been to lay up money enough so that she might never suffer.

And yet it was a grief, too, for there is something of a woman's life goes out of her with every child and death is an amputation that never ceases aching. And I couldn't be sure that the poor child survived the shock of death and won through to a life in which she will have a better chance than she had in this life.

I meant to come and see you then, and talk with you, for after all, her friendship with Amado was the only thing that gave me any assurance that her life did not go out here like an unfruitful flower.

I wonder if Eve ever showed you the letter I wrote her just after Amado's death? In any case, I suppose she would have taken the letter away with her and you might like to have it written here, for it is by mysteries such as these our life is kept from sterility.

It was the night Amado passed, and I had put Ruth to bed with the door open a little crack so that I might hear her if she called. And unexpectedly, absolutely unusually, I heard her laughing and talking to herself. It was so unusual that I wondered if some one might not be in the room with her, but when I went in, I found her laughing in bed.

"Amado is here," she told me in her broken words. "He want me to go a walk with him, a long, long way off."

I didn't understand of course, I took it for a sign of developing intelligence, so I said, "But you wouldn't leave mother would you," and left her, laughing and answering back to what I thought her imaginary visitor. After a little time I heard her say "Good-by, Amado." And two days later I had Eve's letter telling me that at that hour Amado had indeed gone "a long way off."

We do not know what these things mean, but to me it has always meant the faith that back of her poor, imperfect body my child's soul waited its deliverance, and I am glad she will find one child who loved her in that country where they both have gone.

I wanted very much to come and talk with you, there were so few people who ever had the courage to know about my Ruth, even my own family found it easier to speak of her as lost. But you like me, have eaten the bread of sorrow on which the gods feed those they specially endow. . . . And now this long unhappy incident is ended in this life at least. I suppose that many women will have to suffer before society arrives at the place where women who give their bodies to the service of Life can hope to be protected from things like this. . . . I believe that I am regarded as a fortunate and successful woman, I wonder will we ever find any criterion of true values in this life.

I am working here as hard as ever, waiting until conditions in Mexico will make it advisable for me to go there for a month or two. The epidemic of influenza is still raging.

I have been asked to write a chapter on Aboriginal American Literature for the Cambridge History of Am. Literature, the first time the work of the Indian has received recognition as part of our literary wealth, from conventional scholarship. If you have any suggestions, I would be glad to hear them. They pay nothing, but I am glad to do the work as a tribute to a neglected race of artists.

We often speak of you here and wish that you could be one of us in fact as you were the pioneer.

One thing also that I wished to tell you of, and have forgotten in speaking of myself. At Pacific Grove there is a curio dealer, W. A. Silliman, who has searched out of all the Mexican homes, many interesting and valuable relics of Mission days. He has very little idea of their value, but agrees with me that these things should be in a museum. I think the Southwest Museum should look into this. If you write he will give you a description of his things. I meant to tell you earlier of this, but my own affairs drove it out of my mind.

With sincere regards, and best wishes for the years that are left to us.

MARY AUSTIN

THE CARMEL WAY

II

In her autobiography, *Earth Horizon*, Austin records her life-long interest in theatrical activities, from playacting as a child to later protesting against her Methodist upbringing which forbade dancing and acting as forms of sinful physical display. She states that in 1898 and 1899, when her husband was county superintendent of schools at Lone Pine, California, she organized a community theater to perform Shakespearian plays. Efforts of the Austins brought entertainment not only to families in the town and on the farms, but also to miners and Indians who came into the hall used for exhibits at the Inyo County Fair. That her dramatic exploits developed into something more professional is clear from the exchange of letters with Elmer Harris between 1906 and 1918. He is the author of *Letter 12*, the first in a series of ten which date from 1906 to 1918. The letters began in friendship but ended in open and declared estrangement.

Elmer Harris (1879-1966) was among the innovative and resourceful playwrights and producers of the early decades of the twentieth century. He was the son of a well-to-do manufacturer in Oakland, California, who encouraged him to enter courses in playwriting at the University of California at Berkeley. Following graduation in 1901, Harris wrote and directed plays in the Department of Drama at the University of California at Los Angeles. A play he wrote was produced in 1903 by Rudolph Schildkraut at a playhouse in Hamburg, Germany. Harris served in World War I as entertainment director for the Army at Camp Bowie, Texas. After the war, he returned to the stage in San Francisco and New York City. Between 1908 and 1941, he was the author or coauthor of fourteen plays or musicals, the most successful being "So Long Letty" and "Johnny Belinda." He also wrote screenplays for Hollywood and became drama critic for the *New York Globe*. His association with Mary Austin began when they were collaborating on a play called "The Coyote Doctor." *Letter 12* was sent to Mary Austin early in her days at Carmel-by-the-Sea, a place with which she was to be associated for nearly two decades.

Harris wrote his letter before the middle of April in 1906, for he refers to the appearance of Sarah Bernhardt in a San Francisco theater at this time. Her performances were interrupted by the terrifying earthquake on the eighteenth day of that month. Harris must have written from Oakland to Mary Austin in Carmel shortly before that catastrophic event. She was in San Francisco on the day before the quake, and then in a suburban area when the shock occurred, as she describes it briefly in her autobiography and, as previously reported, in David Starr Jordan's *The California Earthquake* (1907). Harris refers to nothing more threatening than a neighborhood fire from which he pretends to save the play they were working on, Austin as writer and Harris suggesting stagecraft. A copy of this manuscript supplies an outline of the plot, and since the script was a matter of concern to Harris and Austin for a period of twelve years, a brief synopsis seems justified.

The setting for "The Coyote Doctor" is a Paiute campody, a word employed by Mark Twain for an Indian village and favored by Austin because it conjures up the communal way of life. As the plot develops, the heroine Sina faces the choice of obeying her father or defying him in the selection of a mate. The prospective man is a Paiute named Bill Bodry, who has been educated in a government Indian school. Bodry pays a medicine man to cure Sina's father and then asks for the hand of Sina in payment of the debt. A conflict develops when he is accused of practicing "coyote" witchcraft upon her and is threatened by his enemies with death. When his supposed witchcraft is disclosed as true devotion, Sina turns to him, but the two are forced into exile by the tribe. Action on the stage is heightened by Indian dancing and threats of violence.

Annotation to *Letter 12* includes reference to Charlotte Hoffman, who was an English teacher in the Anna Head School for Girls at Berkeley. She wrote poetry and articles for numerous magazines and was a frequent visitor to the Carmel colony. Additional information about her friendship with Mary Austin will be found in the introduction to *Letter 13*. Dorothea Moore was identified previously in Ina Coolbrith's *Letter 1*. Both women were firm allies of Austin as crusaders in feminist programs.

_____ 12

1175 Market Street
Oakland, Undated
(April, 1906?)

Dear Pard:

There was a fire in a coal-yard across the street this morning at six o'clock, and the engines have just gone home. The crowds trickle away down side streets. The danger is over. But for a while I hugged our manuscripts closely to a troubled breast. These bad Wednesdays! This is the second time my rest has been disturbed at an ungodly hour in the morning by disasters of this kind.

The third act arrived safely, and ever since I have been intending to acknowledge it, but I thought you might come up today or tomorrow to see Bernhardt. You say nothing about it in your letter so I conclude you are not coming. I send you Act 2 today. The same criticism that I made of the first act applied to this, in the main. I have made several additions, which, I think should be elaborated. This act is inferior to the first, there is so much of interest in that, and we will have to make more of the scene between Bill and Maggie, suggest the idea of the coyote doctor so that our play will preserve its unity in that direction, and develop by description and dialogue the feeling which I have emphasized of the hopeless condition of the Indian whom the progress of humanitarian ways is leaving far behind. Your wizard pen will arrange that.

I will go down toward the end of next week. I do not know whether Charlotte can be there, but I will do my best to persuade her to come. You shall hear at once. Dr. Moore left for Los Angeles this morning.

Hopefully yours,
E. B. Harris

In Elmer Harris's *Letter 13*, the name of Charlotte Hoffman is again introduced, this time to tell of her taking a ship in New York with a traveling companion who was a young woman from Berkeley. Hoffman was en route to marry Vernon Kellogg when both arrived in Florence, Italy. Kellogg taught entomology at Stanford University. Both he and Hoffman were early members of the colony of artists and writers who assembled at Carmel-by-the-Sea. Austin, in her autobiography, tells of meeting the Kelloggs after their marriage in Florence and before she traveled on to Rome in the summer of 1908. Florence Roberts, to whom Harris read the lines of *The Coyote Doctor*, was a New York actress and investor in the theater. David Belasco (1855-1931), also mentioned by Harris, was both an actor and a producer. At the age of 19, he became stage manager of a San Francisco theater and in the following year toured the country in a play he wrote entitled *Hearts of Oak*. He continued to compose and produce plays for the best-known actors on the American stage. Minnie Maddern Fiske (1865-1932), who may have been approached for the role of Sina, grew up in a family of actors. She made her first stage appearance as the young Duke of York in Shakespeare's *Richard III*. No other actress in the American theater played in a greater number of roles, ranging from characters in plays by Shakespeare to those in plays by Sheridan and Ibsen. Four letters from Minnie Maddern Fiske are in the Mary Austin Collection. The first is from Santa Cruz, California, June 28, 1906, in which she says that she is resting and unable to pay a visit to Mary at Carmel. The last was on October 21, 1921, in response to Mary's inquiries about a dramatic school for a young woman. Mary names Fiske among those she met at the Stage Women's Division of Suffrage in New York City.

The advice Harris gives not to start another novel probably fell on barren ground, for Austin was writing *Santa Lucia* (1908), a story about life in a college community which might be one of any number of small towns with private educational institutions in California. A new professor on the faculty awakens interest among the faculty wives, and a scandal develops which ends in suicide. Except for an old physician, concerned about his daughter's romance, all the significant characters are women, whose lives explore outlets and meet frustration by the limitations imposed upon them. Like Elmer Harris, Mary Austin was interested in exposing the faults of society, but her pen flows more convincingly in narrative than in dramatic form.

_____ 13

Gerard Hotel, New York, 9 June [1907]

Dear Mary:

Charlotte came and "has went"! I saw them off. The day was warm, balmy; the harbor shimmered in the noon-day sun. I missed your name from the list of out-going passengers and your face from among those that were absorbed into the general bulk as the vessel backed and steamed away. You would enjoy nothing more than touring Europe with Charlotte and I hope nothing may interfere with your plans for joining her in the Fall.

Something may, however. I read the Indian play to Florence Roberts the other night and since have been camping on her trail. One way or another I shall do her a play for next season. We have three in mind. She does not see herself in The Coyote Doctor. The part is not varied enough for her. But she nevertheless loves the piece and has suggested that I let her bring it out in San Francisco around Christmas time. I am to spend the night at her out-of-town house next Wednesday to talk over terms. Her plan is to try someone else in the role of Sina and then, provided the play rings the bell, send the production on to New York. She calls it the most beautiful and complete Indian story she has ever read. My idea is to elaborate Sina's character a little, making her a little more winsome and prominent in the beginning of act one and more of a woman in the beginning of act three with perhaps a little more to say of a positive nature. I intend to ask Miss Roberts a thousand dollars for one year's option and ten per cent of the gross. These are the maximum. In case she takes it, you will have to be on hand for rehearsals. In fact, it may be well for you to plan to remain in New York for a while during September, if Miss Roberts is to be here still, and make the necessary alterations then.

Belasco has his hands full for two years to come. He is prejudiced against Indian plays. This proposition of letting a Western actress play a Western drama by Western writers is more to my liking. I am sure she will make a hit in the West. I am going this afternoon to see my friend Loomis, Charles Battell's brother, who writes Indian music and see what the entre'act and incidental music will cost. Miss Roberts may be depended on to spare no cost in mounting the play and can command first-class talent.

Mary, the only way to write plays is to be here on the spot, take their orders and bake accordingly. You and I can do modern white skin plays as well as we have done this. There is nothing in New York that can stand up against the depth of interest, the simplicity, the beauty and the humanness of this dearest of your children. Here are opportunities on all sides. A year in New York would make you a rich woman. Why don't you plan to do as I suggest, spend a couple of months here before going abroad? I shall be returning from Prince Edward Island about the time you would arrive and we could then turn out some work. Meanwhile send me your scenarios. Don't bother elaborating them. All the ideas that you sent me are lost, I suppose; jot down as fully as you remember and let me have them too. Henry Miller wants a play, Grace George want a play—they all want plays. Now, don't waste any more time with Stanford or amateur performances but lets get into harness and make some money.

Just now I am breaking the ice for two social plays, one dealing with child labor and the other with the juvenile court. (Don't advertise this please. If I dropped this hint on Broadway tomorrow morning, the managers would be buried beneath manuscripts on these topics within twenty-four hours.) This is taking a good deal of time, all of it in fact; but I hope to get together enough material during the next six weeks for both plays. I am visiting the factories and the courts, the tenement districts and the jails. It makes your heart bleed, some of it, and if I can but pour some of the tears on paper I'll make a killing. I have always felt that the social drama was my medium; now I am sure of it. It takes time and money to get at the bottom of these problems, for they deal as much with facts as with poetry and romance, and I hope to have both time and money next season. My little one-acter for Mr. Stevenson has proved to be a precocious little lovable thing and the income from that alone, if he plays it in vaudeville as he plans, will be ample for my purposes.

What have you done with Mrs. Fiske?

For heaven's sake, don't settle down to the writing of anything so tedious as a novel when there is so much money to be made here in plays.

Yours,
El.

Letter 14 tells a good deal about the New York theater at this time. Plays are in demand, and there is no lack of playwrights. The business details of agents, writers, and producers are presented. Furthermore, Austin receives some practical enlightenment about stage action and dialogue, which (the evidence suggests) she was unwilling to accept. At least, the prospects for production of *The Coyote Doctor* still appeared to be good, with a sidelight that western American audiences were more susceptible to Indian plays than a metropolitan center in the east.

Harris was also collaborating at this time with another woman dramatist, Geraldine Bonner, who helped him to write a play called *Sham*. This drama was in the mold of social criticism, and was successfully produced in 1907 at the Alcazar Theater in San Francisco and at Wallack's Theater in New York. Austin gives no hint that she was disturbed by this fact, but some disagreement with Harris occurred, for on July 18 she sent him a telegram in which she withdrew all authority to execute any contract as her representative. Then on October 18, she notified him through an attorney that she had another play, *The Arrow Maker*, for which she was trying to arrange a production, and that all agreements about *The Coyote Doctor* were suspended between them.

_____ **14**

Gerard Hotel, New York, 16 June 1907

Dear Mary:

Miss Roberts has her letter to her manager all written and we are waiting to hear from you. Delays are dangerous. She is besieged with playwrights. I have never visited her without hearing of a new one and seeing the pile of possible plays grow taller and taller in the library. I am sorry we are so far away from each other. I think for convenience's sake one of us should assume entire control of the play, and as I see no reason for losing the agent's fee in this offer of Miss Roberts and since I am here on the spot and have so far steered the fortunes of it prosperously, I propose that you give me that control according to the original understanding. The expense of telegraphic communication and the delay both make this a more profitable way to transact our business. Write me, therefore, that you give me power of attorney and authority to arrange the business end of the production.

Now, as I understand Miss Roberts' proposal, she offers $500.00 advance against the royalties of which she wants one third as her share for placing the piece and securing for it the best terms possible. She practically becomes our agent. She further proposes to bring out the play, under Court's direction, since he is advancing all the money and taking all the risk, and, if it makes a hit, she will give the role of Sina over to someone more suited to it in appearance and talent and allow the production to continue en tour aside from her repertoire. She does not think a production possible before the holidays, but is confident of a large Western success.

As to the changes she would require, Sina must be pushed a little to the fore in act one, made more winsome; and, in act three, she must be shown to be more of a woman when the act opens. Besides this, here and there the dialogue must be quickened—I don't mean altered materially, but changed from its present literary form to the form dramatic. Fewer words and more suggestion is what this means. In writing a play, the understructure should be conveyed in pantomime and only enough words added to carry the story.

I think we have struck a very good thing with Florence Roberts. At present an Indian play is not favored in New York, with the exception of "Strongheart." The West, I imagine, would be very keen over any legitimate Indian production. And if Miss Roberts makes a success with The Coyote Doctor out West, she will bring it into New York and our original ambition will in the end be attained. This, too, just as profitably as if the production were made in New York to begin with, because the big money is always made touring.

I hope my telegrams and letters are not being sidetracked while you are off somewhere gathering material. I want to wind this business up and get away from New York. The days are growing unbearably hot and sticky, while almost every mail brings renewed invitations from Mr. Stevenson to join him on his Island and enjoy the fishing which is the best in years. If I were well enough I should weather it out here for July at least, in order to listen to the lectures on Philanthropy and visit the institutions of the Charity Summer School. Already I have done considerable nosing about among them, collecting material for my new opus, but cooped up here on the twelfth floor of a sky scraper, where the sun pours in like white hot slag, I have little inclination to sweat over a typewriter. I hope to make my headquarters in New York next fall and then plunge into the work I have begun head first.

Yours always,
Elmer

Either pride in his own contribution or conviction that Mary Austin's plot would interest an audience caused Harris to write on December 29, 1909, offering to purchase her interest in the play, an offer she refused. Nine years later, in *Letter 15*, he again manifested enthusiasm for the script, calling it a "remarkably fine piece of work," but Mary Austin had already turned the play into a story and sold the version to *Sunset Magazine* under the title "The Divorcing of Sina." Publication occurred in June of 1918. She did not, however, destroy the play; it remains in the collection of her manuscripts.

Blanche Partington, to whom Elmer Harris read the play, after the passage of the years, was the dramatic critic for the *San Francisco Call*. She also was a poet and may have appreciated the sweep of Mary Austin's lines, lines that lacked stage brevity and effect. Reference to Austin's wickiup permits an excerpt from a letter by Charlotte Hoffman on March 19, 1906 in which she describes a costume appropriate to a visitor to Mary's writing perch:

I didn't climb up to the wickiup, and I'm going to take the morning train back and surprise you. You will find me there when you go to superintend in the afternoon. Then

I shall stay and dress in an Indian shawl or two, with strings and strings of beads, and toast mushrooms for you under the wickiup, and send you up baskets of berries and roots and all the things you ought to have instead of currant buns.

In some of Hoffman's later letters, she addresses Austin as "Dear Chisera," the medicine woman in *The Arrow Maker*, Mary Austin's second effort at play-writing (see *Letter 16*). The conclusion is inescapable that the authoress saw her-self in the roles she wrote about and may have acted out the lines accompanied by dressing for the part. "Wickiup" is an Indian word for a shelter, but there is no reason to affix it to a shelter in a tree. Mary Austin, however, thought that she could, and she did.

As a friend of both parties, Partington might have smoothed out the mis-understanding between Austin and Harris. That she failed to do so, cor-roborates their correspondence as an alienation between "friends" and "friendly foes." A degree of loss occurred to both parties. Mary Austin was to try again, but she would select another collaborator for her next play.

_____ 15

Highland Ave.,
Pelham Manor,
New York.

Dear Mary:

I read The Coyote Doctor today for the first time since reading it to Blanche Partington in your wickiup at Carmel over ten years ago. Much water has gone under the bridge since then, yet it remains a remarkably fine piece of work. I doubt whether anything finer has been written for the American stage during this period. Certainly nothing at present before the public can compare with it.

In your last letter, written five years ago, you suggested that I send you my next manuscript for criticism. That was a very friendly offer and I appreciate the spirit in which it was made. I did not avail myself of it, however, because shortly after I learned the trick of success and the rest was easy.

Reading the Coyote Doctor has reawakened my interest in it, and I write to know if you would care to consider a proposition to produce it at this time. It is much too fine and too beautiful a thing to be left to collect dust on your shelf or mine. I believe I can find a producer who would give it the sort of production it requires and deserves.

If you do not care to engage personally in this enterprise and will place your interests in the hands of a reputable theatrical agent like John W. Rumsey, of the American Play Co., New York, I shall be glad to do the rest.

With kind regards,

Sincerely yours,

15 December 1917 *Elmer Harris*

One of the patrons of the New Theater in New York City was Winthrop Ames (1871-1937). He belonged to a group of cooperative playwrights and producers who encouraged contemporary experimental plays. Among the papers in the Mary Austin Collection is a registered envelope sent from Ames's office at 244 West Forty-fourth Street. The envelope holds a manuscript of *The Coyote Doctor*. There is no date, but the manuscript must have been returned before Ames wrote *Letter 17* in which he refers to sending copies of Mary Austin's new play, *The Arrow Maker*, to a "Miss Crawford" who was considering a role in the play. Ames stresses the need for the right "chisera" in the cast.

The Arrow Maker found its way to the stage of the New Theater on February 27, 1911, with George Foster Platt as director. As indicated in *Letter 17*, the central figure is a "chisera," or medicine woman, who by her spells and dancing can arouse the nature gods to bring victory to the Paiutes in war or cause the rain to fall on their crops. Medicine women were not customary among Indian tribes, and Austin tells the audience through the dialogue that chiseras were not supposed to marry or to live in a family once they had assumed the activity of prayer and prophecy. Her chisera has great success at the outset of the play as the Paiutes triumph in battle with neighboring Indians. Chisera, as she will now be called, has given her love to Simwa, the Arrow Maker and War Chief, who has been protected by a charmed arrow she has given him. When Simwa turns to another woman, Chisera's power begins to fail. When her downfall threatens Simwa, he turns the charmed arrow against Chisera and slays her, bringing the downfall of the Paiutes as well. The message of *The Arrow Maker* seems to be that even among primitive peoples the gifts of women are belittled when they strive to compete with men or fail to sacrifice themselves to men's needs.

The play held dramatic moments of drum beat, dancing, and song, but the characters failed to arouse an emotional response from the audience. Reviewers of the performance stated that the plot gave opportunities for spectacle, but the actors spoke in diction and rhythms reminiscent of the Old Testament prophets. Austin defended her writing by stating that the director did not know whether she had written verse or prose. Elmer Harris was right four years earlier when he said that New York did not favor Indian plays (*see Letter 14*). Nevertheless, Austin wrote another Indian play called *Fire*, which enjoyed a successful staging at the Forest Theater in Carmel during August of 1912. The same group in 1914 gave *The Arrow Maker* a second public showing.

Ames kept in contact with Austin, for on December 28, 1916, he sent her a letter saying that he saw her playlet *Merry Christmas, Daddy*, at the Children's Theater and found it really charming. This is the play called *Christmas Island,* or *How Christmas Came to the Colonies*, which was produced at the Goodman Memorial Theater of the Chicago Art Institute on November 12, 1927. In brief, the story tells how a skeptical father learned of Christmas customs in many countries and, to his daughter's joy, was converted to having a Christmas at home. Thomas Wood Stevens was then director at the Goodman Theater, and he wrote that the play would work out "wonderfully" for the children's audience. *Fire* was presented for the second time in an amphitheater near Palm Springs, California, on November 5-6, 1921. Garnet Holme of the University of Nebraska was the producer.

Mary Austin's plays caused only a ripple in the professional theater. She argues in *Earth Horizon* that "folk theater" was being created in the Midwest and Greenwich Village, and identifies her plays with more successful dramas, such as *The Green Pastures* and *Porgy*. She lectured on folk theater at the University of California, both northern and southern branches. George Pierce Baker, Director of the Yale University Department of Drama, in 1930 invited her to speak upon the religious folk dramas found in New Mexican Spanish manuscripts. Alexander Dean produced some of the plays. Her folk dramas as well as scripts for stage plays remain in the collections catalogued under her name at the Huntington Library. One of these manuscripts, entitled *The Vacuum*, was given a premier by the *Delight Makers* of New Mexico Highlands University on July 5, 1935. The play presents the conflict between a newspaper editor and a business man who has bribed a City Council member in order to obtain a street car franchise. The editor's public conscience is stronger than his personal morality, which presents a weapon to his foes in dealing with relationships among the characters in the play. If Mary Austin had learned from the expertise offered to her by Elmer Harris, Winthrop Ames, George Foster Platt, and Thomas Wood Stevens, she might have become a leading playwright. However, whatever the cause, she failed to profit sufficiently from her successes or disappointments. *Letter 16* records a moment when her optimism was justified.

_____ **16**

THE NEW THEATRE
Sixty-second Street and Central Park West,
New York   September 13th, 1910.

My dear Mrs. Austin:
    I have received the last act of THE ARROW MAKER. To my
thinking this is thoroughly successful. I get a real throb and dramatic
thrill, and I feel perfectly sure that it is now all right. I sincerely congratulate you. I will have some copies made immediately, as you suggest
and will give one to Miss Crawford.
    That lady is very busy at present with THE BLUE BIRD rehearsals
which are now coming thick and fast, but I look forward to seeing you
again before long.
    Ought you not to be sending me an account for your passage money
and expenses while at work on the play? I am quite ready to remit at
any time.
    Please don't forget to continue to "make medicine" that we may find
the right "Chisera."

                              Sincerely yours,
                              Winthrop Ames
Mrs. Mary Austin,
Baldwin,
L.I., N.Y.

_____

        Lincoln Steffens (1866-1936) visited the colony at Carmel after
the San Francisco earthquake and fire in April of 1906. Like Elmer Harris, he
was a graduate of the University of California at Berkeley. He had already
earned fame through his book *The Shame of the Cities* (1904), in which he told
the story of crime and poverty in urban centers of the United States. He had just
completed his manuscript exposing corruption in six eastern and midwestern
states under the title *The Struggle for Self Government* (1906). Four years later,
Mary Austin wrote a novel in which she placed a reformer who could be identified with Steffens and the outlook he held toward governments and their aims.

The book was called *Outland* (1910). It was published in England when she made her first visit there. The setting for the novel is a beautiful place on a seacoast where artists and intellectuals have formed a community. They encounter the Woodlanders, who are the natives already living there. The new colonizers plan a life in harmony with nature. If Steffens is the sociologist named Herman in the novel, he speaks for a society which is founded on such principles as Steffens espoused, that is, a system adjusting wealth, labor, and the means of production to the common good.

As a companion for Herman, the author introduces a woman English professor named Mona. Identification of Mona with Mary Austin is easily made. *Letter 17*, written by Steffens, has a tone sufficiently intimate to support friendship between the two writers. However, Mary Austin in a later novel created a character that also has been identified with Steffens and the portrait is not as complimentary. This fictional creation is Adam Frear, the lecturer and reformer in *No. 26 Jayne Street* (1920). In this story, Frear is presented as a social radical and war correspondent, who in the opinion of two women characters in the novel fails to translate his proclamations of social democracy into personal relations with either of them. In *The Letters of Lincoln Steffens* (1938), there is a document dated December 25, 1910, in which Steffens states to one of his sisters: "I've been seeing Mary Austin, the author of *The Land of Little Rain*, *The Flock*, *Lost Borders*, etc. She is an odd but interesting woman." The letterhead is "Little Point" at Cos Cob, on Lond Island Sound, where Steffens was living with his first wife, Josephine Bontecou. She died there on January 7, 1911.

Letter 17 must have been mailed to Mary Austin when she arrived in New York to attend rehearsals for *The Arrow Maker*. George Sterling wrote to her in New York on June 28, 1911 (see *Letter 15*). Steffens' account of the Sacramento River conveys his nostalgia for the stream as it flows through vineyards and fruit orchards. He was born in San Francisco, but grew up in the capital city of California, where his parents moved when he was a child. The *Autobiography* (1931) describes his boyhood in considerable detail; then develops less fully the postgraduate years in Europe; and expands his professional life in the eastern United States and again in Europe. How curious that the period he spent in Carmel is never mentioned!

Mary Austin's correspondence has only a few addiitonal items from Lincoln Steffens. One is a note addressed to her at "The Players," 16 Gramercy Park, New York, October 28, 1914, in which he informs her that he may be out of the city when she arrives, but will return in a week. Another note, marked "Wednesday," without a date, acknowledges hearing from her and expresses regret that she is not feeling well. He offers to call upon her whenever she is ready to receive him. A final postcard, dated December 23, 1914, bears a cancellation mark "N Y P O Hud. Term. Paquebot," but carries no message at all. On the picture side of the card is a scene marked "Entrada de la Alameda, Veracruz."

So ended a friendship which had begun in Carmel, found renewal in New York City, and apparently ended there. Lincoln Steffens, with his second wife, Ella Winters, returned to Carmel in 1927 to work on his autobiography, which appeared four years later. He does not mention Mary Austin in the book. When her autobiography appeared one year after his, she refers to Steffens only by name in a list of those who arrived at Carmel when the community began.

_____ 17

Sacramento, Cal.
May 8, 1911

My dear Mary Austin:

There are poppies, fields of them, and there's a blue flower which sometimes blushes through the blush of red, which is lovely as any other conflict of emotions. And I have seen miles upon miles of such beauty. It is California—in the country. But I am here in a small city, and here the impression is one of roses, all sorts of roses, and in all shapes and conditions. They front the little houses, trimmed and prim, and then again they have got away and scramble all over the place. I saw one old neglected garden, where the roses had filled the whole yard and worked all up through all the trees till the whole place was a mess of loveliness. No doubt some gardener will some day come along and tame it all. He certainly will have to do something if he is to save the orange trees and the palms. But, as it stands, this place is the most winning argument for anarchy that I ever saw.

You are wrong about me and the sorrow. I do not want to nourish it. I felt the temptation to do so. There was, there is a pull off in that direction. But I didn't want it so, and I don't. No, we shall never talk of that.

Brother Lawrence has come. I took off the wrappings, but I have not read the book. I'll wait till I am off on my travels again. And that will be tomorrow. I go down to San Francisco, then, by the boat, so as to see the old river; and the fruit lands along its banks; and the coolies, and the East Indians, who have come here, I think, since you went away. They are new to me. I am to ride with the pilot, and hear his stories of the olden days and the new. It will be pleasant to listen when I know that I need not sit down afterwards to write. And after a few days in San Francisco, I am going South to your country; no, to the enemies of your country—to Los Angeles. I shall take a week there, then start for the East again via S.F. and Portland. Oregon has some great men for to see, but I want really to see that cut of the land which the Oregon Short Line goes through. I want to see the United States before I die, and I mean the land; the country; the face of the good earth.

There is one passage in your letter which I wish very explicitly to answer or, rather, to respond to. It is that about writing to somebody. I know what that need is. I used to have it. I haven't it now; I don't like to write letters. And I think I know the reason why; or the two reasons. I'll tell you what they are someday. But they are peculiar to me; I mean that I have them and you have not. But I have left a deep sympathy for the feeling you express, and I wish you to know that I shall read all that you care to write, especially in that mood, with more understanding than may appear. For I think I can understand. I certainly want to understand. I'd rather a thousand times understand than be understood. For which again there are reasons; and not merely smart ones either. One of them is that my whole training has been to understand; to get things that are outside myself. We are opposites in this respect. But I must say to you sincerely, and earnestly, that if you wish to put yourself down on paper you may do so with me and be sure, oh, absolutely sure, that you will be read as I would be read—with the wish only to understand.

And I do not show letters, of course; nor do I keep those that should not be kept. Letters are a place for half-thoughts.

As for me, I am feeling better, but I have not yet had that itch to write which is the sign of health. You know.

> Yours, warmly,
> *Lincoln Steffens*

The poet George Sterling (1869-1926) receives more attention in Mary Austin's autobiography than any other personality in the Carmel community. For her, he seems to have symbolized the spirit of freedom and inspiration which was spurred by the rugged beauty of the Monterey peninsula. He was almost Mary's age, but her descriptions of his boundless energy and soaring spirit make him seem to be ten years her junior. Sterling was the son of a well-to-do physician in Sag Harbor, Maine. He attended private as well as public schools and persevered for three years in a small college in Maryland; then came to Oakland, California, to serve from 1898 to 1908 as secretary to an uncle who had succeeded in the business of insurance and real estate. During that time, Sterling established himself as a writer of poetry that was widely published and soon collected in two volumes, *The Testimony of the Suns* (1903) and *A Wine of Wizardry* (1908). Later works were to include *Lilith* (1919) and *Rosamund* (1920), both dramas written in verse. He was a charter member of the Carmel colony, building two houses there, the second of which had a large central room with a high ceiling and a big fireplace, a wide porch in front, and an assembly place in back enclosed by a ring of trees marked by animal skulls.

Sterling dressed in shirts with open collars, loose-fitting jackets, trousers with long, heavy hose and boots, and an omnipresent cap, a type of headpiece that seemed to appeal to Jack London and a number of other men who appear in the photographs taken of outdoor groups. His activities ranging the forest, climbing cliffs, challenging the surf are dramatized in *Outland*, where Mary Austin portrays him as Ravenutzi, one of the original natives of the place, who looked like a faun and had the instincts of a wild creature but the intellect and will of a man. In *Letter 18*, Sterling tells Mary Austin that the players of the Forest Theater would like to dramatize her successful first novel. He implies that he might develop the script from the plot of *Isidro* (1905), but he is confident that to find lines for actors in the book would be preferable to devising a play entirely by himself. Since the novel deals with a neophyte priest in the days of the old Carmel Mission, the outdoor setting of the Forest Theater would be ideal. The book was not used because eager playwrights showed up to volunteer their plays. Sterling was called upon to appear in some of them but not to supply dramatic material.

Ambrose Bierce (1842-1914), who visited Carmel in the summers, was mentor, guide, and friend of younger men in the San Francisco literary set. He grew to manhood in Meigs County, Ohio, but left to serve in the Civil War. When that conflict ended, he went to San Francisco where he first worked in the United States Mint, then began a newspaper career on the *Argonaut* with assignment as correspondent for the Washington *American*. Professional advancement led to a column on the *San Francisco Examiner*, where he began to write stories about mining camps, tales about soldiers, and comments about humanity in general. His biting wit earned such fame that he became literary dictator to a coterie of young Bohemians. Author of such iconoclastic works as *The Cynic's Word Book* (1906), later entitled *The Devil's Dictionary*, he earlier had written books of great sympathy, such as *Tales of Soldiers and Civilians* (1891). Austin indicates in *Earth Horizon* that Sterling felt that Bierce was not her type. She does not challenge the statement, contributing her own opinion that Bierce often exaggerated his points of view, presenting them with what she called "apocolyptic gestures."

Bierce's quarrel with society was personal. He was a malcontent. Jack London revolted against society from an ideological position. He had become a socialist and planned to control capitalism with socialistic programs. Bierce and London, therefore, were not compatible. Sterling's friendship for each was often strained. Ambrose Bierce retained a loyal following until the time of his strange journey into Mexico. This trip was made in 1913, during the time of the glorified Mexican bandit-leader Pancho Villa. Bierce may have been the victim of one of Villa's raids. Carlton or Carlt Bierce was the nephew of the famed journalist and storyteller, and Lora was the nephew's wife. Sterling had often urged Bierce to build a house in Carmel, but the man was forever on the move, sending his letters from San Francisco, Washington, D. C., New York, London, and elsewhere.

There are no letters from Bierce in the Austin Correspondence, nor any from Gertrude Atherton (1857-1948), also mentioned in *Letter 18*. Atherton's stories, collected in *Before the Gringo* (1894), and her novel *Rezanov* (1906) drew successfully upon Spanish life in California for her fiction as did Mary Austin for *Isidro*. Atherton was older than Austin and had married into an aristocratic Spanish family that had transferred a fortune from Chile to California. She pioneered in writing biographical novels, such as *The Conqueror* (1902), which tells the story of Alexander Hamilton. She also wrote fiction of wide appeal, of which *Black Oxen* (1923) is the best-known novel. As a regional task, she completed two volumes dealing with her home state, *The Splendid Idle Forties* (1902) and *California, An Intimate History* (1915). Her autobiography, *The Adventures of a Novelist* (1932), appeared n the same year as Mary Austin's *Earth Horizon*. In their life stories, neither of California's most distinguished women mentions the other.

"The Jinks" reference in *Letter 18* names the annual entertainment presented by members of the Bohemian Club of San Francisco to other members and guests. Three years before this letter, that is, on July 27, 1907, the Bohemians produced a play written by Sterling. His theme was the triumph of good fellowship over Mammon and the Spirit of Care. Such entertainments as these were offered at an encampment on the Russian River in Sonoma County north of San Francisco. Herman Scheffauer, a guest at "The Jinks," was a young architect who qualified for the Carmel group because he was a protégé of Bierce. Scheffauer had traveled in Europe and was bohemian enough to enjoy life at Carmel. James Hopper, mentioned in this letter, is the author of *Letters 22* and *23*, which will make his place among the Carmelites (as they chose to call themselves) abundantly clear. Nora May French, a San Francisco poetess ill with tuberculosis, was befriended by Hopper, Sterling, and their families. She visited often in Carmel, where she found surroundings more congenial than at home with her sister. Unhappy in her love affairs and depressed by failure to win fame as a writer, she committed suicide at Carmel on November 14, 1907.

Time has dated the diction and imagery in Sterling's poetry. A disciple of Coleridge, he failed to match his master's literary background or sophistication in taste and judgment. The poetic dramas composed by Sterling fare better today as reading matter. Exaggerated lyricism may be accepted as emotional release. Theodore Dreiser, in his introduction to *Lilith*, calls the drama richer in thought than any dramatic poem with which he is familiar in American literature. The heroine, a beautiful and ageless siren, who betrays the hero, along with his father, wife, and friend, views all of life as illusion, and truth as just a dream before life ends. A troubador sings that only love is rewarding and only lovers know what it is to live. Yet the tragic thread of love for Lilith brings only death and destruction. This doctrine of disillusionment is explicit in *Letter 18*.

_____ 18

Carmel, Cal.,
Sept. 1st, 1910

Dear Mary:

I'm so glad that you'll let us use "Isidro"! I have been telling our crowd here that it's just the thing we want. Had we been unable to obtain it, I fear I'd have had to write some sort of mission-play myself, a thing I've little or no time to do, as I've been loafing all summer.

I'm awfully glad that the gods, great and small, *have* been good to you. They show discernment. I suppose you came to New York to put on a play. You have my heartiest wishes for its success, though it is likely to be too good for the public pig of America.

I fear I don't take as much interest in our Forest Theatre project as I should—probably because I don't care for acting as an art (if it be one). But they seem to want my advice; and the Lord knows that that is inexpensive. The main trouble here is that we've so small a community to draw on for actors and actresses, and even such as are available are pretty bad. We had a mighty pleasant summer. Ambrose Bierce came here in May, and we spent ten days with him, his brother, and Carlt and Lora Bierce in Yosemite: I'd never been there.

I found the place overwhelming, and sha'n't attempt to "handle" it. It's plain to see why no one else has ever come within ten thousand miles of doing so, either. Hundreds of years may not bring the man.

Gertrude Atherton was there just before we arrived, and was afterwards quoted as saying that the place was "much over-rated," a statement that gave me gooseflesh. She'll never get a chance to say that of Heaven (as no doubt she would), for that remark bars her.

I've thought too much about the interstellar spaces to be stampeded by mere size; but when beauty and majesty meet, the effect is tremendous. Coleridge gives just an inkling of it in his noble "Hymn before Dawn in the Valley of Chamouni."

I took Ambrose to the Jinks with me—he was the Club's guest—and he enjoyed the grove-play, saying that it was a thousand times better than he expected it would be. While there he met and became friendly with Jack London, to my joy and surprise—as he'd been knocking some of Jack's ideas and practices rather vigorously. But he said to Lora and Carrie: "I tell you, London's all right." He remains implacable in his hostility to Scheffauer, though.

We had him here for a week, last month, and he was enthusiastic over Carmel. He seemed to like especially Point Lobos and its rock-pools, though perhaps steamed mussels (as he's a bit of a gourmet) ran them a close second. He's back in Oakland now, reading proof for the fourth volume of his "Collected Works," which are rocks on which Time's sea, I think, will go white for many a century.

There's no special news. We are all extremely well. Bob Haughey is dead: he leaned too far from a second-story window, fell, and got concussion of the brain, never regaining consciousness—at least while alive. He was sober at the time. This was up in Fruitvale.

Jimmy Hopper is (as doubtless you know) on the French coast for the time being. He says he "wasted" two months this summer on an essay he calls "The Suicide of Man." I'd like to read it. He seems gradually to be reconciling himself to his matrimonial fate, probably because nothing is ever as bad as a man expects it to be. (I've heard that *women* are disagreeably surprised by child-birth.) He has no notion as to when he'll see Carmel again, but wants very much to see it.

Dear woman! it was good no end of you to try to sell my poems. But I don't remember actually asking you to do so. If I remember correctly, I merely asked what show you thought they might have with the English magazines, as I expected to send a few to them. If I really asked you to try to sell some of them, I must have been partially intoxicated when I wrote, as in my sober senses I'd not dream of putting you to such trouble, and still less dream of having my adored Wells be bothered by such matters. It was this way: some of my friends had been selling poems (already sold in America) to the "Thrush" and other periodicals, and it seemed to me a shame to throw away money that at the time (not *now*) I really was in need of. So I sent out a few of my best, and got one of them back; but the magazines for the most part didn't even send *back* my verses, though I enclosed stamped and addressed envelopes. That I didn't mind, except in the case of the "Thrush," which is said to be "run" by poets, and which had accepted work by friends of mine which was infinitely inferior to that which *I* sent them.

Well, it's all right. I was only after temporarily needed money. As for any extension of my local and rather tenuous fame, I must own to more than apathy, as I find what I have flatly a nuisance. So real fame, I think, would be torment.

Probably the trouble is that with me my art is entirely secondary. To live and be happy are my only real concerns, and when I write what it gives me joy to write, I care to get it published because it's *mine*, and I don't want someone else to steal it some day. No one could, if I were not addicted to giving away MSS to my friends, who, doubtless, occasionally pass them on to *their* friends.

I'm not surprised that the English editors don't take to my verses, for when I see what they print I notice that they run mostly to stuff that treats mainly of the scenery or traditions of England and her possessions. It's only to be expected.

As to what *you* write of my work, I've no doubt you're correct, at least from your point of view; and I'll not start a discussion as to "what is Truth." So far as *I'm* concerned, I try to express only beauty, beauty unattainable and unimaginable, and in art your words "efficiency" and "achievement" are meaningless to me, except insomuch as they apply to such success as I may have in glimpsing that beauty—call it sterile if you will. Of course I may be suffering from incurable immaturity, and I cheerfully confess I'm leagues less human than you—and Wells, and Browning. But I'm doing (so far as my endowments permit) just what I want to do, and I know just about what that is. I took the liberty of reading to Mr. Bierce what you said in your letter of those things, and found him in entire accord with what I've written on this page and the page preceding. I suppose that he's naturally a bit biased in my favor; but still, I've not yet found anywhere such a judge of poetry as he. And we agree that we find in what to us is the highest poetry an absence of "purpose, end or care." Take Kubla Khan or the Eve of St. Agnes, for instance.

I did get a theme into "Duandon"—a big theme to the man of forty or less; but I'm about ready to apologize. After all, what really mattered is only some of its phrases.

I've read Outland again, revelling in its beauty. As for its esoteric part, I fear I get only hints. So I must wait till we can talk it over together, unless you care to be, in black and white, more definite. An article in the S. F. Call speaks of the book as being satiric. Yet it seemed far from being bitter enough to be that: gently satiric, maybe.

I know well enough what Wells' trouble was—Agnes Tobin told a friend of mine. As *she* is a so-called aristocrat, she is not a friend of H. G. W. I've no ethical quarrel with what he did; but I think he was a chump to take such chances of letting the pack at his throat. It's always waiting, always prepared to leap at the exposed flesh. Human beings make me think of a rock-rolling episode of my early days. One of the rocks went farther than we dreamed it could, and smashed the knee of a cow's foreleg. The other cows promptly began to gore her.

We've sold about 300 of the 500 copies of Nora May's book. I've personally sold over 90, and am taking another 100. I hope you got the copy I sent to you. We receive enthusiastic comments on her work.

Autumn is here, and the poison-oak's "burning bush" is everywhere, almost. The days are divine. No one, nothing, can ever get me away from Carmel. The rest is illusion.

But good hunting to *you*!

George Sterling

Sterling's career as a poet reached a peak with the publication of his third book of poems, *The House of Orchids* (1911), to which he refers in *Letter 19.* All told, there are twenty-three items from Sterling in the Mary Austin correspondence. They cover a period from September 1, 1910 to January 12, 1913. Eighteen of the documents are poems. The letter dated February 14,

1910, also contains a note from Upton Sinclair addressed to Sterling, who has penciled at the end, "You needn't return it." Sinclair states that he has dispatched the manuscript of a novel to Jack London for his reading and is sure London will tell Sterling about it. This assumption may have been based upon the knowledge that Sterling read many of London's manuscripts and reread them in publisher's proof. Sinclair mentions having articles accepted by *Cosmopolitan* and *Contemporary Review*, articles dealing with his experience in fasting. He asks Sterling to tell Austin that her *Land of Little Rain* puts all the nature books he has ever read "out of court."

Edwin Markham (1852-1950)—whose verses devoted to "The Man with the Hoe" and "Lincoln, The Man of the People" may have been as effective in bringing social change as Sinclair's prose—became a member of the Charles F. Lummis circle when Austin taught in Los Angeles. He remained her friend, as his *Letter 24* testifies. Why he urged Sterling to read the poetry of Anna Hempstead Branch (1875-1937) is unclear, for the quiet Connecticut versifier wrote chiefly of humble tasks that can glorify a life of order and discipline, as the titles of her books, *The Shoes That Danced* (1905) and *Rose of the Wind* (1910) illustrate. However, she had published a highly imaginative narrative poem called "Nimrod," in the year before Markham wrote his letter, but the plot of an Old Testament monarch who struggled against the wrath of Jehovah was scarcely the story to inspire Sterling however skilled the performance. The news in *Letter 19* that Hopper had sold a novel to the *Saturday Evening Post* must have cheered all his compatriots, for Hopper was well liked, as *Letters 21* and *22* will establish.

———— 19

Carmel, Cal.,
May 9th, 1911

Dear Mary:

My best thanks for your delightful "Arrow Maker"! I've read it but once, so far, as it arrived only last night; but even that preliminary reading shows me how big, dramatic, basic, vital and vividly human a thing it is. You have certainly "delivered the goods." Some of the sentences are unforgetable; the play as a whole is entirely unified, and its spiritual impact irresistible.

I should have sent you my congratulations two months ago, when you were so kind as to write to me. But at the time I was at London's, whither I had retired to endure a siege of uncommon mental stress, and I was not in a writing mood. Besides, I knew that you were being inundated with congratulations, and mine would hardly have been missed.

Yes, it's a big play, and I'm so glad it "landed." I saw but few criticisms; but I'm impervious even to those of praise. A criticism is almost invariably an indecent exposure (personal and monologic) of congenital ignorance. So why waste any more time on them than on other insect afflictions?

But so far as the critics went in laughing at Redding's absurd libretto, I'm with them. It is the holy limit.

I truly hope you can get out here this summer, if only to help Heron with his play. We've a pretty good crowd here now, though some of them fight shy of *me*, because they think I'm immoral—or unmoral: Grace Cooke, Vachell and the Bechdolts are the worst. I mean at disliking me.

I don't know *why* Mike Williams didn't answer your letter. He has been away from here since last autumn, however—mostly in Arizona and Mexico, and seems to have corresponded but little. My third book (which I had to give the rather decadent title of "The House of Orchids," etc.) came out last month. I'd send you one were I sure of your address. But the one I have is over two months old, and you move around pretty freely—and 3rd class mail isn't forwarded. If you'll let me know if this letter reaches you, and if I've the correct address, I'll forward a book at once.

I'm glad you saw Upton; but I can't discuss him. He's an amazing creature, and in good and bad ways. Wait till you see his last book, "Love's Pilgrimage"! Probably "sincere but not sound" is a good estimate of him. His wife has just sent me a lot of her poems to criticize. I prefer her work to his.

We were absent from Carmel during all March and April, and I'm only now getting back into the traces. I hardly know what to begin on— I was considering some short-stories—but for a while my neglected correspondence will fill many idle hours—I mean hours otherwise idle.

Markham wrote me a fine letter, mostly about that big poet, Anna Branch. Scheffauer has also sent me a most interesting letter from London, whither he's fled for good. New York's commercialism was too much for him, he says. He's having great success over *there*, if I'm to judge from his letter.

I've been owing Jimmy a letter since February. He's still in Paris, I believe, though one often hears rumors of his being in New York. He *did* write that his *wife* might spend the summer in California. He was doing well financially, at last accounts, and got $2,000, from the Sat. Even. Post for the serial rights of a novel he called "The Freshman."

Carmel is as beautiful as ever. The river, thanks to destructive floods in March, now disgorges at Mission Point—close up to the bank. This is an extremely late spring: I got wild strawberries on Apr. 23, last year—none in sight *now*. I've three acres put to potatoes—half a crop! I enclose a clipping that you may not have seen.

Well, I hope you'll find time to let me hear from you soon. In the meanwhile, "good hunting!"

George

More than eight months passed between *Letter 19* and *Letter 20* in George Sterling's correspondence with Mary Austin. Both of these letters were sent to her in New York City recovering (can it be said?) from the failure of her play *The Arrow Maker*. However, she was preparing the play for publication, and that was some satisfaction in the literary sense of the word. The play is eloquent on the printed page, and in the preface to the printed book, Austin says that she wrote the play to awaken the public to "the enormous and stupid waste of the gifts of women," an admission that concealed in the chisera's career was Mary Austin's own view that women were forced to become too subservient to the needs of men.

In *Letter 20*, Herbert Heron, whose last name appears in paragraph five, was a Los Angeles actor and playwright who helped to establish the Forest Theater at Carmel. He managed to construct the stage and to design the outdoor amphitheater. He also wrote a play called *Montezuma*, which provided opportunity for open air spectacle, but arguments among the members of the committee in charge delayed production of this play until 1914. Some of the others at Carmel who are mentioned in the letter are: Grace MacGowan Cooke and her sister Alice MacGowan, free-lance writers and survivors of Upton Sinclair's experiment in socialized living at Helicon's Hall, Englewood, New Jersey; Arthur H. Vachell, an English artist in residence at Carmel; Frederick Bechdolt, who had moved to Carmel in 1907 after prospecting in Alaska and Death Valley, but was now a married man settled into pounding the typewriter for a living; and Michael Williams, one of the most talented and fascinating characters in the community. Williams was called the "wild Irishman," but he settled into family life, pursued a search for soul fulfillment, and found it in conversion to Roman Catholicism. Ultimately he became the editor of *Commonweal*, the Catholic weekly journal. Williams is mentioned in a number of letters written by members of the Carmel inner circle. He seems to have been well liked and the subject of much conversation. His spiritual odessey is detailed in his account entitled *The Book of the High Romance* (1918).

Letter 20 was written from the home of Frank C. Havens, Sterling's uncle, at Sag Harbor, Maine, where Sterling spent his youth. The letter again underlines the tie to Jimmy Hopper, both during and after their comradeship at Carmel. Mary Austin's suffrage work, to which he alludes, is fully described in *Earth Horizon*, where she first writes of walking with suffragettes she met in England during 1908. She states that Anne Martin, an American, got herself arrested for obstructing traffic and had to be bailed out by Herbert Hoover, who maintained an office in London while engaged in worldwide engineering activities from 1901 to 1914.

Sterling in *Letter 20* reflects his continuing admiration for Ambrose Bierce and H. G. Wells, plus his contacts with Michael Williams and Upton Sinclair. In addressing Mary Austin as "Coyote Woman," he is harkening back to her play about the Indian medicine man as discussed in the letters from Elmer Harris. This is the first of Sterling's letters to Austin in which he signs his nickname "Greek," as conferred upon him by his friends. The "O'Hara" to whom he refers may be John O'Hara Cosgrove, editor of the San Francisco weekly called *The Wave*, in which some of Jack London's early stories had appeared. The novelist, Frank Norris, before his rise to fame, was Cosgrove's editorial assistant on *The Wave*.

Upton Sinclair (1878-1968), one of the most effective and prolific advocates for social reform in modern times, visited Carmel in 1908 during the period which Sterling reports in *Letter 20*. Such followers as the MacGowan sisters, Michael Williams, and Sterling himself were drawn to Sinclair. Others were alienated by his zealotry. Sinclair's exposé of the management and operation of the Chicago stockyards in his book *The Jungle* (1906) was followed by exposure of journalism, *The Brass Check* (1919), education, *The Goose Step* (1923), the Teapot Dome scandal, *Oil* (1927), the Sacco-Vanzetti case, *Boston* (1927). So effective were Sinclair's campaigns that in 1934 he received the Democratic nomination for governor of California. He failed, however, to be elected.

_____ **20**

Sag Harbor, N. Y.,
June 28th, 1911.

Dear Coyote-Woman:

I'm very glad you're still in New York, but sorry your letter announcing so had to go to Carmel, as otherwise we could have seen you on the 16th, when we were in N. Y. for the day.

We hope to go up again before long. My uncle is a jealous host, so we must stick here till he makes one of his flying trips to California. What about *you* coming *here* then (it will be *very* soon) for a few days. We will let you write daily if you wish. It's cool and pleasant, and we have two fine powerboats (one 87 ft. long) to go on cruise with. I can have O'Hara here too—met him on the 16th. He has just sent me a noble sonnet, written to *me*, of which I'm mighty proud.

I didn't send you my book because I wasn't sure of your address. I've one here for you; also one for Jimmy. I hope it's true he's coming, but don't know anything about it, as I've owed him a letter for five months, and surmise he has a mad mit me. Yes—I saw reports of your suffrage work. You're a heroine, all right! Better try to convince *me*. I saw that Collier's article too. Oh! the critics are brain-whores, all right! I got a *good* review in the last Times, and if it hadn't been for some advertising of the book that my publisher had given them, I bet it would have been a roast, as they hate all us Biercians. I sent the book to Wells and got a kind letter from him. He's now in France.

I've just exchanged letters with that erratic "flame" (as Jimmy calls him) Mike W. Don't understand what you mean by saying his wife is successful—yes I do too! Sinclair sent his book to me too—also to Bierce and to London (*they* will not even notice it and him!). I wrote him a long letter about it, but it was such a roast that he'll not dare quote it. Of course the advt. was all he really wanted from us: for such an uncompromising idealist he's a pretty fair business man. Most reformers are, I suppose. Carrie joins me in hoping you will come. Please write soon.

Faithfully as ever,
Greek.

George Sterling and his wife Carrie, after happy years at Carmel, were divorced in 1914, and both suffered from severe depression afterward. Carrie remarked to Mary Austin in a letter dated December 16, 1914, after discussing her life with Sterling: "We are too near the cave-man state yet to have a perfect or even near-perfect mate." She expressed good will for her former husband and happiness in her new found work and way of life. She had been offered employment by her husband's aunt, Mrs. Havens, who owned a picture gallery and frame shop. She had met many old friends in San Francisco. She thanks Mary for offering her the Carmel house, adding that she may be able to go to Carmel at some future time. But four years later she committed suicide by swallowing cyanide. Sterling took the same means to end his life in 1926.

Such parallelism seems to confirm the song of the troubador in *Lilith*, but scarcely could be construed as the outcome of the years of companionship the Sterlings enjoyed or the measure of Sterling's capacity for friendship, or the charm of his personality. Lines in his poetry reflect views of the fleeting beauty in nature and an austere view of fate, but both his life and work contradict this pessimism. His letters, as well, refute this view through expressions of generosity, sympathy, and love.

The Sterling letters belong with those of James Hopper (1876-1956), for the two men exchanged a friendship that was like an invigorating tonic for both of them. Sterling was the older, but in some ways he seemed younger, for he was slender, even ascetic, in appearance. Hopper was athletic and rugged. He had won fame as an athlete in both football and rowing at the University of California at Berkeley. Yet he also had edited the college weekly magazine and published his first short stories there. Despite a law degree and having been admitted to the bar, he took a job as reporter on the *San Francisco Chronicle*, later joining Will Irwin as a reporter on the *The Wave*. When the earthquake came, he was working on the *San Francisco Call* and left a record for reporting that for timelessness and skill has never been surpassed. In his literary career, he produced six novels and 450 short stories. *The Letters of Lincoln Steffens* contain several written communications which refer to Hopper. On May 3, 1913, Steffens confided to a friend:

I am to dine with James Hopper, the shortstory teller, who writes like Conrad, and a lot of his artist friends. They come up from Carmel and Piedmont, Marin Co., and the tenements, and at some queer Mexican joint, meet and talk and play. I have been with others of them before. They are pleasant; they are exhilarating. But so is San Francisco.

Hopper collaborated with Fred Bechdolt in writing a novel about prison life. The title, *9009*, was drawn from the address of the cottage he built at Carmel. The book was published in 1908, and republished in 1968 when Clarence

Gohdes, a professor at Duke University, wrote an introduction which identified the story as one of a group which he called "muckraking novels," those that dealt with political and social evils in the United States. The term "muckraker" became current after President Theodore Roosevelt used it in 1906 referring to those in American society who used corrupt means to acquire political and economic power. Roosevelt borrowed the figure from the Second Book in *Pilgrim's Progress*, where the wife of the hero, Christian, beholds a man absorbed in raking through the filth of material things for his profit. Reformers, such as Lincoln Steffens, and novelists, such as James Hopper, reversed the meaning of the term, as they raked filth and muck to clean it up.

Hopper's novel vividly portrays the need for reform in the prison system of the country. Prisoner 9009 has been sentenced for burglary and assault. His name is John Collins, and his term is for eight years in a prison built in the Bay area of northern California. 9009 resolves to become a model prisoner and to shorten his term by good behavior. His good intentions are frustrated by a vicious guard and by trusties who are stool pigeons. He discovers that the whole prison is a vast center of espionage and torment, of stalking, spying, treachery, and betrayal. The action in the plot shows how the experience of Collins turns him into a monster who, in desperation, contrives to escape and is hunted down and killed by the same law officers who placed him in confinement. The book ends with the flight of Collins into the high Sierras, where golden-hazed valleys, dark canyons, and snowy summits form a beautiful backdrop to the cruel and tragic end.

James Hopper's *Letter 21* continues the friendship established with Mary Austin years earlier. Just what "invisible line" she may have crossed is not explained, but he makes clear his fondness for her and continues in the most informal way. The "autobiographical novel" she was writing was probably *A Woman of Genius*, which was published the next year. The book enjoyed considerable success, as it traced the life of an actress whose unconventional behavior destroys one marriage, complicates a romance, and ends in a marriage of convenience that adjusts to her career. The story was as close to the expression of sex in fiction as Mary Austin ever came. In *Letter 21*, the names of Carmelites appear who have been introduced previously in letters by Sterling.

One of those named who was not a Carmelite was Joseph Conrad. Mary Austin received an invitation to visit the Conrads at their home south of London. Herbert Hoover drove her there, and when Conrad greeted her he said that she was one of the few who had written to him from America. The jackets of some of her books quote him as saying, "I stand on the shore and make my cry into the dark, and only now and then a cry comes back to me." She corroborates this in *Earth Horizon*. She also saw H. G. Wells and Bernard Shaw. For a report of her conversation with Wells, see Mary Austin to H. G. Wells, *Letter 107*.

Although she did not meet Rudyard Kipling, she would have enjoyed him more than Hopper's comment warrants, for in *Earth Horizon* she indicates that Kipling's tales were an inspiration for her, probably in such stories as those found in *The Trail Book* and *One Smoke Stories*.

———— **21**

American Express Co.   Paris, France
11 rue Scribe   September 1911

Dear Old (this is affectionate and not taking you at your word)
Mary:

I have your letter of the 17th— which I was mighty glad to get. I've been wondering a good deal about you the last year. I still am for that matter—though I don't believe you have passed that "invisible line" as completely as you say, in that your heart is broken as thoroughly as you believe. You can't make *me* sentimental, Mary Austin; and I know very well that you ain't got no heart—only a typewriter, just like me.

I'm glad it has been clicking (and palpitating) so well, anyway. The Lost Borders I know. I think it's a *fine, fine* thing and with The Land of Little Rain and The Flock will make a trilogy of which any writer, past and present, would be proud. Santa Lucia, which I read since we parted, I did not like. But I'll bet that autobiographical novel will be corking. You're intensely subjective, I think—guess I'm making you mad; so will change subject.

I've been doing *rotten* work or no work at all this year. I suspect, in fact, that I haven't done anything worthwhile since I left Carmel. I need some fanatical fool admirer like George near me or I lose all faith in myself. I've started five stories this month, none of which I've finished— from sheer disgust. I've been morally and intellectually lonely ever since I left the Outland. Remember what good talks we used to have, you and I and George? And later there was Nora May and Bechdolt—good old Beck. You'd like him. He's coming through in great style and I found him.

Paris isn't doing anything to me (I haven't the time) nor I to it. I like it though—I like the liberty you have here and the ferocious intellectual *frankness* of the French mind. But I have but to poke my nose in the newspapers to feel rightly humble. Everyone can write here better than I can or ever will—And, say, don't the American magazines look *funny*, eh, Mary?

Mike Williams, a temperamental, irresponsible whom I imported into Carmel (and who burns secret incense to your art, by the way) got out a paper there which he sent me. It was chuck-full of poetry! Real poetry.

I wonder if you've seen Conrad. I've always had a secret and tense desire to tell that man some time what I think of his work. He must be a singularly *lonely* soul. And Wells—have you seen Wells? At present he seems to me the star of hope for the whole world. Bernard Shaw must be interesting; but I wouldn't care a D. D. for James—and not much for Kipling (that's heresy, I suppose).

I haven't quite decided what to do next. At present I'm *Busted*. But I may leave Mrs. H. and the children here (Elizabeth is beginning to talk French) for the winter and take a jump to New York to stir up my editors and my agent. If I do, I may go via London and go call on you—. How would that be? We'd have a good pow-wow; you could poke me head-first into the den of your lions; I'd bum a week and then off for the U. S. Tell me what you think of that.

I expect to become a father again in February. Guess I was meant to be a Father, not an artist—which makes me mad as hell. However, it won't matter ten thousand years hence (you see that I'm leaving a margin of a few milleniums for the survival of my books).

I'd like to go back to Carmel and live in a little cabin and have a horse and work. (Carmel is the center of the world to me.) And then once in every year or two sally forth and bum over the world. But I guess I can't.

I've written a darned sight more than you've written to me—so no more. Be of good cheer—and go back to Carmel when you're through the book—or aren't you ever going back? Anyway, let me know of your movements.

> Yours,
> *James Hopper*

Letter 22 is dated only by month and day, but the year may be added from events to which the letter refers. The Carmel theater group produced the play *Fire* on July 26, 1913, which is close enough to the August he cites for the year of writing. John Hilliard was briefly associated with the drama group, and Bechdolt is mentioned in Sterling's *Letter 19* as a permanent associate of the Carmel colony. Hopper was Bechdolt's close friend, as illustrated by their collaboration in the novel *9009*. *Letter 22* may have been forwarded to Austin at the National Arts Club, an address in use before she located an apartment in the city. The early group at Carmel was breaking up about 1913. Mary Austin went to San Francisco to write publicity for the Panama Pacific Exposition which opened in 1915. Hopper had been away but returned in 1915. Sterling's wife separated from him, returned and left again, then filed for divorce on January 5, 1914 after which Sterling went to New York.

———— 22

Carmel, California, February 26 [1913?]

Dear Mary Austin—

I wrote to you a month ago on this same matter, but addressed you Tucson, Arizona, and probably you have not received the letter.

The matter is this. There has been here a change in the theatrical situation. A new society has combined and taken in all the other societies and individual elements in an effort to have a real community theatre. Everybody is in and pulling to make this a success.

The Play Committee, elected at the first meeting of this new Forest Theatre, and which is given much power by the constitution, consists of John Hilliard, Fred Bechdolt, and myself (chairman). Among our powers are those of choosing the plays to be put on, and the producers thereof.

We would like to put on in August your play Fire. And we would like still more to have you come out to produce it.

Please let us know what you think of this. If you can give us a definite answer (affirmative, we hope) could you wire it to me to save time? We are anxious to get our year's program all settled early.

I am addressing this Carmel, to have it forwarded by the local office.

We are not able to pay much for producing this year, but I think we can offer you one hundred dollars.

Sincerely, and hoping to have soon a favorable answer.

James Hopper

A twelve-year period elapses between *Letter 22* and *Letter 23*. On February 21, 1924, James Hopper wrote *Letter 23* from the Hotel Lafayette in New York City and addressed it to Mary Austin's home in Santa Fe, New Mexico. The letter conveys information about the burning of George Sterling's house at Carmel with everything he had left in it. Hopper was selling stories and sketches to both the *Saturday Evening Post* and *Collier's*, with several novels appearing as well. An anthology of Hopper's work, entitled *Pepe*, was sponsored by the Book Club of California in 1937. All of these stories deal with the California scene. Hopper was chosen a council member of the Authors League of America and elected as president of the Authors Guild from 1929 to 1931. He and his family returned to live at Carmel, and to participate in the life of the community until the time of his death in 1956. Of the three associates, Sterling, Hopper, and London, Hopper was the most stable in exercising his talents and assisting his friends.

———— 23

Hotel Lafayette   Feb. 21, 1924
University Place
New York

Dear Mary:—
                    I have now the address of
George's sister
                    Mrs. Guy Liliancrantz
                    2936 Mc Clure St.
                    Oakland, California
        And I remember now you asked in your letter about pictures of the Carmel place.
    The house burned down two years ago and with it everything we had in it (which was everything he had) including all pictures. Yes, he took it over in 1914. We've been rebuilding it and Mattie writes the new place is about finished.
    Some day I'm going to take a look at that Santa Fe place and call on you. I don't know when that will be.
    Elizabeth is married—to a Stanford boy. They were both still in college when this happened. Maryan has just finished an extra year at

college (California) and is home resting up. She has one more X to take in May for a High School Teachers certificate. Jim is at the Monterey High School—a big boy—on the basket ball and track teams. Jane (nine years) is a little blonde devil, going to Sunset (Carmel) school.

With love,

J. H.

Austin affirms in *Earth Horizon* that Sterling, she, and London initiated the colony at Carmel, but Gertrude Atherton, the San Francisco novelist, Vernon Kellogg, a Stanford University scientist, and Arnold Genthe, a San Francisco photographer, were also residents in the area at the time. Genthe, in his autobiography, *As I Remember* (1936), relates one of the amusing incidents about Mary Austin in those early days. He offered to escort her home late one evening after a party in the neighborhood. The direction led through brush and trees, but Mary refused to be guided. She insisted that she had eyes like a cat and could see in the dark. Despite bumping into obstacles and plunging through the shrubbery, she refused to accept any help, insisting that both her instinct and eyesight were faultless. Genthe was amused, but resisted any further attempt to save her from blows or falling.

Neither Jack London nor his wife stayed at Carmel for any length of time. Charmian and he came down from their ranch called Valley of the Moon to visit on occasion with friends but they never owned a house there. Letters from the Londons in the Mary Austin Collection are dated in the period when she made her residence in New York City. These letters will, therefore, be presented in the next section of her chronology, entitled "The New York Projects." The same manner of dating will explain why letters from others who at one time lived in Carmel will appear in later sections of this book. These names include those of Sinclair Lewis, Edwin Markham, Percy MacKaye, Ernest Thompson Seton, the Robinson Jeffers, and Van Wyck Brooks. Brooks was a visitor in 1911, stayed through the summer, and in *Scenes and Portraits* (1954) described Carmel as "a wildwood with an operatic setting" which was inhabited by "every sort of anomalous type." He reported incidents of violence outside the immediate community which shattered the ambient calm.

Two visitors arrived at Carmel in the spring of 1910. They were introduced to the Sterlings by a friend, with the result that George and Carrie invited them to stay in the guest house. The guests, it turned out, were journalists from the *Los Angeles Times*: a literary editor, Willard Huntington Wright, and a woman cartoonist named Gale. Wright was a sophisticate who graduated from the *Times* to become editor of *Smart Set*. He subsequently wrote detective stories under the pseudonym of S. S. Van Dine and created the Philo Vance crime series. Little did the Sterlings suspect that the young woman who was their guest would cartoon George chopping wood while his mother called, "Come in, George, and help wash the dishes"; nor would Mary Austin have extended a welcome to strangers who would portray her in braids and a nightgown wandering through the piney woods; and Upton Sinclair may not have laughed to see himself holding a single tomato as a bird overhead uttered the word "Humph." The tomato must have satirized Sinclair's vegetarian diet.

Nicknames are always enlightening as sidelights upon personalities. Sterling and London signed themselves in letters as "Greek" and "Wolf"; Bierce was designated publicly as well as privately as "Bitter Bierce"; Harry Leon Wilson, a sojourner who does not appear in the Austin Collection, was cordially spoken of as "Old Ironsides"; and Mary Austin's associates sometimes spoke of her, inaudibly of course, as "God's mother-in-law." The entire group was covered in visual as well as written imagery by Huntington Wright's article entitled "Hotbed of Soulful Culture, Vortex of Erotic Erudition: Carmel in California, Where Author and Artist Folk are Establishing the Most Amazing Colony on Earth." That Mary Austin held no such view is shown by her tribute in *Earth Horizon* to Carmel as "a place that nurtured genius through its dramatic landscape and seascape, the mornings directed to work and the afternoons freed for climbing, walking, or swimming; the evenings brightened by driftwood fires, mussel roasts, and talks." Not many of the original Carmel group stayed there longer than a few years, but when they departed, others arrived. Jimmy Hopper stayed, and Lincoln Steffens returned when he wrote his autobiography a few years before his death. Robinson Jeffers came in 1914 and, once married and a father, never left his home, High Tor, for any length of time (see *Letter 97*). When some creative spirits left, they were replaced by others of like interests, but many of the newcomers were drawn by recreational ways of life or for retirement pursuits. The mixture of motives for living at Carmel-by-the-Sea still exists.

THE NEW YORK PROJECTS

III

New York City presented challenges to Mary Austin. Could she support herself by the use of her typewriter? Would she find a place in the numerous organizations there with outlets for lectures and publications? She had fought one battle against a metropolitan area, Los Angeles, and lost. New York was much larger and the need for battles much greater. She had lived in San Francisco, but at heart she was not a city-dweller. Most of her life had been spent in small communities: Carlinville, Illinois; Independence and Carmel, California. When she moved to New York City in 1912, the environs of Greenwich Village appealed to her. She could hardly build a wickiup there, but the park at Washington Square was a touch of nature. She remained a resident at various times in the National Arts Club at Gramercy Park; but institutions and small shops in the Village had much in common with groups everywhere. The schools, clubs, and churches were like those she had always known. She rented an apartment on Barrow Street not far from Washington Square.

One of the groups she joined was the National American Woman Suffrage Association. The president at this time was Anna Howard Shaw (1847-1919). Dr. Shaw was both a minister and a physician, as well as a champion of women at the polls. She had been, and remained, a feminist who knew the hostility toward women in professional life. Others who were members of the women's political front were Frances Perkins, represented by *Letter 56* in this collection, and Anne Martin (see the introduction to *Letter 38*). Mary Austin was active in publicity campaigns during this period, pursuing a career as journalist in the process. She renewed acquaintance with Will Irwin (1873-1946), who had used his background of newspaper days in California to write up the San Francisco earthquake for the *New York Sun*. Ryan Walker (1870-1932), when he edited the rotogravure section for the *New York Graphic*, became a new acquaintance. His cartoons adorn the many letters he exchanged with her. He contributed an interview to Mary Austin's *Everyman's Genius* (1923), as did Robert Edmond Jones, Fannie Hurst, Marianne Moore, and Bill Robinson, each of whom is represented by a letter in this book.

As a writer of fiction, Mary Austin developed eight novels: *Isidro* (1905), *Santa Lucia* (1908), *Outland* (1910), *A Woman of Genius* (1912), *The Lovely Lady* (1913), *The Ford* (1917), *No. 26 Jayne Street* (1920), and *Starry Adventure* (1933). Six of these narratives were written between 1912 and 1920, and were therefore created while she was living in New York or during occasional stays at Carmel. The letters in this period include correspondence with the novelists Jack London, William Allen White, Fannie Hurst, and Sinclair Lewis. Mary had known "Red" Lewis from the early Carmel period, and she continued to be on penmanship terms with him during her lifetime. He visited her on a number of occasions after she moved to Santa Fe. It can be pointed out, however, that the majority of letters she preserved during the early Carmel years were concerned with literary matters, whereas beginning with her life in New York her interests were of a broader sort, that is, political and social projects that occupied a larger part of her activity and writing time.

In *Earth Horizon*, Austin refers to Dr. Shaw as a reformer who lived with the old restrictions upon women, and was unable to keep pace with the younger generation of females. Austin ignores the fact that there would have been no younger suffragettes without the labors of such an extraordinary forerunner as Dr. Shaw, who became assistant to Susan B. Anthony (1820-1906), founder of the American Woman Suffrage Association, and took her place as president when Anthony retired in 1904. Anna Shaw learned early in life the lessons of self-reliance. Her father was a Scottish physician who came to Lawrence, Massachusetts, in 1849, and two years later brought his wife and six children to this country. He filed for a homestead in 1859, sending half his family to live in northern Michigan in a log cabin in order to prove the claim. His wife, two daughters (of whom Anna was the older), and a younger brother lived in the wilderness while Dr. Shaw and an older brother returned to Massachusetts. Anna first earned laurels as a public speaker in midwestern Methodist churches, defying the opposition to women ministers. In her autobiography, *The Story of a Pioneer* (1915), she tells of a venture in which she was required to hire a driver with a wagon for a long drive at night. She carried a revolver in her satchel as protection. Before she reached her destination she had to draw the revolver and hold it in the driver's back to force him to proceed to the log hotel in the settlement where the church was located. The congregation that turned out for her sermon was the largest in the history of the church, and among the listeners were many lumbermen who had heard about her from the driver.

After graduating from Albion College, she returned to the East and earned degrees at Boston University in both theology and medicine. She continued to preach and also to practice her profession as a doctor among the poor of Boston until she felt called to enlist as a lecturer in the broader field of women's rights. Her *Letter 24* was written just three days before the suffrage referendum was held in California. She was 64 years of age and was making arrangements to travel from New York to San Francisco in order to celebrate the victory of women's right to vote in that state. According to the *New York Times* for October 11, the returns were incomplete, but on October 14 the *Times* reported that the suffrage amendment had won by 2,500 votes. Anna Shaw had every reason to be present for the jubilee. Austin does not record that she also was there.

_____ 24

National American Woman Suffrage Association
PRESIDENT, Anna Howard Shaw, Moylan, Pa.

National Headquarters,
505 Fifth Ave., New York
October 9, 1911

Mrs. Mary Austin,
Cambridge Hall,
456 Riverside Drive,
New York City.

My dear Mrs. Austin:

As you have probably heard, we are hoping to hold a Jubilee meeting over the vote in California on the night of Friday, October 13th. Of course we do not yet know whether it will be a Jubilee or a Consecration meeting. If they win it will be a Jubilee. If they fail it will be a Consecration to begin again. But having heard that you are a Californian and deeply interested in the success of the State, we are very anxious to have you speak a few words on that occasion. I am sure that having lived in California you cannot fail to feel a deep interest in the success, even more so than most suffragists who have never been in the State.

I am enclosing two platform tickets which I hope you will use on that occasion and that we will have good grounds for rejoicing.

Will you kindly let me know by return mail, or telephone 6855 Bryant, our National Headquarters, whether or not it will be possible for you to take part in the meeting. We have not made any announcements in regard to it because we do not want the papers to get hold of it until we hear what the results are.

Sincerely yours,
Anna H. Shaw

2 Encls.

Edwin Markham (1852-1940) was on familiar terms with some members of the Carmel colony, as witnessed by Sterling's *Letter 19* and Markham's own *Letter 25*, written to Austin when both of them were sojourners in the state of New York. By temperament and background, Markham was like the themes of many of his poems, a toiler, farmer, hunter, and worker at menial tasks. By means of study and conviction, he found his voice in poetry. His expression was unique in rhetoric and power. After completing a degree at San Jose College and teaching in Oakland at the Observation School of the University of California, Markham sent a poem to the *San Francisco Examiner* in December of 1899 that electrified readers and became perhaps the best known poetic utterance in American literature. He called his verses "The Man with the Hoe," borrowing their title from Jean Francois Millet's painting of a peasant outlined against a bleak landscape and standing in the rows of earth he had tilled. Such descriptive phrases for the workman as "bowed by the weight of centuries" with "the emptiness of ages in his face" and "stolid and stunned, a brother to the ox" made the portrait unforgettable. This single poem foretold the rise of Markham to front rank among the poets of his time.

Edwin Markham's first book of poems was published in 1899 and took the title of his famous poem as a title for the book. Four editions of his poetry followed between 1901 and 1920. He became the founder and president of the American Poetry Society, and was honored by degrees from New York University, Baylor, Syracuse, and St. Lawrence universities. He moved to the New York City area, and in 1909 began a titanic undertaking called *The Real America in Romance*, a history planned in thirteen volumes and later expanded to fifteen. Preparation of these volumes occupied eighteen years of his life. The title page for Volume I refers to him as "Editor," and only Volume xv indicates that any mind other than his own was involved in the writing. The series of books may be the most comprehensive history of the country ever completed by a single individual.

Francis Grierson (1847-1927), who was to be a guest at the Christmas dinner to which Mary Austin was invited in *Letter 25*, was an English pianist and critic. He had published widely in both England and the United States, and is mentioned in a letter from Mrs. Herbert Hoover to Austin as having played for several musicales at the Hoover's home in London during 1916. Grierson and a companion named Tonner came to Los Angeles where they founded the Romance Fellowship for Lovers of Nature, and were the center for a coterie of musicians and fellow critics of literature and music. *The Valley of Shadows, Recollections of the Lincoln Country* (1909) is perhaps Grierson's best known book.

Reference in the Postscript, *Letter 25*, to Doubleday's request for a book on California was, no doubt, satisfied by Markham's *California the Wonderful*, which appeared in 1914. The book must have received the "energetic support" the author requested, for Mary Austin was in charge of the Panama-Pacific Publicity staff. The full title of Markham's book ran to forty-three words which included such terms for California as "romantic, picturesque, wild, glorious, resourceful," in addition to "wonderful" and "expanding." In the same year, Mary Austin herself produced a travel volume entitled *California, The Land of the Sun.* This book was first published by a British company, and then reissued in the United States by an American publishing house, using only the subtitle but pluralizing it as *The Lands of the Sun.* The author states that she drew upon a Spanish proverb to the effect that the lands of the sun expand the soul. Revised and reissued thirteen years later, this beautifully written account of the mountains, seacoast, cultivated lands, deserts, gardens, birds, and animals contains the strongest statements of Mary Austin's conviction that nature inevitably governs man instead of the reverse.

———— 25

Mrs. Mary Austin.   92 Waters Avenue
                                               West New Brighton, N. Y.
                                               December 17, 1913.

Dear Mrs. Austin:

I thank you heartily for your good letter. I must pull my foot out of the rut here and get over to see the Doubleday and other publishing houses at an early date. I fancy that a publisher likes to know about his year's books at the beginning of the year.

My chief reason for writing this moment is to tell you that Mrs. Markham and I would feel happy and honored to have you come to our little Christmas dinner—everything as informal as a squirrel's holiday. Mr. Francis Grierson, the essayist and musical genius, will be one of our company. We sit down at table at one-thirty.

You know the way hither—take Silver Lake Trolley at St. George and get off at Waters Avenue.

> Yours with high regard,
> *Edwin Markham*

Postscript
I am planning to see the Doubleday people in a few days about the book on picturesque California. I have made up my mind to write the book pro-

vided your Panama Publicity Forces will give it their energetic support. Of course it will be up to me to write a book that will be worth while. Let me say that I have searched thru my mind and can find no fear on this head: I feel that the reading and the experience of my whole life have made me ready for such an undertaking.

Edwin Markham

Probably the best known journalist in the United States during World War I was William Henry Irwin (1873-1948), better known just as Will Irwin, who was a correspondent in Europe with the armies of Germany, Britain, and Belgium, and after April 6, 1917, with the army of the United States as well. He had previously been a reporter on newspapers in San Francisco and New York City, and had written twenty books dealing with subjects as diverse as *Old Chinatown* (1908), sketches of a corner of San Francisco, to *Stanford Stories* (1913), tales of a young university. The latter may be in line with Irwin's own career, which included a period of probation for pranks holding up his degree in 1898 until the following year when a faculty committee on student affairs reconsidered his case.

Irwin was born in Oneida, New York, an industrial town near the lake by that name. Before he was 6 years old, he moved with his parents and his brother to Leadville, Colorado, a mining town where he lived until his family chose Denver as their home and Will graduated from high school. In his autobiography, *The Making of a Reporter* (1942), he describes the school days at Stanford University. He seems to have earned fame mostly in campus politics, theatricals, writing, and some forms of misbehavior that caused his expulsion three weeks before graduation. His multiple talents enabled him to write forty books, which include works of fiction, nonfiction, and drama. In addition to his autobiography, the best known nonfiction books are those dealing with his profession as a journalist: *A Reporter at Armageddon* (1918), *The Next War* (1921), *Propaganda and the News* (1936), and *The Making of a Reporter* (1942). Two of his nonjournalistic books are biographical accounts: *Theodore Roosevelt: Letters to Kermit* (1915) and *Herbert Hoover, A Reminiscent Biography* (1928). In Herbert Hoover's *Memoirs* (1951), the author describes Irwin as a college classmate who remained a lifelong friend, and on a visit to the Hoovers in Paris during Hoover's term as chairman of the Commission for Relief in Belgium helped to furnish "the never failing rays of sunshine."

Letter 26 was written in answer to a request from Austin for help in defeating a bill which would legalize titles to Indian lands held by Spanish and Anglo-American settlers. The bill was introduced in 1922 by a senator from New Mexico, and was rejected following the efforts of such groups as the one mentioned here.

_____ **26**

240 West Eleventh Street   March 7th
New York City   1923

Dear Mary Austin:

If my poor name is of any use to the American Indian Defence Society, I shall be glad to have you use it. But I don't think that just now I should be put on the publicity committee.

I have just undertaken a big and important job in connection with the International Cooperation and the League of Nations which is going to keep me extremely busy for at least two years; and my general idea is that when a person starts out to reform things he ought to emulate the rifle, not the shot gun, and shoot at one thing at a time.

In saying this I perhaps do not have to reassure you how much my heart is in your movement to stop the theft of Indian lands.

Yours as ever,
Will Irwin

The date for *Letter 27* may be determined by the content which deals with an edition of Austin's book about the life and significance of Jesus Christ. An investigator can choose between 1915, the date when the book was first published, and 1925 when it appeared in a revised edition. The title in 1915 was *The Man Jesus*, and when reissued in 1925 the title was *A Small Town Man*. Examination of the two volumes will not show a great deal of change, except that the author has tended in the latter to stress even more her persuasion that the nature of Christ was essentially human and that his insight into men's lives was more humane than theological. Since all letters from the Irwins bear dates between 1923 and 1930, the likelihood is that Irwin's short word of praise is directed at *A Small Town Man*, the second date for the book's appearance. Two years earlier, he had written *Christ or War*, a powerful indictment of the failure of religion to determine the causes of war or eliminate them from the human heart and society. This effort may reinforce his support of Mary Austin's theme: that Jesus wrote and taught the significance in humble experiences— God in the surface of the common life; harmony symbolized by the candle and the bushel; the housewife's measure of yeast; the children playing in the street; and the multitude fed by faith. *Agnosco* is Latin for "I do not know."

_____ 27

Sixteen Gramercy Park   Undated, 1925 (?)
New York

Dear Mary Austin:

I haven't acknowledged the book before, because I've just lately had time to read it. It's a wonderful piece of writing. I know few things as fine in contemporary workmanship as that opening paragraph. And you've made a human figure out of Jesus the man. As for your whole view of him—I reserve my judgement, as I shall reserve it, I suppose, until the end. The apostles and those who came after were such poor reporters! It's one of the things which you must accept on faith, or keep forever in the world of speculation. As for me—*agnosco*. The testimony is too imperfect.

Yours very truly
Will Irwin

The date for the writing of *Letter 28*, from Ryan Walker (1870-1932), presents a problem similar to the dating for Will Irwin's *Letter 27*, as both letters express the writer's interest in Austin's biographical story of the life of Christ. Ryan Walker was a cartoonist whose story-pictures were seen in the *New York Graphic* during its period of publication, 1924-1932. When living in New York, he stayed at the National Arts Club on Gramercy Park, a frequent home for Austin during New York visits. There are forty-one letters from Walker in Austin's file, most of them dated after 1925. Many contain enclosures of cartoons which present a unique interchange for ideas and points of view. The *Bookman* magazine published a group of Walker's cartoons in December of 1903, under the title *Leaves from a Barn-Stormer's Sketchbook*, and another collection appeared in 1914 as *Adventures of Henry Dubb*, which were praised by Bernard Shaw. Walker also contributed an interview to Austin's *Everyman's Genius* (1925). He explained that his best ideas came about five o'clock in the morning and the drawings began as random marks on paper which gradually developed into figures.

The cartoon illustrating *Letter 28* shows a devil with a curved tail sitting on the left side of the page. His horns protrude above big eyes and a turned down mouth as he fixes his attention on the book he holds. The label on the book is "The Man Jesus," and the caption below the cloven hooves is "R. W. Before." On the right side of the page there is the side view of a man in a frock coat, holding a book, "The Man Jesus," and crowned with a halo. This caption, however, is "R. W. After." Other letters show Walker on a treadmill or at his desk with papers flying in all directions. In one of the last letters, October 22, 1929, he says that he has talked to God and the Great Spirit, informing each that he wanted to visit Mary Austin in Santa Fe and would draw pictures of the Indians if his wish is granted.

Mrs. Ryan Walker was Marjorie E. Smith, whose name appears on the letter-head of "Ryan Walker and Marjorie Smith, Publicity, 205 Mark Strand Theatre Bldg., New York City." On June 27, 1932, she wrote to Mary Austin that Ryan Walker had died of pneumonia in Moscow and been given a communist funeral: "cremation . . . a beautiful service . . . red lacquer coffin . . . with one large wreath of deep red roses, and the organ played the Internationale. It was most impressive." She sent Austin a copy of her third book *From Broadway to Moscow* on February 2, 1934.

———— **28**

RYAN WALKER

TELEGRAPH ADDRESS:	NEW YORK ADDRESS:	POST OFFICE ADDRESS:
Little Falls, New Jersey	National Arts Club	Great Notch, New
	15 Gramercy Park	Jersey

October 23 [1915?]

My dear Mrs. Austin

    See what wonders your book is working for me.

"The Man Jesus" is as you know a splendidly written book—perhaps when I shall have finished the reading I will know the personage that I have never known. Who knows?

Enclosed please find two seats for Monday night at The Comedy Theatre. I hope that you may be able to go.

Mrs. Walker joins me in all good and sincere wishes.

Yours hastily

Ryan Walker

    Jack London (1876-1916) was one of the most brilliant and provocative writers ever to appear in the United States. He rose from a background of adversity to the heights of popularity and affluence, yet collapsed at the age of 40 in physical and mental exhaustion resulting from overwork and intemperance. In his letters, the reader will encounter again members of the Carmel colony who belonged to "The Crowd," as London referred to friends and acquaintances he had known during his youth in Oakland, California, and the suburban Piedmont Hills. He had known James Hopper from grade school days, and George Sterling was the nephew of the real estate developer from whom London and his first wife, Bess Maddern, rented a dwelling shortly after he began to sell his short stories. In 1901 and 1902, this dwelling, called the Villa Capricciosa, became the gathering place on Sunday afternoons for Hopper, Sterling, their mutual friend Ambrose Bierce and his protege, Herman Scheffauer, Edwin Markham, and Xavier Martinez, an artist who moved his studio to Carmel and left portraits of some of the notables who lived or visited there.

Letter 29 was written at the pinnacle of London's fame. He and his second wife, Charmian Kittredge, the author of *Letter 31*, were then living on London's ranch at Glen Ellen in Sonoma County north of San Francisco. Here he planned to establish a model community with farms, grazing lands, vineyards, and all the equipment to process their products. Such novels as *The Call of the Wild, The Sea Wolf, White Fang*, and *Martin Eden* had brought him the money to make this possible, but his Beauty Ranch was never profitable. Plans for producing grape juice, marketing dairy products, and selling ranch stock failed either from mismanagement or neglect. London's world was really in his imagination, based upon experiences in the Yukon where he began his first serious writing;

the trip to London where he lived in the slums; the service in Korea as a war correspondent during the Russo-Japanese War; and his voyage with Charmian and the crew of the *Snark* from San Francisco to Hawaii, Tahiti, and the islands of the South Seas from 1907 through 1909.

Author of forty-four books published during his lifetime and six more published after his death, London's personality and his life were as dramatic as anything he wrote. The autobiographical memoir he entitled *John Barleycorn* (1913) is an extraordinary mixture of fact, imagination, mysticism, exultation, and depression. After discoursing about hardships and rewards during his life and lecturing by analysis and illustration on the evils of drinking hard liquor, he reaches the last chapters in which he personifies alcohol as a figure of demoniac reason with whom he conducts a dialogue in what he terms White Logic. Tags of German philosophy mingle with squibs of Chinese wisdom while the screen of reality fades into the abyss of the unknown in interstellar space, "pulseless and frozen as absolute zero." That a Prohibition tract could explore the mystery of man's place in society and the universe discloses the depth of Jack London's thinking and experience. His remarks in *Letter 29*, as he discusses themes in his narratives, inspire deeper interest in the romances as storytelling. By "Christ story," London refers to an episode in *The Star Rover* (1915) which tells of a Roman centurion who witnessed the crucifixion of Jesus and was moved by the serenity of the man in the confusion and harshness which surrounded him.

_____ 29

Jack London
Glen Ellen
Sonoma Co., Cal.
U.S.A.   Glen Ellen, California, November 5, 1915.

Dear Mary Austin:

In reply to yours of October 26, 1915:

Your letter strikes me that you are serious. Now, why be serious with this bone-head world? Long ere this, I know that you have learned that the majority of the people who inhabit the planet Earth are bone-heads. Wherever the bone of their heads interferes there is no getting through.

I have read and enjoyed every bit of your "Jesus Christ" book as published serially in the "North American Review." What if it does not get across?

I have again and again written books that failed to get across. Long years ago, at the very beginning of my writing career, I attacked Nietzsche and his super-man idea. This was in THE SEA WOLF. Lots of people read THE SEA WOLF, no one discovered that it was an attack upon the super-man philosophy. Later on, not mentioning my shorter efforts, I wrote another novel that was an attack upon the super-man idea, namely, my MARTIN EDEN. Nobody discovered that this was such an attack. At another time I wrote an attack on ideas brought forth by Rudyard Kipling, and entitled my attack THE STRENGTH OF THE STRONG. No one was in the slightest way aware of the point of my story.

I am telling you all the foregoing merely to show that it is a very bone-head world indeed, and, also, that I never bother my head when my own books miss fire. And the point I am making to you is: why worry? Let the best effort of your heart and head miss fire. The best effort of my heart and head has missed fire with you, as it has missed fire with practically everybody else in the world who reads, and I do not worry about it. I go ahead content to be admired for my red-blood brutality and for a number of other nice little things like that which are not true of my work at all.

Heavens, have *you* read *my* "Christ" story? I doubt that anybody has read this "Christ" story of mine, though it has been published in book form on both sides of the Atlantic. Said book has been praised for its red-bloodedness and no mention has been made of my handling of the Christ situation in Jerusalem at all.

I tell you this, not because I am squealing, which I am not; but to show you that you are not alone in this miss-firing. Just be content with being called the "greatest American stylist."

Those who sit alone must sit alone. They must continue to sit alone. As I remember it, the prophets and seers of all times have been compelled to sit alone except at such times when they were stoned or burned at the stake. The world is mostly bone-head and nearly all boob, and you have no complaint if the world calls you the "great stylist" and fails to recognize that your style is merely the very heart and soul of your brain. The world has an idea that style is something apart from heart and brain. Neither you nor I can un-convince the world of that idea.

I do not know what more I can say, except, that, had I you here with me for half an hour I could make my point more strongly, namely that you are very lucky, and that you should be content to receive what the world gives you. The world will never give you due recognition for your "Christ" book. I, who never read serials, read your serial of the Christ and turned always to it first when my "North American Review" came in. I am not the world, you are not the world. The world feeds you, the world feeds me, but the world knows damn little of either of us.

Affectionately yours,

Jack London

Mary Austin
  National Arts Club
    New York, New York
JB/JL

The joyous references in *Letter 30* bring George Sterling and James Hopper out of the pages of literary history into moments of lively fellowship as three men anticipate revelry with other members of the Bohemian Club at the summer Hi Jinx on the Russian River. Founded in 1872, the Club by 1916 had lost some of its most illustrious members, such as Bret Harte and Mark Twain; but everyone who was active in San Francisco creative arts and society belonged and attended the annual satires on the state of the world. The year before, however, the Bohemians had rejected Jack London's drama in verse which he called *The Acorn Planter*. Its poetry was of questionable merit, and perhaps the music was equally undistinguished. In any case, London and his friends attended the entertainment in the following year, and the Macmillan Company published the script six months before *Letter 30* was written. Although Mary Austin does not record that she accepted London's invitation to visit the Glen Ellen ranch, there is every indication that she found London a challenge, as she certifies in *Earth Horizon*, and disagreed with his theory that genius justified men's sharing their biological necessities with a number of women. There are only three letters from London in the Austin Correspondence, but thirteen letters from his wife Charmian define the relationship between Austin and London to an even greater degree, as *Letter 31* will confirm.

———————— **30**

Jack London
Glen Ellen
Sonoma Co., Cal.
U.S.A.   Glen Ellen, California, August 8, 1916.

My dear Mary Austin—
        You were right. You did reply to my letter, and the date of your
reply is December 18, 1915. I was just sailing for Hawaii at that time. In
some mischance my Secretary included your letter in a bunch of finished
correspondence. I am back just now on the ranch and just now have I
discovered your letter.
        George Sterling and Jimmie Hopper are with me and I can hear their
laughter from the next room, and we are starting to-morrow for the
Mid-Summer Jinks of the Bohemian Club.
        Oh, anyway, next time you come to California try and plan your
itinerary so that you can come and visit Charmian and me on the ranch.
It is a dandy place to work; if you want to, you can stay in your own
room all the time you are here and work your head off. We make no
demands upon our guests, and we refuse to permit our guests to make
any demands on us. We get together or we do not get together just as
our hearts list and as our work dictates.
        And when you and I do get together let us quit all dallying and spar-
ring. Let us get down to real talk and real stuff as you and I should be
able to get down to.
        When I first met you the world was too much with you. Now let us
really get together and the world with us, but not too much with us.
        I shall be in New York next October and shall hope to meet you there.
Address me, with your address, care of The Macmillan Company.
                                Sincerely thine,
                                  Jack London
JB/JR

_____

        Jack London ended his life on November 22, 1916, a little more
than three months after *Letter 30* had been written to Mary Austin. The doctor's

certificate stated that his death resulted from gastro-intestinal uremia. However, the evidence supplied by two empty bottles of pain-killing narcotics found at his bedside confirmed a decision to end the pain and depression which had developed in recent months. Emotional concern for the Allies in World War I and the failure of the United States to enter the struggle heightened anxieties about his home and his work. He left a note to his daughter Joan inviting her and her mother, Bess Maddern London, to join him for lunch on the following Sunday and a sail boat trip if the weather permitted.

Letter 31, written by Charmian Kittredge London, is a summary of not only her life with London but of her relationship to his friends and to his literary career. Her offer of three books, *Love of Life, Theft,* and *The Acorn Planter*, points to three eminent characteristics of her husband: hardiness, honesty, and camaraderie. The last term embraced his glorification of village life in contrast to urban and industrial society, a theme he shared with Austin. Her novel *Outland*, in which she portrayed London as Persilope, leader of the Outliers, describes a socialist community similar to those in *The Acorn Planter* and *The Valley of the Moon*.

Other letters from Charmian London, some with the heading "National Arts Club" and other "Glen Ellen," reveal a confidential and affectionate relationship with Mary Austin. On June 6, 1920, Charmian invited Mary to visit the "paradise on Sonoma Mountain"; on May 2, 1925, Charmian expresses interest in the house Mary is building in Santa Fe; and on October 30 of that year she wrote from the liner Matsonia that when London visited New York in August of 1916 he was not himself, because of alcohol and the artificiality caused by the city. The tribute Charmian pays to her husband in *Letter 31* is a moving and fascinating appraisal of a most gifted man. She inspires the reader to seek out her own books, *Our Hawaii* (1918) and *The Book of Jack London* (1921), as well as those of her husband.

———— 31

Mrs
Jack London
Glen Ellen
Sonoma Co., Cal.
U.S.A.   Oct. 30, 1917

My dear Mary:

How good to hear from you again. And of course I shall send you something to represent Jack—indeed, I should be hurt, for him, if you did not appeal to me. There is so little to send that breathes of his personal touch—why, woman, he had so few personal possessions. Of course, many have asked for pens. I gave away three,—one to his surgeon, Dr. Will S. Porter, one to his sister, and one to a friend. And I cannot give any more—indeed, I use them myself. The very touch of them seems to give me spirit to do my work. So I've been thinking—there are, of course, not so very many of his autographs, and, after looking about me, I have put a different, original signature of his into each of three of his books, LOVE OF LIFE (collection of splendid short stories), THEFT, a play, and THE ACORN PLANTER, another play. I have put above each autograph, a small but good photograph of him—one, a recent snapshot in his cow-boy hat, one of the "Wolf Head," as he called it, his favorite picture, and one, a full-face, that is a very beautiful thing and shows the Greek in his face. Will these books be acceptable? Will they do, Mary? It seems to me there could be nothing much more intimate of him than his own name written by his own hand with his own pen. If you differ from me, I'll try to do better.

"A well-thumbed book" would not be characteristic of Jack! He read so many books, read them so fast, read them in such droves and slathers and thousands, that they never got thumbed! Bless him, bless him! I bless him every hour of every day I live.

I am glad you think of me. I want you to. I need being thought of. Oh, I am well—fat, for that matter; and, not being a quitter, I intend to live to the best of my ability. And speaking of "OUR HAWAII"—the story of our many months spent in Jack's beloved Islands, ten years ago, and the past two years. The publishers pronounce it "admirable," and so of course I must believe there is a modicum of merit in the stuff—although, in the past eight months that I have worked night and day on it, alone here in the country, many's the night I've gone to bed devoutly believing I was writing absolute rot that no one would publish or read! However, it seems turning out well. I hope you will like it.

What are you doing? And you are more than good to suggest my putting up at the Club. I may be in New York before very long, but expect to visit friends. But if the visit should not come about, through their possible absence, the Club certainly would be exactly the thing I would love, because there are few persons I care to "visit." You understand— the lack of independence, etc. So you may be hearing from me. You will do that, of course, in any event!

By the way—pardon a hayseed Westerner, but what Club is it? I think

of Authors' League, but don't know that this is that kind of a Club!
Let me know if the books arrive in good order.

> Faithfully yours,
> *Charmian London.*

Walter Prichard Eaton (1878-1957), author of books about
plays, actors, gardening, New England towns, poetry, and stories about Boy
Scouts from Maine to California, joins the numerous correspondents who found
Mary Austin's book *The Man Jesus* an extraordinary achievement. Perhaps she
could have written this study of Christ only in a complex urban community
such as New York, for her thesis in the work is that religious serenity and vision
are more likely to appear in rural surroundings than in a congested environment.
The environment in which she wrote supplied contrasts to the world of nature
where visions of reality had come to her. Eaton's citation of Moody, Sankey,
and Sunday embraced three of the noted evangelists at the turn of the nineteenth
century into the twentieth. Dwight Lyman Moody (1837-1899) made Chicago
the center of his city missionary work. Associated with him was Ira D. Sankey
(1840-1908), composer of Gospel hymns. William Ashley Sunday (1862-1935),
better known by the nickname "Billy," carried on the crusading through the
next three decades. Moody and Sankey were active in providing seminaries and
educational institutions for young people.

———— 32

Walter Prichard Eaton
Stockbridge
Massachusetts   Nov. 20 '15

Dear Mrs Austin

   I'm sorry, but I can't get up even a little quarrel with you over
your life of Christ! Having been brought up a Unitarian in childhood, I
very early began groping myself for some such human interpretation,
though I never really achieved it clearly in my own mind. I think the
sense you give of the *small town man* bringing his simple, clear, efficient
vision to the life of his time and people is splendid—what a shame you
couldn't have used your original title!

I must admit ignorance of a great deal which has been written about Christ, so that I don't know how far your explanation of the appearances after the crucifixion is shared by others. It opens up considerable ranges of speculation, including the material question, when and how did Christ actually and finally die?

There is one point in your account which, to my own way of feeling, you do not enough insist upon. At the very end you say, "The Kingdom—must be entered into by personal determination." Wasn't it this very element of "personal determination," this conversion of the will, that made Christ's teachings so unintelligible to the Jews, even unpleasant to them, because not the conversion of the will but the obedience to external law was bred in their minds as the way of salvation? And haven't the so-called Christians all through the ages—the great ones, I mean—after their age and kind, all felt this conversion element, even though over and over it has been perverted into Moody and Sankey or Billy Sunday excesses and grotesqueries, and over-laid with dogma and atonement theories? Isn't it necessary to a living of the Christian life today—for most of us? A redirection, a readjustment, a *conversion* of the will? So it seems to me, at any rate.

There! That's the nearest to a quarrel I can get with you. I shall always treasure my copy of the book, with your presentation.

Truly
Walter P. Eaton

For Henry Ford to invite Austin to join the pilgrims on the Peace Ship that embarked for Europe on December 4, 1915, is a tribute to the contacts she had with women's organizations that were capable of spreading the message of peace. Mrs. Herbert Hoover's comment in *Letter 35*, however, indicates that little hope was held for the success of this venture. The story of the so-called "Peace Ship" begins with Henry Ford's background of pacifism growing out of his mother's opposition to war. Of Mary Ford's three brothers, one was killed during the Civil War and another suffered wounds which later led to his death. Her son opposed World War I on both moral and economic grounds. After a German submarine sank the English passenger ship *Lusitania* on May 7, 1915, American preparations for intervention in the war were speeded up. Ford gave an interview to a reporter for the *Detroit Press* in which he stated that he would do everything in his power to stop militarism in America and the whole world. At this time, the Carnegie Endowment for International Peace and other organizations were trying to stop the war by negotiations. Two of the leaders of the movement were a Hungarian lecturer, Rosika Schwimmer, and a former secretary of the International Students Federation, Louis P. Lochner. They went to Detroit on November 18, 1915, and persuaded Ford to help form a neutral mediation committee that would assemble in Europe. Ford contributed the idea of chartering a ship to convey the members of such a group to Stockholm where the war could be ended by sitting around a table instead of dying in the trenches. Hundreds of invitations were written or wired to leading men and women throughout the United States. The telegrams reproduced here are an exchange between two New York City addresses: 15 Gramercy Park and 17 East 38th Street.

In *Earth Horizon*, Austin writes that she knew too little of the conditions necessary for peace to commit herself to such a conference. Her reply shown in *Telegram 34* expresses sympathy with Ford's idea but rejects his invitation to join the group which sailed on December 4 aboard the *Oscar II* of the Scandinavian American Line.

A good deal of ridicule at the time the boat sailed and newspaper reports beforehand helped to doom the mission. Titles like "Flivver Ship," "Ford's Ark of Peace," and "The Floating Chautauqua" jeered at the vessel escorting the peace makers. Prominent figures such as Jane Addams, John Wanamaker, and Thomas A. Edison withdrew at the last moment. A state governor, a congressman, Judge Ben Lindsey, and William Jennings Bryan were among the prominent delegates who sailed, along with students, newspaper correspondents, and several hundred Scandinavians who were going home to spend the Christmas holidays.

Disunity among the delegates erupted on shipboard and broke out again at the conference held in Stockholm. Ford fell ill on the boat and carried his cold and fever to the hotel where the delegates were lodged. He was kept incommunicado after the first conference, and left the hotel to find passage on the next boat returning to America. The cause of mediation to end World War I died in Stockholm, followed by announcements in the neutral capitals of Europe and in Washington, D. C. The Peace Ship was stage for a minor tragedy with comic dimensions, but a tragedy nevertheless.

———— 33

WESTERN UNION TELEGRAM   NATIONAL ARTS CLUB
MISS MARY AUSTIN   DEC 1ST 15

IT GIVES MR HENRY FORD A GREAT DEAL OF PLEASURE
TO INVITE YOU TO BE HIS GUEST ON THE PEACE PILGRIM-
AGE WHICH STARTS FOR EUROPE DECEMBER 4TH. IF YOU
ACCEPT YOU SHOULD ARRANGE FOR AT LEAST SIX WEEKS
ABSENCE APPLY FOR PASSPORT AT ONCE AND THE COUR-
TESY OF AN IMMEDIATE ANSWER WILL BE APPRECIATED
                              KATHERINE LECKIE
                                        530 AM

———— 34

WESTERN UNION TELEGRAM
To Katherine Leckie
17 East 38th St., N. Y.   [December 1, 1915]

Deeply sympathize with Mr. Henry Ford's ideal of permanent peace   I
regret that I have neither the knowledge of conditions nor capacity
which would justify interference with the European situation.
                         Mary Austin

          On December 6, 1911, William Allen White, the editor of the
Emporia, Kansas, *Gazette*, employed the editorial "we" and used the columns
of the newspaper to state: "What we want, and what we shall have, is the royal
American privilege of living and dying in a country town, running a country
newspaper, saying what we please, how we please and to whom we please."
White (1868-1944) made his journal the sounding board for the Republican
party in Kansas, and through his editorials, reports, and news columns, he
became an influential figure in both regional and national thought. On August
15, 1896, he wrote an editorial "What's the Matter with Kansas?" that was
reprinted in 3,000,000 copies and distributed in the campaign to elect William
McKinley as president on a platform to preserve the gold standard and a high
tariff on imports to the United States. When the election was over, William
Jennings Bryan had carried Kansas, but McKinley had been elected president.

White's influence, however, grew both in his party and as a spokesman for the midwestern states. After becoming integrated into politics, he became acquainted with six presidents of the United States: McKinley, Theodore Roosevelt, William Howard Taft, Woodrow Wilson, Warren G. Harding, and Calvin Coolidge. In his autobiographical comments on these men and their associates, he reveals a grasp of journalistic reporting that is both factual and creative. His objectivity shows in writing about himself as well as about others. Few autobiographers have employed such adjectives for themselves as "fat, clumsy, sly, chunky, insensitive, tricky, smart alecky," and "rash." Most of these appear in his description of himself at various periods of his youth, but he selectes a few that are equally frank about his actions in maturity. This may explain the realism in his novel *A Certain Rich Man* (1909), a narrative which has been proclaimed one of the outstanding achievements in American literature. In telling the story of John Barclay, a boy who becomes a banker, prospers on the misfortunes of farmers, and sacrifices his friends to his insatiable desire for wealth, White draws upon his knowledge of the economic and political morality in midwestern America during his lifetime.

Letter 35 recalls a dinner Mary Austin arranged at the National Arts Club when the Whites and the Herbert Hoovers were visiting in New York City. Vernon Kellogg, a former classmate of White at the University of Kansas, had moved to California as a professor of biology at Stanford (see introductory notes to Elmer Harris's *Letter 13*.) He sent Will and Sallie White autographed copies of two of Austin's books, *The Land of Little Rain* and *The Flock*. In this way, Mary had been introduced to White before they met in New York at the seventy-fifth birthday party for William Dean Howells, held on March 2, 1912. She said that they enjoyed "folk talk" about the Middle West, but she added that he had little information about Indians, her own reservation. Elsewhere in *Earth Horizon* she states that the Whites spent their honeymoon in 1893 at the Santa Fe Railroad resort hotel near Las Vegas, New Mexico, and returned to the state for a wedding anniversary in 1931. At this time they visited with her at her home in Santa Fe.

White's comments on Austin are to be found in his *Autobiography* (1946). He said that she had a "tough-fibered brain, was vainer than a wilderness of gargantuan peacocks," and was "a strong, overbearing woman." However, he adds that he and his wife "loved her and took her to their hearts." He also thought that her novel *A Woman of Genius* (1912) was one of the great American novels. He concludes: "Always we left her presence feeling that our minds and hearts had been kindled with new energy and refreshment."

——————— 35

THE EMPORIA GAZETTE   December
                                                      Fourteen
                                                      1915

My dear Mrs. Austin:

   Since we have got home and the horizon of our visit is taking a
definite shape, we find that the highest peak of our visit was the night
with you and the Hoovers. For that, we have you to thank. What a
wonderful evening it was! We can only offer you in return the peaceful
vale of Emporia. Come and visit us and let know you and love you better.

   Mrs. White has insisted upon me writing this letter for ten days or
two weeks, but a man is tremendously slow and does not get around to
things.

   I am sending you herewith a blank check, for which I wish you would
buy me two copies of your book, "THE MAN JESUS," and inscribe
them something like the inscription on the enclosed list.

   The more I think of that book, the better I like it.

                                      Truly and sincerely yours,
                                          W. A. White
Mrs. Mary Austin,
The National Arts Club
Gramercy Park,
New York City.
WAW:FH.

   During 1917, White was designated an inspector of the Red
Cross activities in Europe. He and another Kansan, Henry Allen of Wichita,
each went as a lieutenant colonel to learn of the scope and success of this international organization. Upon his return, White's personal appraisal of their
performance consisted of a humorous account devoted to a pair of heavy-set,
middle-aged men who left their wives at home, bought a pair of Red Cross uni-
forms in New York, and took a ship for Paris, where without knowing any
French they tried to get their garments altered to fit them. The outcome of
expanding their pants at the waist and trimming the shirts elsewhere was as
haphazard as their experience at the battlefront. This is the "blithe little war
book" mentioned in *Letter 36*, and it sold 50,000 copies in the United States,
but failed to amuse the British; nor is there any record of it amusing Mary Austin.

_____ **36**

THE EMPORIA GAZETTE
Emporia Kansas   April 12, 1918

My dear Mrs. Austin:

I am getting out a blithe little war book called, "The Martial Adventures of Henry and Me," and I am taking the liberty of sending it to you. As the man said of Kentucky whiskey, "There is not a headache in a barrel of it." Yet I have tried to put in it an undercurrent of a rather serious interpretation of the war as I saw it. I hope some time when you are weary and cannot sleep, you will take this as a nightcap and lie down to pleasant dreams.

Truly and sincerely yours,

Mrs. Mary Austin,   *W. A. White*
Arts Club, Gramercy Park,
New York City.

On June 1, 1922, from 10 Barrow Street, New York City, and on letterhead paper belonging to the *Bookman,* Mary Austin wrote to William Allen White about the literary programs planned by John Farrar, editor of the magazine. Farrar had invited White to serve on a committee to recommend study groups in fiction, poetry, and drama for women's clubs throughout the country. Austin was named chairman of this committee and she sent the names of thirty-three writers for White's approval or protest. On her list were both White's name and her own, but she explains that Farrar said that he considered committee members to be representative of their profession and if their names were left off he would put them back. In her lists she includes the names of Robert Herrick, Joseph Hergesheimer, Harry Leon Wilson, Ellen Glasgow, Emerson Hough, Edith Wharton, Booth Tarkington, Kathleen Norris, James Branch Cabell, Sherwood Anderson, Willa Cather, and in a group she calls "Novelists of Ideas" adds her name and White's to those of Theodore Dreiser, Upton Sinclair, and Dorothy Canfield. Among the younger writers she places F. Scott Fitzgerald and Edna Ferber. She omits the name of her California rival Gertrude Atherton from all of the groups. In this frame of reference, *Letter 37* needs no further introduction except to underline White's preference for *The Virginian* by Owen Wister to her nomination of titles by Cabell (see also *Letter 116*).

——— 37

THE EMPORIA GAZETTE   June 15, 1922.

My dear Mary Austin:
I am enclosing your memoranda. It seems to me all right except I cannot see any earthly reason for James Branch Cabell being in any list of authors, who amount to anything. If he had not had his book suppressed, he would not have been heard of, whereas Owen Wister has written a real book that will be known a hundred years from now, because it tells a real story of real life, and preserves for history a social condition, which was virile, and interesting, and even though it is past, is still a part of our American tradition. Otherwise, I agree with your list.
                                            Sincerely yours,
                                            W. A. White

The William Allen White letters are an introduction to those from Herbert and Lou Henry Hoover, for in *Letter 42* Mrs. Hoover sends greetings from London to the Whites. White was a supporter of Hoover in his 1928 campaign for the presidency, and he remained Hoover's supporter through the economic storm which broke six months after Hoover was inaugurated as the thirty-first president of the United States. White quotes his father's epitaph on the downfall of Hoover's term: "He will be known as the greatest innocent bystander in history. But history will also write him down an earnest, honest, intelligent man, full of courage and patriotism, undaunted to the last."

Herbert Clark Hoover (1874-1964) and Lou Henry (1874-1944), who became his wife, met at Stanford University in the fourth year of that institution's life. In 1895, he was a graduating senior and Miss Henry an entering first year student. As an impromptu assistant to the professor of geology, he became acquainted with the laboratory problems of the young woman who also was born in Iowa in the same year as he was born. They became friends, maintaining contact by correspondence after Hoover left college, and when he had established himself as a mining engineer through assignments in Nevada, Colorado, and Australia, she accepted his proposal to be married at the home of her family in Monterey, California, and to travel to China with him on their honeymoon. Herbert Hoover and Lou Henry were married on February 12, 1899, and took passage on a steamer for the Orient the next morning.

During this first year in China, Hoover's explorations for mineral deposits and their possibilities for development led him to travel in Manchuria and Mongolia as well as to many other parts of the Chinese interior. Mrs. Hoover went on many of these expeditions. Before they left their home in Peking, it was looted by Russian mercenaries who had been called there to quell the revolt staged by a Chinese secret society called "The Boxers." After European and American forces arrived, the Hoovers were able to leave for London, having survived a siege that lasted through the winter into the spring of their second year in China. Arriving in London, Hoover in November became a partner in a British firm with mining interests all over the world. In the first volume of his *Memoirs* (1951), Hoover lists professional visits made between 1901 and 1908 to fourteen different countries in addition to the trips in England and the United States. London having become their headquarters, Mrs. Hoover found a delightful old house and garden on Horton Street in west London. They named it the "Red House" and were living there when Mary Austin made her first visit to Europe, which lasted from December of 1907 until September of 1910. In *Earth Horizon* she describes her first contact with the Hoover family. She arrived for tea after a visit with H. G. Wells and his wife, and she reported that Wells had told his wife that a friend was going to bear him a child (see Mary Austin to H. G. Wells, *Letter 107*). Mrs. Hoover admitted that she had heard this story and Hoover expressed irritation that people talked about such things. In the weeks that followed, Austin made trips with the Hoovers to Stonehenge, Stratford-on-Avon, and the cathedral towns. She recorded that Lou Henry Hoover and she would gladly have lingered in such places, but that Hoover was bored by sightseeing and always wanted to go on to the next place scheduled. A second event reported on this trip by both Austin and Hoover was the arrest of Anne Martin, an American feminist, who was a classmate of Mrs. Hoover at Stanford University. During a suffrage parade, she assaulted a policeman, and Hoover bailed her out at the police station.

The drama of Mary Austin's friendship is a minor episode in the extraordinary lives of the Hoovers, but after the rewarding visits in London, the relationships among the three resulted in an exchange of seventeen letters from Mrs. Hoover and sixteen from Hoover during the same approximate dates, 1916 to 1927. Only five of these are reproduced in this book, but excerpts from others will fill in gaps in the story as outlined in Austin's *Earth Horizon*.

Letter 38, written from London probably in the spring of 1916, presents Hoover as a man interested in plays and playwriting. The lines are typed on the same letterhead paper used by Mrs. Hoover in *Letter 42*, which is dated March 23, 1916. References to the theater in both letters may indicate the period in the undated one by Hoover. Mary Austin, evidently, had written a play in which villainy was provided by an engineer and carried out by means of a blast furnace. Her correspondent can scarcely be blamed for shifting the crime to a member of a vocation other than his own! Although Hoover did not mail pages of a book on "real engineers," he did send two pages from the *Engineering and Mining Journal,* New York City, showing details of furnaces at the Tezuitlan, Mexico, smeltery which he had marked for use as a stage setting. He also included two pictures of copper furnaces and a "Sierra type" hoist. The letters from former President Hoover and his wife, Lou Henry Hoover, are printed by permission of the Herbert Hoover Foundation, Old Oaks Route, Box 369, Leesburg, Virginia 22075 and their son, Alan Hoover.

_____ 38

The Red House,
Horton Street.
        W.   Undated: Spring, 1916 (?)

Dear Mrs. Austin
    I send you a print of a proper copper furnace; those are big machines: a front elevation would fill the whole back of the stage and would be up to the "furnace stage"—be thirty feet—above that line it could be painted. It would not be hard to imitate the lower works out of stage material. A copper furnace is a noisy beast—it "blows" like ship boilers. Some smoke spitting out; with light streaming through doors and spouts would be effective enough!
    The equipment of these great copper mines has been in progress for two or more years. The one has hitherto to all other comers resisted treatment. These men have tackled it on novel and bold lines involving new departures in furnace construction. A furnace has been built, cooling pots (?), and will treat 5,000 tons a day—employ 10,000 men. Their professional future and the financial success of the enterprise depends on this furnace. The criteria of success will be the actual flow of metal from the furnace. The day arrives when the smelter is to be "blown in." It has been charged some hours before. They stand by and moralize on their future and the probabilities of the monster chewing up metal. They evince proper stage anxiety. All the dramatis personae are there to see the first tapping of the furnace. Enters the female and does her stunt.
    Suddenly the foreman from up on the furnace stage (screams) announces she is ready (furnaces are also females). The chief engineer takes the honor (or delegates it to the ultimate victim) of the first tap. Everybody stands on one foot. He dashes along, opening the spouts

(there are about 40 of them). The glowing metal ripples out, sparks; (water over red light). Everybody cheers, dance a minuet. *But* at the last hole a breastplate blows out. Great cloud of fumes, yellow smoke; victim dies either on or off the stage as you like.

Seriously, I am interested in this matter; I've whiled away many idle hours constructing a drama to represent to the world a new intellectual type from a literary or stage view—the modern intellectual engineer—there're more possibilities than you think. But you are trying to make a villain out of him, which won't do; the successful man's intellectual, educational, and physical circuit en route to success never produces a villain: given a weakness in intellect or education or professional experience it would or might. You should put the real engineer on the stage as the general manager. The metallurgist could be your semi-civilized villain; the foreman, the man who maltreats his wife.

I'd send you two pages of a book on real engineers if I thought it would do you any good—

Yours faithfully
H. C. Hoover

From 1915 until 1919, Herbert Hoover served as chairman of the Commission for Relief in Belgium. The United States entered World War I on April 6, 1917, and on May 9 he was asked to assume added duties as director of the United States Food Administration. The responsibility entailed coordinating activities of the Department of Agriculture, the War Council, the Department of the Interior, rail transportation, and volunteer groups of educational and other public agencies. Mary Austin, in her autobiography, writes of her participation in public relations and in organizing community kitchens in New York City. She became a member of the Mayor's Committee for National Defense. From *Letters 39* and *40*, it would appear that she engaged in a discussion of matters broader than food, such as women's and children's labor problems and community welfare in general. Her point of view is clearly presented in *Letter 41*, which would appear to be a reply to *Letter 40*. On June 23, 1917, Ray Lyman Wilbur, on leave as president of Stanford University, wrote to Austin asking her to become general advisor on psychological propaganda for Food Conservation, and on July 18 she sent "Chief" Hoover a list of fourteen national women's organizations with the names of the leaders of each. In August of 1917, the *New York Worker* carried a picture of Mary Austin surrounded by boys who were carrying garden tools for a war garden in Van Cortlandt Park in New York City. Both of these letters are in the Herbert Hoover Presidential Library, West Branch, Iowa. The only explanation for "Miss" in the salutation to *Letter 40* is a secretarial error.

_____ 39

UNITED STATES FOOD ADMINISTRATION WASHINGTON

14 March, 1918
IN REPLY REFER TO
1-H-S

Mrs. Mary Austin
    48, West Tenth Street,
        New York City.

Dear Mrs. Austin:
    Many thanks for your letter of March 12th. I have set up the principle ever since I came here, of taking no interest in any matter except food. I do not like to see the limitations on women's and children's labour—that have been built up through the pains of so many years—taken off. However, I can take neither the time nor the energy to enter this dispute.

Sincerely yours,
Herbert Hoover

_____ 40

UNITED STATES FOOD ADMINISTRATION WASHINGTON

11 April, 1918
IN REPLY REFER TO
1-H-AGS

Miss [*sic*] Mary Austin
    48 West Tenth Street,
        New York City.

My dear Miss [*sic*] Austin:
    Many thanks for your letter of April 8th.
    I would be glad indeed to have a discussion with you next September as to the policy of the Food Administration for next year. We cannot

intelligently discuss the question in any event until the harvest is in hand.

Generally, I think you have never grasped the basis of conservation. Any spiritual aspect of this matter is secondary to the very material aspect of accomplishing directly the object which we have in view.

Being an engineer, my natural aspect in mind in building a railway is never to buy more locomotives or railway cars than are needed for the traffic.

Out of the 1917 harvest year we have had a certain burden to carry in regard to the Allies. It becomes a matter of specific pounds and ounces of various commodities. The measures that we have adopted are accomplishing this purpose, and therefore, from my own aspect and from the aspect of the fundamental objective of carrying on the war, the Food Administration is succeeding.

Furthermore, the Food Administration is succeeding in these matters by implementing purely voluntary forces, and in this it has diverged entirely from any experience hitherto known in such matters, and in consequence of using this particular implement instead of many others which were at our hands, it is succeeding with the least injustice on any method of reduction in consumption. The voluntary sacrifice of food comes from plenty and not from nourishment.

So far as having the cooperation of the American women is concerned, we feel that we have secured this. In any event, we have secured it to a sufficient degree to accomplish our objective.

In my capacity as Food Adminsitrator, I have no general reforms, no spiritual movements to undertake, but simply a purely practical end to attain. If I succeed in the practical end, that is what I shall be judged by, not by any outside attitude towards citizenship which I may hold. Beyond this, again, the tax on my time and ability is sufficiently large in carrying out the very definite object with which I have been entrusted to preclude interest in any other objective.

I fear your memory is short on some particulars. You seem to overlook that the statement I made at Mrs. Astor's was a direct appeal to these ladies to rectify "the households above Forty-second Street."

Furthermore, I think you have been influenced by some current hysteria as to the imminence of famine. So far as I can see from a war point of view the question of community cooking is a famine measure, and as I do not contemplate the imminence of famine, I see no particular object in entering upon a social experiment as a matter of war administration.

I do think if you will sit down and contemplate this whole matter from the point of view of only one issue, you will take a different mental attitude towards it. That one issue is to win this war, and my part in winning this war is simply a question of intelligent handling of the supplies which we have available, and doing so with the very least interference in the normal life of our people.

There are infinite injustices and wrongs in the United States and an infinite amount of social evils. Like every other citizen who loves his people, I would truly like to see these things remedied. But it is a job that I cannot undertake and at the same time successfully fill my niche in prosecuting the war.

Yours faithfully,
Herbert Hoover

Letter 41 was written in advance of Austin's appointment as member of the propaganda corps of the Food Administration, which may explain her roundabout apology for crediting her performance to that branch of the war effort. In a letter she wrote on July 18, 1917 (found in the Hoover Presidential Library, West Branch, Iowa), Austin had asked Hoover for a contribution of 300 words to go into a book being compiled for war relief purposes. She said that the statement would help to present him as a thinker with a world outlook and she offers to help him to prepare it. In conclusion, she states in this letter: "I am busy going about the country assisting at the opening of community kitchens. . . . What the women want, *what your whole movement needs* is the sense of social directions. That's what I'm doing with it. *If I can't do it with your approval*, I'm going to do it anyway." The tone of this letter may indicate the source of the discord which later occurred in the relationship between Austin and the Hoovers.

—————— 41

356 South Occidental Boulevard
Los Angeles, California
June 4, 1918

Mr. Herbert Hoover
Food Administration
Washington, D. C.

My dear Chief:

I have arrived here by various stages, stirring up the country on the food problem as I came. I haven't always been able to avoid having my lectures credited to the Food Administration, especially West of the Mississippi. At this distance all conservation propaganda looks alike to them. However, you need not worry. Everybody tells me that it is the most interesting food talk that they have yet heard. Everybody seems to be doing all you tell them, though they are not doing all that they could, or that most people think ought to be done. Everywhere I find the same feeling about the need of constructive propaganda, which I have been trying to make you understand. Of course, there is a good deal of constructive propaganda going on, either in connection with the Department of Agriculture or sporadically in separate communities. It is most of it in the nature of community enterprise, community gardens, community storehouses, community markets and kitchens. The community kitchen is now so well established that I do not feel the need of doing anything more about it. There are quite a lot of them working, some as co-operative enterprises and some as commercial enterprises.

What I do want to call your attention to, is the growing realization of the need of centralized cooking, not only as a food and fuel conserving measure, but to meet the labor crisis. In nearly every city I go to I find people more and more convinced that something of the kind will have to be undertaken officially, and hesitating to undertake it until you at least give it the sanction of official experimenting. The great problem to be met now is the accommodation of labor, the housing and feeding, not only of the people who have to be taken from one place to another to work, but the accommodation of families where both the father and mother are now engaged in war work. The women who are interested in the Women's Land Army idea are working out some kind of a land army mess, portable kitchens and methods of feeding the laborer without invading the private home of the former, and something of the same sort will have to be applied to nearly every industry in which large numbers of women are taken out of their homes and put to work in places of insufficient accommodation.

The textile strike in the east is the thing I tried to tell you about a year ago, where skilled women workers are absolutely indispensable, and yet so many of them, with the improved wages, have married and had families, that they are extremely unwilling to surrender. This is really the source of much of the unrest of labor. For awhile this can be satisfied by increased wages, but the limit of possible increase will be soon reached. Then if there is no other method of accommodation at hand, there will be more—and still more—disorganization. You remember that I told you that I am on the Publicity Board of the Women's Trades Union League, and that I have inside information on the nature of these strikes, and the possibilities of future strikes. It is not going to be very long before the general public itself becomes aware of the fact that the accommodation of living conditions is at the bottom of much of the difficulty.

I am writing this all out to you, because, as you will agree with me, the kitchen is the pivot of family existence, and becomes a question of national importance. I don't think it is necessary for the Food Administration, if you do not wish to commit yourself to the constructive propaganda, to actually initiate experiments of this kind, but I do think it really important that you should show yourself aware of the situation in advance, and friendly toward it. If you want more information about it, I will be glad to supply it. I do know that there exists among the people who will be charged with the management of such adjustments, a feeling of irritation with the Food Administration for not recognizing the importance of these adjustments, and for not lending to them that high engineering skill for which they have learned to look to you.

As a representative of organized labor, I want to say that I consider it immensely important for the winning of the war that changes in methods of feeding the working classes must not seem to come as a necessity of famine or the result of inadequate wages. I assure you that the labor leaders see this very clearly, that it would be far more acceptable to them, and go much further toward the winning of the war if any adjustments that are necessary could come under the head of Social Experiments, Constructive Experiments, or any other of the phrases so dear to labor in America.

This is probably the last that you will hear from me for some months, as I am not [now?] having my vacation, and in August and September I expect to disappear from public view for a matter of six or eight weeks.

Sincerely yours,

Mary Austin

MA-L

If Lou Henry Hoover (1874-1944) had chosen to write her memoirs, she could doubtless have related when she and Mary Austin first became acquainted. Mrs. Hoover's father had been a banker in Iowa, but when his wife developed a severe bronchial cough, he moved his family to Los Angeles. Later he opened a bank at Monterey, neighbor to Carmel. Lou Henry Hoover left Monterey before the artists and writers had begun to colonize the peninsula, but after her marriage to Hoover, her visits home may have brought her in contact with Austin who in 1912 dedicated *A Woman of Genius* as follows: "To Lou Henry Hoover and some Pleasant Memories of the Red House in Horton Street." Four years later, the earliest letters written by Mrs. Hoover to Mary Austin are found in the Austin Collection. One of them is a long undated account of the London social season for the Hoovers, with a descripton of the plays they had seen and the musicales held in the Hoover drawing room with Francis Grierson as the soloist (see note on Grierson as introduction to Edwin Markham *Letter 25*).

"Pomona" is an admiring term for Mary Austin as it is used by Lou Henry Hoover in *Letter 42*, since it identifies Mary with the guardian (in Roman mythology) of apple orchards and other fruit trees. Lou Henry's friend Anne Martin is the suffragette introduced before *Letter 38* by an episode in her acquaintance with the Hoovers. The previously written introduction to *Telegrams 33* and *34* deals with Austin's part in the Ford Peace Expedition. On the margin of the next to last paragraph in this letter, Mrs. Hoover wrote "and the Wells" to her list of greetings. Ida Tarbell (1857-1944) was an American author and lecturer who became associate editor of *McClure's Magazine* in 1894 and served until 1906. President Wilson appointed her to the Industrial Conference in 1919, and during the administration of President Harding she attended the Unemployment Conference. Mollie Best was also a leader in progressive causes and organizations working for women's rights. The Whites are, doubtless, the William Allen Whites of Emporia, Kansas (see *Letters 35, 36,* and *37*). Vernon Kellogg, classmate of White at the University of Kansas, taught entomology at Stanford University from 1894 to 1920; he was a director of the American Relief Commission to Belgium, 1915-16, and assistant to Hoover in the Food Administration. He is mentioned in the Elmer Harris *Letter 13*. In 1920, he authored *Herbert Hoover, A Biography*. "Bertie" is, of course, Herbert Clark Hoover.

_____ 42

THE RED HOUSE
  HORTON STREET
    LONDON, W.   23 March 1916

My Dear Madam Pomona,
        You don't know what an utter joy your letter was,—the very nicest one I have had for months and months. Quite aside from all the interest about you, was the delightfully breezy news of the outside world! It is so good to know that there are Beaux Arts Balls, Mrs. Fiske, Shakespeare Celebrations even though they do fiasco, and Suffrage Conventions! And it is the crowning of Anne saying that *you* are *also* getting middle-aged and conservative,—she dubbed me that years ago! Please do it again whenever you can spare the time.
    I do tremendously wish you were here to talk things over with often. The psychology is really getting very interesting,—I think much more so than at the beginning of the War. Things are becoming more crystallised perhaps. Sometimes I am much more than tempted to tell you to come along, but be sure whenever you do come that you have a very good reason for coming, as the mere sightseer is not very welcome these days. Also don't come if the Germans decide to blow up all the neutral boats. Thank fortune you were not on the Ford Expedition. And yet as a human study, it would have doubtless been absorbingly interesting. And about Peace propaganda or Preparedness, I really suppose they have to go on together until all the great Powers accept the former. But alas! if this thing goes on for a few more years, Spain, Portugal, and Scandinavia will be the great powers of Europe. Holland, we hear from people who are coming over, is really in a state of furious exasperation.
    But where are those humorous tales? I have not seen one of them.

Here we have not a great bookstall full of American magazines, to turn over the tables of Contents, and pick out our friends from,—and the result is that I see very few American magazines, and when I happen to pick one up, the names I most want to see are not there that month.

And I did get the Belgian Cook-book for Xmas, but I thanked another lady for it! There was not any name in it, and I happened to have a letter about it just as I was leaving New York, from a lady I did not know, but who had been helping prepare it. And so I supposed that she had sent it. However, many thanks to you now just the same. We will cook a dish from it tomorrow and call it "Mary Austin Pudding."

Do remember me to that extremely nice Miss Tarbell, and Mollie Best, and also those very nice Allen Whites if they turn up again. Did you catch a glimpse of Dr. Kellogg when he went through New York? He did very good work in Belgium and France, but I am afraid was pretty tired out by the time he left. He had a good article about it in the March Atlantic Monthly.

Now I am being interrupted, so I will finish this some other time, but don't forget, between plays, to write another letter like this one.

With much love from us all—Bertie is in Belgium at the moment.

Yours

Lou Henry Hoover

An undated letter written by Mrs. Hoover on the California Limited, a train of the Atchison, Topeka, and Santa Fe Railroad, covers thirty-six pages of the company stationery and details the trips she has taken with her husband to many parts of the world. The letter is, in fact, a brief biography of Herbert Hoover's professional career as a mining engineer. Although *Letter 43* is undated, the jars that have arrived are mentioned again in a letter written on April 26, 1919. In this letter, Lou Henry Hoover expresses a desire to see the Indian dances of New Mexico, but she states that a trip then would conflict with the Easter vacations of her two sons. On May 18 of the same year, she writes in the same vein but makes no promise for a specific time to bring the visit about.

_____ **43**

March or April, 1919 (?)

Dear Miss Austin:

The box of jars arrived simultaneously with a couple of boxes from Washington. But I will let you guess which one we opened first! They came in perfect condition,—three Santo Domingo, one Zuni, one Tewa, and the San Ildefonso water jar,—all beautifully packed around with grass. They were promptly put in the bathtub to see if they were "self-cooling,"—we hope they don't put soup in the foodbowl, it loses about a quarter of an inch an hour through its skin! Now they are all over the living room, and we look extremely picturesque, and are extremely pleased with ourselves, and you. And are spending thought on what should be the artistically correct branches to put in them, which of course we must have, even if we have to rob the botanical cactus garden. I was interested in the quaint smaller bowls, one of which will go to Mrs. Rendtorff according to your drawing, because I did not realize they made many so small. Do they make them even larger than the two Santo Domingo jars you sent? Some day when you are writing to me about something else, tell me about how tall the largest you happen to have seen.

And the shining black water jar is quite the loveliest thing I could imagine! It sets me to planning all sorts of appropriate backgrounds for it—I shall have to have an Indian room some day,—or perhaps better an Indian porch. It is a household possession to treasure and has given me a lot of joy in the last twenty-four hours! Just at present it stands on a mahogany table, full of bronze leaves, and looking at itself in a mirror, and you might think it had been civilized all its life.

I am keeping your letter, and as soon as I have a more concrete idea of how many jars my California house can hold, and what kind, I shall let you know.

An since we have promised to land on your doorstep—if you have one—when we come to New Mexico, you will probably know almost as soon as we do when the Hoovers are coming!

Yours,

Lou Henry Hoover

On December 17, 1922, Mrs. Hoover wrote discussing a bill introduced in the United States Senate by Senator Holm Bursum of New Mexico. The intent of the bill was to settle claims to Indian lands held by non-Indians through intermarriage or direct negotiations with individual Indians. Mary Austin happened to be among those who were strongly opposed to the bill. After the Bursum Bill had been sent back for amendments, it was finally defeated. On June 14, 1923, a letter written by Mrs. Hoover from 2300 S Street, Washington, D. C., states that she has been requested to answer her husband's mail when it comes to the house during his absence. She replies, therefore, to a letter sent to him by Mary Austin on May 26 in which Austin asserts that Hoover had privately informed citizens of Phoenix, Arizona, that Austin was not reliably informed on the Indian question, or any other. Mrs. Hoover replies that as Secretary of Commerce, her husband was not connected with Indians in any way, but that from the time he was a small boy and spent months at a time with his uncle on one of the largest Indian reservations, he has always had a passing interest in their development. She knew without asking him that Austin's statement was without foundation, but to be certain she asked him whether he had discussed her in relation to Indian affairs when the Hoovers were in Arizona and New Mexico. He replied that to the best of his knowledge he had not mentioned her name while he was out there. She concludes with the advice: "Don't spend so much time or energy or vital force over the Indians, or any other subject, and become so obsessed with it that you lose your sanity or sense of values, or that better sense of humor!"

The subject of the native Americans had previously caused some annoyance to Secretary Hoover as shown by a letter to Mary Austin on January 30, 1923, which he had annotated with words at the bottom of the page: "How are you anyway—outside of Indians?" Only one letter followed the exchange between Lou Henry and Mary in June of 1923. On September 8, 1927, Mrs. Hoover answered a note sent to her by Mary Austin with information about Henry Seidel Canby, editor of the *Saturday Review*. She expressed "her love for Santa Fe and all that country" but made no mention of a plan to visit the Pueblos with Mary Austin as a guide. Comments in Mary's *Earth Horizon* indicate that the disagreement about the Indians led to the alienation. That something ended a friendship lasting over many years is confirmed by Hoover's failure to make any mention of Austin in his *Memoirs*.

The Hoovers were a team in their public activities, working in the labors of the American Committee to assist their countrymen stranded in Europe at the outbreak of war in 1914, and continuing in their cooperation until the last day in the White House on March 4, 1933. They collaborated in the study and translation of a Latin work called *De Re Metallica*, which was written in 1556 as an early treatise on geology and metallurgy. In 1909, Hoover had published a pioneering textbook called *Principles of Mining*. Following this labor, he published a dozen more books, consisting of biography, politics, and public addresses. His literary style combines the quiet virtues of his personality, which were straightforward statements, good-humored comment, and resourceful learning.

The United States Senate on November 11, 1973, authorized a $5 million federal contribution to construct and equip a memorial building in honor of Herbert Hoover. This educational building and library is planned for construction adjacent to the Hoover Tower on the Stanford University campus near Palo Alto, California.

Letter 44 was written in the year after Edgar Lee Masters (1869-1950) published his *Spoon River Anthology* (1915), a book of poems that immortalized the author in the story of American literature. Masters had been writing poetry for thirty years before he sprang into fame with this book. In his autobiography *Across Spoon River* (1936), he pays tribute to his high school English teacher in Lewistown, Illinois, where he was for a time an apprentice printer for the local paper called the *News*. Lewistown was just north of the *Spoon River* bottom lands, a farming area of ramshackle homes which were often flooded by the stream. Earlier Masters had lived in Petersburg, near New Salem, where Lincoln spent his early manhood. *Spoon River Anthology* assembles 214 epitaphs for people in a cemetery. Each poem is a verse portrait of an individual who is alphabetically listed, but then presented in no perceptible order, just as the burials occurred on the hill. An entire community relives its life as the stories are told.

The name of the writer of *Letter 44* is printed in a masthead of ornate Old English type, and the Marquette Building designates a location where a lawyer's fame is eclipsed by his fame as a poet. In fact, Masters states that he had to notify associates that he was still practicing law in order to reassure his clients in the legal profession. Later in this year he was to publish two more books of poetry, one called *The Great Valley* and the other entitled *Songs and Satires*, the first oriented to themes of nature and the Illinois environment and the second to subjects suggested by Chicago and its people and localities. Critics felt that both books were below the drama and excitement conjured by the collection in *Spoon River Anthology*.

Masters was a prolific author. The bibliography of his writings will list more than sixty titles, consisting of twelve plays or dramatic poems; sixteen books of poetry independent of reprints and the revision of *Spoon River Anthology*; four biographical studies; and books on political and legal matters. He was a close friend of the novelist Theodore Dreiser and the poets Carl Sandburg and Vachel Lindsay. Among his contacts were Harriet Monroe and Alice Corbin Henderson, coeditors of *Poetry, A Magazine of Verse*; Amy Lowell, the apostle of Imagism as a poetic creed; and many others in the literary scene, including Mary Austin. Masters stated that Amy Lowell thought he was obsessed with sex and wrote too much about it. Had she lived to read his autobiography, her opinion would have been confirmed. He concludes the autobiography with the comment that his last book, *The Invisible Landscape* (1935), contains an imaginary figure much like himself. It is "mad Frederick" in a poem called "The Star." The mad one pursues a star imaged in a pool, searches through hills and rocky headlands, crosses valleys by old houses and windmills, through cities and fields until he has a vision of something universal and deathless which broods upon earth and reflects itself in it.

In *Letter 44*, Masters inquires, indirectly, whether Austin had visited the Holy Land in order to write so convincingly about the places in *The Man Jesus*. Her reply would have been in the negative. His question about her "one smoke stories" was answered when she published a number of these Indian folktales some years later in the *American Mercury, Nation, Bookman, Atlantic Monthly, Southwest Review,* and other magazines, collecting them all in a volume called *One Smoke Tales* which was printed in 1934, a few months before her death.

_____ 44

LAW OFFICE
Edgar L. Masters
Marquette Building
Chicago   Chicago, Ill., Jan. 8, 1916.

Mrs. Mary Austin,
    C/o National Arts Club
      New York City, N. Y.

Dear Mrs. Austin:
    Your kind letter of the 6th reached me to-day. Since I wrote you last, I have read your book and I find it so wonderfully vivid in its descriptive passages, that I wonder if you have been over the ground yourself. What you say about the crowds in Jerusalem on the day of the crucifixion brings it home to me with a new significance. Altogether, I think your book a beautiful piece of work, even though it sags a little in places. I addressed my letter to you at Carmel-on-the-Sea, California, and I meant to ask you in that letter something about that place and whether you liked it, etc. etc. I have thought a good deal, particularly during the last year about leaving this city, largely because of the hideous winters that we have here so frequently, but there you are sojourning in

New York and leaving the summer of California, and New York is not much better than Chicago in winter. Can you not tell me something about the one smoke stories of the American Indians and where I can find some of them? I would like to look into this.

With many thanks for the book, which I enjoyed greatly and for your kindly letters, believe me,

Very sincerely yours,
Edgar L. Masters.

Glancing through *Letter 45*, as written by Mary Austin to H. G. Wells, the reader gets the impression that there have been previous letters between these two individuals. Austin says "I shouldn't be writing at all," a comment that implies previous exchanges. Her last paragraph refers to an observation by Wells that she could not write novels. Anyone who knew Mary Austin would be skeptical that she ever really agreed with this opinion, for she had sold five novels successfully to publishers before this letter was mailed, and she produced two more at later dates. No letter from Wells is to be found in her correspondence, but a letter written by him to her publishers on November 14, 1932, became the cause for her to write *Letter 107* in which she defends herself from reporting a conversation with him in which he stated that he was to become the father of an illegitimate child. This incident in 1909, however, caused no rupture in their friendship as *Letter 45* makes evident. The state of their relationship fifteen years later, when she revealed the conversation in *Earth Horizon*, will be more fully presented in the introduction to her *Letter 107*, printed in this volume.

Mary Austin, in her less renowned career, shared many of the attitudes and points of view held by H. G. Wells. She found herself a rebel to her religious and educational background. She was unfulfilled in her experience of marriage, though she took no radical measures to readjust it. Her mind and writing crossed the lines between politics, science, and fiction, and she was quite as much a reformer as the all encompassing English author who quite obviously found her stimulating. Otherwise he would not have provided the statement printed by her publishers that her work "would live when many of the more portentous reputations of her day would have served their purpose and become no more than fading names." H. G. Wells, using the pseudonym "Reginald Bliss," placed these words in his book *The Mind of the Race* (1915).

The *American Magazine* for October of 1911 printed an article entitled "An Appreciation of H. G. Wells, Novelist," written by Mary Austin. In her testimonial, she identifies Wells as a genius, and associates his directive force with the "waiting powers" behind it, a favorite concept of hers for energy expressed in both nature and man. She points out that he has written both novels and social science in the form of fiction; that he has been called both a socialist and a revolutionist; that he is not what she would call "a University man," but a scholar of human conditions; and that in all the time she knew him in London, he never "clouded his genius with the obscurations of an 'Art Atmosphere'," but has been devoted to the broader concerns of scientific discovery and social consciousness. She lists a number of his works of fiction, such as *Love and Mr. Lewisham* (1900) and *Tono Bungay* (1909), but makes no mention of *Ann Veronica* (1909), a sensational story about a young woman who defies her father, becomes a zealous suffragette, and lives with her lover unredeemed by any ring or law or statute.

It was upon the issue of freedom from sexual restraint that Mary Austin and H. G. Wells can be said to have "locked horns," as illustrated by their dialogue described in *Letter 107*. The comment with which she concludes her "Appreciation" may be pertinent as she states that Wells understands the male characters in his novels better than he understands the females he creates. She adds that it is conceivable that of his women "the best of them might have known the novelist better than he knew them." However, she pays tribute to him as an avowed feminist, and claims that by his writing he has raised himself to a citizenship in the world of human understanding unattained by any Englishman since Dickens and by few before him.

Some annotation is warranted as an introduction to *Letter 45*. The "family affairs" to which Austin alludes were associated with the death of her brother James, which caused family dissension and raised problems concerning a niece who was christened with her name and chose to live with her in Carmel and later in Santa Fe, New Mexico. Austin's remarks on God as a "Power and Presence moving in the affairs of men" could be compared with Chapter 5 of *God the Invisible King* published by Wells in 1917. His view of an ideal Divinity calling for activism in his cause is much more specific and less mystical than the Presence invoked by Austin. Her reference to "Mr. Britling" calls to mind the novel *Mr. Britling Sees It Through* (1916) in which Wells records the bitterness of a famous English writer towards World War I and the loss of his son in Flanders' fields. Her novel mentioned in the final paragraph of the letter is *The Ford* (1917), a study of the clash in northern California between farmers and the members of a city water district committed to buying and removing the water from a river that has supplied their needs. The narrative in the book is skillfully handled and the characters are vividly drawn. Social consciousness is in the background but not obtrusive. By the "Mexican matter," she shows concern over the punitive expedition led by Brigadier General John J. Pershing against

Pancho Villa in reprisal for raids upon American border towns, one of which occurred at Columbus, New Mexico, on March 9, 1916.

The reader of *Letter 45* will applaud the courage and competence with which Mary Austin defends the course of the United States against European critics during the period of World War I from 1914 through 1918.

_____ 45

National Arts Club, New York
Jan. 24, 1917

My dear Mr. Wells:

I have read much of yours lately and I have more than once begun a letter to you, and left off, wondering if after all I could reach you through all the clamor of things nearer home. If you haven't seen me there in England it is because just at first when it seemed the whole thing was to be simply a stupendous drama, quickly done, it was because family affairs kept me in the West. After that I had a sort of feeling about going to look on, as if one should go to a funeral uninvited. It didn't seem quite the thing. Later still I have been convinced that the only thing people like myself could do would be to undertake to bring about a better understanding between my country and yours and I doubted my ability to do that at close range.

I have been afraid that some of those admitted family likenesses which we so detest in one another might come between our profounder realizations.

I shouldn't be writing at all tonight if I didn't feel that I represent, or at least interpret, a much larger class in America than you English are aware of, that I stand in a frame of mind unrealized by you and with an outlook which you only half understand. Perhaps I should say here and now that one of the heaviest silencers which falls across the lips of people like myself is the general unwillingness of English people like yourself to believe that we can speak for ourselves, interpret our own motions and locate ourselves in our own time. I should have written this letter to the English instead of simply to an Englishman if I had not felt that most English are a little surer that they understand us than that we understand ourselves.

Personally, if it had been left to me, I think I would have had my country fling itself bodily into the break of the Belgian boundary, not perhaps with blood and iron, but with those modern instruments which come more handily to our industrial temperament. But you must not make the mistake of thinking that our failure to do so was wholly due to apathy nor even to a deep rooted ideal of Peace. *You* let this thing happen, you people over there. Was it apathy or idealism that kept you sunning yourself on the doorstep with your dog scratching fleas, while a basilisk hatched under your walls? Well, whatever it was, much the same thing is holding us here, and I do not think it wholly discreditable in either case. I think it is the thing you just skimmed in saying that men must more and more learn to acknowledge God as a purposeful force in human affairs.

Over here we really believe in God—oh, not in that funny old tribal God who is always sitting on our banners or being jockeyed off the banners of our enemies, but we believe pretty generally in a Power and Presence moving in the affairs of men. After the first shock and surprise of the war, you could feel all over America, like the tightening of a ship's cordage in the rain, the common consciousness of the Power overseas. I was on the California coast when the war broke out, and I came back three months later to meet that consciousness as the profoundest social experience I have known.

People discussed the political, social and industrial contributing causes of the war, and then would be struck with silence. . . . Something Doing over there, one would say. . . . Something Doing . . . which was our way of saying that we saw in the War something larger, more mysterious than the clash of political entities. But to believe in God the way Americans believe in Him you must first have arrived at the conclusion that you are not in any way indispensable to Him, and we don't know, *we honestly don't know whether He needs us in this war*!

This is a primitive, picture-writing way of saying something so subtle that perhaps the language for saying it just precisely hasn't been invented yet. But if you can understand it, it will account to you for me and thousands like me, I might say millions like me who say little, but think much and wait—wait even in the face of things like the Lusitania—and relieve the strain of waiting by getting up bazaars for Belgian Relief and rolling bandages for the Red Cross.

I don't mean to say of course that there isn't apathy and financial interest and all sorts of vicious shirking, just as there is in England, but there is also something else which the pinch of present anxiety with you shouldn't permit you to miss in us. I admit that the obvious arguments seem to me all in favor of our throwing our influence where the weight of our sympathy is, on the side of the Allies. *But*—though we have an almost British aversion to talking of anything less than obvious, nothing about this is more American than the certainty of our acting, when we act, in the least obvious direction.

I notice among English writers—in particular yourself in *Mr. Britling,* a tendency to scold because we haven't reacted in a characteristically Anglo-Saxon way to this crisis. You have gone on thinking of us as English in the main, and bound in the ultimate reaction to come back to our allegiance, while the fact is that we are not even predominantly Anglo-Saxon any more, and mustn't be expected to be. That is what the war has brought us, the realization that we are not step-children of Europe at all—and I think it has surprised us, rather—but somehow have suffered a sea-change. Even the much quoted German-Americans are discovering after the lapse of the first shock that there is much more American than German.

If we come into this war—and as one close to the sources of knowledge I am not at all certain that we won't—, it will be the Americanism in the English and French which draws us to them much more than the French and English in us drives.

I am particularly anxious that you shouldn't miss knowing that our Pacifism isn't just the love of comfort, nor yet the spectacle of waste and loss which this war has shown us.

It goes deeper than that:—it comes to a profound distrust of fighting as a *means of getting something done.* War, in the vernacular, "doesn't get us anywhere"; and the profound, the controling American impulse is to "get somewhere." I believe in Europe you call it "materialism." Really it is our idealism and it is the inner meaning of phrases not always the happiest I'll admit—which puzzle Europeans, "too proud to fight" "Peace without Victory."

And that of course brings us to President Wilson. Nature undoubtedly designed him for such a crisis and society thwarted her by bringing him up in a University. Rail splitting would have served better. In America for a man to become a University Professor means that he is too early removed from the necessity of making good on his own among his equals.

He becomes the preceptor, the authority who must not take counsel lest he be shown to be weak, nor questioned why. This is one thing which has come to us out of the war, a notable example of the inutility of the "Intellectual life" as a preparation for social service. President Wilson believes profoundly in his own gift for divining in advance the will of the People. He has such a gift. But he is prevented by all his past from "putting it over." Neither is he able constitutionally to call around him and extract from their experience the kind of men who like Hoover—we've plenty of men built on those lines though not of Hoover's capacity—who could carry out his vision. This is the last benumbing trail of the Monastery around our institutions of learning. This is what they do to men who indulge in school to excess.

Nor has the President that use of words which belongs to men to whom words are a means of getting something done. Too many of the things he says are not speaking but writing, even fine writing. He is a man dealing with words as an officer on parade deals with his sword; he has not used it to carve his way through ranks of men. He is entirely sincere; it would be a gross injustice to think otherwise . . . he means what he says without always being able to say what he means. His latest document, read before Congress is a true report of the American point of view . . . such a report as some lately dead American might make through the journal of the Society for Psychical Research.

I have written this just as it comes at intervals, during the recovery from an illness. I think you will see me in England before the year is out. I probably shan't come with my mind made up to more than one thing, and that is that for the new order such people as you and I and Hoover—artists and engineers must get into the game. People with creative vision, with creative capacity must have more power in the processes of government. Civilization mustn't be allowed again to run into a blind alley. And in the meantime if you can persuade your country-men to give over the country-cousin concept of America it will go far to reducing a certain irritation which is occasionally felt by my countrymen.

Personally I am doing not much at present—I have written another novel—yes. I agree with you that I can't write novels, but publishers will have them. Recently I had a one act comedy successfully performed, but the times are too strenuous to write. I've been doing all I can in the Mexican matter.

Did you get the article I sent you clipped from the Times?

With best wishes to you and my express personal regards to Mrs. Wells.

Sincerely yours,
Mary Austin

Five letters in the Mary Austin Collection deal with an extraordinary vision which came to the author in the summer of 1917. This experience was reported in an exchange of letters with Sonya Levien, who at that time was a member of the editorial staff of *Metropolitan* magazine, 424 Fourth Avenue, New York City. Levien's husband, Carl Hovey, came from a very old New England family, and was managing editor of *Metropolitan* until it closed down in 1924. Subsequently, both he and his wife found employment in Hollywood, he as an editorial guide with manuscripts and she as screenwriter. Among her assignments, Levien worked with S. N. Behrman on the screen version of Molnar's *Liliom.*

The first letter, written on September 1, is printed here as *Letter 46.* Mary wrote to Sonya Levien after the two women had met at tea. They had conversed about the use of psychic power, a subject Austin once discussed with the psychologist Henry James, according to her autobiography. In her letter to Levien, she states that she has been under tension because of losing her older brother plus dissension in the family about his estate. She also cites added pressure occasioned by her work as advisor in public relations for the Food Administration (see *Letter 40*). To escape these complications, she had gone to a mountain retreat named "Byrdcliffe" in Woodstock, Ulster County, New York. She confirms this in a second letter which gives additional data. Written on September 4, this letter is recorded on stationery provided by the "Byrdcliffe" lodging house.

The vision, as described in both letters, tells of a light or ball of fire arising in Russia and proceeding southward from a dark wood. Austin calls it "an organizing, revivifying light which will produce far reaching activities and a purging of old ideas." In the second letter she puts the vision into verse, as follows:

A light out of middle Russia,
Out of a dark wood.
An ancient spark . . .
Moving over the mountains,

A light by a sea in the south.

. . . . .

They go over the mountains,
Whose roots are in the mountains.

. . . . .

White towers—four sided towers
By a sea beyond the mountains,
White sails—wing pointed.

. . . . .

Many rivers run together.
They rage in the mountains.
They run to the sea.
A ball of light—

. . . . .

The roots of fire—
A small man with a sword.
A dark man with an ancient sword.
A tree of fire in the south.

On September 7, 1917, Levien replied from Manchester, Vermont, where she was spending a three week vacation at the home of a friend. She said that Mary's engrossing letter, including the second explaining it, interested her very much. She noted that psychic contacts could be misleading, but expressed her ardent hope for peace in Europe and her faith in Mary Austin's vision.

The United States entered World War I on April 6, 1917, so that *Letter 46* and its sequel were written four months later but not before American troops were being sent to Europe. The Russian Revolution, led by Lenin, Trotsky, Stalin, and others, occurred in October of 1917, and could be identified with the ball of fire in Austin's vision. The "military exploit" to which she refers might cover the withdrawal of Russia from the war and the signing of the Treaty of Brest Litovsk on March 8, 1918. The "small, dark man with a sword in his hand" could point to Joseph Stalin, who came from the region of Georgia in eastern Russia and was five feet, four inches tall. His sword, symbolically speaking, was the agent of slaughter for tens of thousands of his fellow Russians.

More than a year later, on October 11, 1918, Mary Austin wrote to Levien from 356 South Occidental Boulevard, Los Angeles, returning to the discussion of her vision. She described it as an illumination that was swift and clear, something like a flash of lightning. She acknowledged that the images she saw could have been tossed up from tag ends of her thinking, and thrown to the surface of consciousness in unrelated moments. She calls Levien the "guardian of her psychic adventures."

Two more letters were written by Levien. The first, on April 8, 1919, consisted of five lines, and informed Austin that Levien had retained the original letters and now had sent all the correspondence to Mable Dodge Sterne, who lived in Taos, New Mexico. The second, written on May 8, 1919, repeats this information and is addressed to Austin in Taos. Mable Dodge Sterne was a famous confidante and patroness of artists and writers in both European centers and in New York City during the decade before she moved to Taos in 1918. More about her association with Mary Austin and other acquaintances will be written as an introduction to her *Letters 57* and *58.* Both she and Mary were deeply interested in psychic research. Both the faith and practices of exponents employing mental power will be revealed to the reader of Sterne-Luhan's letters.

_____ 46

The National Arts Club
New York

Gramercy Park
Manhattan
September 1, 1917

My dear Miss Levien:

You will recall that when I last had tea with you, and we discussed the development of psychic power in the individual, I said to you that I thought if I could get the right contact, I could find out something about the end of the war. Now in a curious way I have had a momentary illumination.

You know what a strain this summer has been for me,—the sudden death of my brother, coming in the midst of work for the government which taxed my powers to the utmost and could not be left off even for so great a bereavement. On Wednesday I finished all I had to do and dismissed it from my mind and gave myself leave to go away into the mountains and mourn for my brother and release my soul.

Of course my mind has been steadily occupied with problems of the war for months, and for the last few weeks I have been concentrated on the problem of peace—not seeing any more than anybody else how it would come or rather how it *could* come. Now for two days I have not thought of the war at all. I have not thought of anything, but I've sat in my room mending the summer's accumulation of silk stockings and this morning when I woke about sunrise I had a singularly vivid impression. If I were really to put it to you the way it came to me it would be something like a free verse poem, in rather obscure imagery. I shall try when I'm a little rested to express it in that way. That is almost always the way foreknowledge comes to me, but I always know myself whether it is just a poem or whether it has a definite meaning.

As nearly as I can interpret it now it is that there will arise help out of Russia—within a few months there will be rumors of it. Soon after the turn of the year it will begin to make itself felt in international affairs. It will be, I think, in the nature of a military exploit which will introduce new and unexpected elements not only into the conduct of the war, but into its solution. I cannot say now whether this help will be expressed in the person of one man or as a national policy, but I am very certain that in some way Japan will be involved. Perhaps it will be a man with Mongolian blood in him, or perhaps he will succeed in bringing Japan to the relief of Russia.

Possibly all this is too explicit. What I really see is a light arising out of Russia, moving southward toward the Southern Seas, centering there,—an organizing, revivifying light, far reaching activities, a purging of old ideas, new forms, center of civilization, all this far away, years away,—ten, twelve, years before it begins to make itself felt. And closer at hand a small man, a dark man with a sword in his hand.

Perhaps this is only the reaction of an over-wearied mind but things like this have come true so often to me that I cannot resist putting this on record. If I get any more definite interpretation I shall write you again.

Sincerely yours,
Mary Austin

VISITS TO THE WEST
IV

Two prominent West Coast friends suggested to Mary Austin that, as a stopover between trips from Carmel to New York City, she would enjoy a visit to the Indian pueblos of New Mexico. These friends were Frederick Webb Hodge, who had excavated some of the ancient ruins at Zuni pueblo, and Charles F. Lummis, who had lived from 1889 to 1892 in the Indian village at Isleta. During his stay in New Mexico, Hodge was associated with the School of American Research in Santa Fe. This may explain how *Letter 47* from John Haynes Holmes came to Mary Austin at that address. Holmes had met Austin somewhat earlier, for in a letter dated November 2, 1916, he mentions a previous meeting and also accepts an invitation to visit her at the National Arts Club. They planned to discuss her appearance before the Unitarian Conference scheduled in Washington, D. C., during the following month.

Mary Austin was a very religious woman. As she grew to womanhood in Carlinville, the Methodist Church was the center of her social and spiritual life. She protested the restrictions placed upon her in both spheres of activity. In small Midwestern towns, the traditional role of women was found in household duties, family occupations, and church obligations. Of course, there were parties in summer, berry picking, fishing, and apple butter making. In winter, the candy pulls, sleigh rides, and spelling bees added variety to church, school, and community occasions. Love for nature and the out-of-doors brought inspiration and beauty to drab moments in Austin's life, as she states in Book Two of *Earth Horizon*. She tells of a childhood experience on a woodland hill near her home. While playing there under a great walnut tree, she felt the oneness of earth, sky, wind, and sunlight with the creatures who shared these elements. A voice within her spoke the word "God" and she answered back "God, God." The episode became an abiding reality in her life.

None of this mysticism is evident in the remarkable career of John Haynes Holmes (1879-1964), who became one of the most famous clergymen of twentieth-century America. From a background of religious training in Malden, Massachusetts, he entered Harvard, earned a degree in theology, and was ordained in the Unitarian ministry. At the age of 27, he accepted an invitation to assume the pastorate of the Church of the Messiah in New York City. Eleven years later he changed the name to the Community Church, having drawn to the congregation worshipers of liberal outlook on theological, social, and political problems. Holmes wrote books on world peace, anti-Semitism, civil rights, and the revolutionary nature of religion. He was a disciple of Mahatma Ghandi, telling of his relationship with the master in both biographical and pulpit memoirs. Holmes was an eloquent speaker, in the great tradition of American oratory. *I Speak for Myself* (1959), written the year he retired as minister for the Community Church, tells of travels during which he met such world figures as H. G. Wells, Bernard Shaw, Kaiser Wilhelm, Harold Laski, and influential people in the Soviet Union. Included among his friends in the United States were two mayors of New York City, Jimmy Walker and Fiorello H. La Guardia, plus such other prominent leaders as Eugene V. Debs, Clarence Darrow, Rabbi Stephen S. Wise, Emma Goldman, and Jane Addams. His letters to Mary Austin indicate that he also thought highly of her.

There is no copy of "letter of the 28th last" as Holmes refers to it, but in his reply he summarizes the contents. He states that, as a minister, he separated from the Unitarian fellowship in the fall of 1919. His intention was to break the tie with any specific covenant in Christianity in order to emphasize his universal concept of religion and his church's ecumenical mission. *Letter 47* underlines the emergence in the churches of a new type of minister, one that extends his ministry into the everyday contracts of his parishioners as they try to demonstrate their Christianity in the world of business, political, and other social relationships.

_____ 47

CHURCH OF THE MESSIAH

Park Avenue and Thirty-fourth Street
New York City

Miss Mary Austin   April 4, 1919
School of American Research,
Santa Fe, New Mexico.

Dear Miss Austin:
        How welcome is your letter of the 28th last, and how earnestly do I thank you for reaching your hand to me through all this vast distance

between New York and New Mexico. I also am sorely troubled about the world, and am groping for companionship and help in the day's task of living and hoping. I am at times tempted to despair by the failure of so many people to rise above their prejudices and to crush out their hates and fears; and when I look Abroad, especially to Paris, I see there the reflection of what seems to be the impotence of the human spirit. At my best moments, however, I am certain that there is no occasion for hopelessness. Man is the creator of his own destiny and he will not be balked permanently. If not by one method, then by another he will reach his goal. But, alas, the hideous and unnecessary price that has to be paid—the waste of time, and energy, and happiness that seems to be involved! At bottom what we now see is, after all, the perfect fruitage of the war, is it not? Men cannot sow widespread the seeds of lust and violence without raising the harvest that we now behold. Lord Dunsany's plays of the gods are constantly haunting me these days. You know how he always seems to have in mind the picture of men flouting their gods, deriding them, doubting them, denying them—and then at the climactic moment these same gods with firm tread come to visit upon men the doom of their ignorance and folly. We are living at that dreadful moment when the gods have come. We must pay to the uttermost farthing, and then begin again.

I like what you say about the need of spiritualizing our social life, and am humbled by the word of confidence that you address to myself. I am in the midst of great experiences in my church, and inwardly in the midst of mighty spiritual throes. I am convinced that if our churches are to accomplish anything, they must throw off all the shackles of past habit and tradition and enter upon the services of a true religion of communal, or social, life. I have left the Unitarian body that I may be entirely free in the service of pure religion. I am eager for my church to leave the Denomination also, and become a Community Church dedicated to the exclusive service of human-kind. I am getting responses from ministers and laymen everywhere indicating that a great new movement of spiritual emancipation is under way; and I am confident that it will soon manifest itself in startling and inspiring ways. The new religion, when it comes, will be indeed a combination of Christianity and Democracy. I am to-day preaching a series of sermons on "The New Religion and the New Democracy," in which I am stating that the church of our time and of the future must be simply that social instrument in which the spiritual ideals of our democratic friendship shall be embodied. How I wish I could sit down with you and tell you all that is in my heart and all for which I am laboring! This is just a hint to let you know that I am trying, and trying hard.

Thanks again for this moment of communion and renewed friendship. When you find the opportunity, will you not write me again and tell me more of what is in your heart.

Sincerely yours,
John Haynes Holmes

Fire destroyed the Church of the Messiah in 1837 and again in 1919. The second church was a magnificent structure. Placed in mid-Manhattan and built in the rare Byzantine style with heavy sandstone blocks, the church had a splendor which survived the encroachment of office skyscrapers and commercial structures. When this second church went up in flames, Holmes was at his summer home in Maine. *Letter 48* records his dismay and frustration as he was faced with the prospect of building what was to become his Community Church. For a while, services were held in the Town Hall. Finally, Holmes was able to rejoice in a new church building just one block from the location of the second church on Park Avenue.

_____ 48

THE COMMUNITY CHURCH OF NEW YORK

Park Avenue and Thirty-fourth Street
New York City

September 22, 1919

Miss Mary Austin,
Santa Fe,
New Mexico.

Dear Miss Austin:

I am cleaning up my desk in preparation for the winter ahead, and I came upon your two letters written me last April. It grieves me to think that I have never answered these, especially, as I have all along had so much that I wanted to confide to you; your second letter, especially, went deep into my heart, and challenged frank confession as to my spiritual experiences; but in the wear and tear of my routine work, I never seem to find the quiet moment for writing, and so time has gone on, and you probably think I have forgotten all about you.

Even now I cannot write as I should like, for alas and alack, I am sitting here amid the ruins of my church, which was wrecked by fire on September 11th, last, overwhelmed with a hundred and one tasks occasioned by this disaster, and facing the melancholy prospect of hard labor for months, and perhaps years, to come on such material things as land and bricks and mortar. The blow is a terrific one, especially coming at a time when my new movement was just getting under way; but I am resolved, if possible, to transform this tragedy into opportunity for greater and better things.

Is there any likelihood of your coming back to New York this winter? I sincerely hope so.

With all good wishes.

Very sincerely yours,

John Haynes Holmes

There is a lapse of nine years in the correspondence between Holmes and Austin. *Letter 49* was sent to her house called "Casa Querida," which he does not identify either by street or number. He addresses her as "Miss," which he does in three of the six letters remaining in the file. In 1928, possibly before *Letter 49* was written, Austin published her book *The Children Sing in the Far West,* her only book of poetry. This collection contains seventy-six poems, divided into such groups as "Songs of the California Coast," "Songs of the Southwest," "Tribal Wisdom," and "Songs of Occasion." Some of these poems had appeared in *St. Nicholas, The Youth's Companion, Delineator, The Forum,* and *The Nation.* She states in the Preface that when she began to teach children in the elementary grades at Mountain View and Lone Pine, California, from 1889 to 1892, she could find only poems written about the eastern United States by Bryant, Whittier, and Longfellow. Titles for some of her poems will show their adaptation to western themes: "Road Runner," "Sandhill Crane," Rocky Mountain Sheep," "Grand Canyon," "Western Magic," and "Winter in the Sierras."

Mark Van Doren, a distinguished poet and literary critic, on reading these poems, thought that Mary Austin should abandon other forms of literary expression in order to write more verse. *Letter 49* invites her to take part in a series of poetry readings by ten of the better known poets of the day. She accepted the invitation, and her reading occurred on Sunday, February 24, 1929. John Haynes Holmes wrote on March 26, following his trip to Palestine, that people in the audience were enthusiastic about her reading and he concludes, in appreciation, that her visit was one of the "most happy occasions in our Church life."

⎯⎯⎯⎯⎯ 49

THE COMMUNITY CHURCH

Park Avenue and Thirty-Fourth Street
NEW YORK CITY

| MINISTER | October 31, 1928 | Church House and Offices |
| John Haynes Holmes | | 12 Park Avenue |

Dear Miss Austin:

For some four or five years past I have been conducting here at my church, in the late hour of Sunday afternoons during the winter, a series of poetry readings. I have gathered together a small group of poetry lovers and we have learned together to be familiar with much of the poetry that is being produced in our time. During the last year or so I have taken occasion to invite one or two of our contemporary poets to read in my place from their own works.

This coming winter I am expecting to be away from my church on an important mission for a period of ten successive Sundays, and I am cherishing the hope that I may be able to arrange a series of poetry readings by ten contemporary poets for these dates. The series of Sundays will begin on January 13 and run through March 17. I am sending this letter to you and to Lenora Speyer, Lola Ridge, Countee Cullen, Sarah Cleghorn, Kahlil Gibran, Stephen Vincent Benet and Brent Dow Allinson.

I am writing to ask, as you see, if you can accept my invitation to take one of these Sundays and, if so, if you can submit two or three dates during the latter part of January and through February, at which time you are to be in the city. I should like as many dates as possible as it is not easy to arrange a successive series of meetings of this kind.

The poetry hour begins here at 5:15 and continues until 6 o'clock. It is held in a quiet corner of the church in the gathering shadows of the evening. I should like you very particularly to read from your own poems with such accompanying comments and interpretations as you may think helpful. I can promise you a group of eager and sympathetic listeners. In the case of this especial series I should plan regularly to advertise the poetry hour in our regular church notices in the Saturday newspapers, together with such reading notices as I can secure. I am confident that the presence of yourself and your associates with us in this especial way would gather a much larger company of my own parishioners and the general public than we have ever had before.

It is my eager hope that I may hear favorably from you. Believe me, with high regards,

Very sincerely yours,
John Haynes Holmes.

Fannie Hurst (1889-1968) wrote *Letter 50* some day in the week before Friday, May 23, 1924, when *Abie's Irish Rose* was presented as a benefit performance before members of the P.E.N. organization to which Anne Nichols, author of the play, Mary Austin who approved of it, and Fannie Hurst who did not approve of it, all belonged. This organization of poets, playwrights, editors, essayists, and novelists was holding an international gathering in New York City. Mary had been appointed to a committee authorized to select a play as entertainment for the group and its guests. Other members of the committee urged the selection of Max Reinhardt's beautiful spectacle called *The Miracle*, then being shown at the Century Theater as it had been remodeled into the likeness of a Gothic church. Mary pointed out that the play was of foreign origin and had been shown throughout Europe, whereas *Abie's Irish Rose* was a folk drama enriching appreciation for everyday life in New York City. Little did it matter to her that the critics considered it a dramatic comic strip, and Jewish theater goers (of whom Fannie Hurst was one) looked upon the play as a carica-ture of their way of life. She won the support of Anne Nichols (1891-1966) and the offer of the theater for the benefit; then appealed to members of the P.E.N. and overcame all opposition. The playhouse was crowded as the audience was treated to the humorous but edifying complications of a Jewish groom with an Irish bride, two families that required three wedding ceremonies, a year of married life, and the birth of twins to reconcile their differences and restore harmony for all involved. In a letter written on May 27, 1924, to A. D. Mac-Dougal, director of the Desert Laboratory, Tucson, Arizona, Mary stated that the performance was a great success and she felt the audience became a part of the play, "the thing for which all the modern producers strive." Carl Van Doren, an ally of Austin's in many ways, is a likely reference in the letter.

_____ **50**

Dear Mary Austin: Undated

I have spent days mulling over a matter which without the imprint of your personality upon it, I could have decided in as many minutes.

All that you say in your fine and logical letters is true—to you—to Mr. Van Doren—to me—but Dear M.A. so far as the unthinking public is concerned any one appearing at Abie's Irish Rose next Friday evening to say a few amiable words on any subject whatsoever, is sponsoring the play!

Perhaps if I were a Mary Austin and sufficiently secure in my remoteness from the feeble aspects of the play in question, I might not feel as I do. It may be just that sort of inferiority complex, although I will never admit that my work at any time had any of the qualities that make Abie's Irish Rose a travesty on life. But I won't bore you all over again with that aspect of the matter.

I know that you would not want even my great admiration for you to impel me to violate convictions that are as strong as mine are in regard to the matter under discussion.

I wish before you flit west and I flit I-wish-I-knew-where, that you would come dine with me.

One day next week?

Faithfully,

Fannie★

During a literary career that included journalism, short stories, novels, plays, and film scripts, Fannie Hurst was always primarily concerned with people, both as she created imaginary characters and as she labored to assist real individuals in the world around her. Her publishing achievement included eight volumes of stories, seventeen novels, plays, and six books of nonfiction, one of which was an autobiography entitled *Anatomy of Me* (1958). The reader of Fannie Hurst's novels will find the analysis she provides of her youth in Hamilton, Ohio, and St. Louis, Missouri, a guide to the social documentation in her books, explaining why she took time to serve on the National Housing Commission, 1936-1937; the National Advisory Committee for the Works Progress Administration, 1940-1941; the Board of Directors for the New York Urban League; and as Special Delegate to the World Health Organization in Geneva, Switzerland.

The florid imagery and sentimental dimension of her early style became more restrained in later writing, but never lost its essential vividness. *Letter 51* reveals her thinking about the way she developed scenes and situations in the highly imaginative content of her fiction. The "last two novels" referred to are *Stardust* (1921) and *Lummox* (1923). The first tells the story of a woman's childhood in a boarding house and the outcome of sacrifice in success for her daughter as a singer. The central figure in the second story is an immigrant woman who as a servant suffers abuse and neglect, but surmounts every circumstance to arrive at appreciation and contentment.

Letter 51 was printed in Austin's *Everyman's Genius* (1925), one of her most widely read books. Individual chapters of this work appeared in *The Bookman* during 1923 and 1924. Except for the first paragraph and the handwritten postscript, the context appears as one of the "Notes on Personal Methods" which were contributed by fifteen individuals who had attained notable success in such varied fields as invention, engineering, literature, theater arts, drawing, dancing, poetry, teaching, and museum work. In addition to Fannie Hurst, four of the others who gave testimonials are also represented in letters selected for this book: Robert Edmond Jones, Ryan Walker, Marianne Moore, and Bill Robinson. The letter appears in the Appendix of *Everyman's Genius*, and is reproduced with the permission of the publisher, Bobbs-Merrill Company.

———— 51

5620 Cates Avenue,
St. Louis, Missouri,
February 9, 1925.

Mrs. Mary Austin,
The National Arts Club,
Gramercy Park,
New York, N. Y.

Dear Mary Austin:

    The title of your book is somewhat disarming, but I take it that in attempting to reach your conclusions regarding that phenomenon of the supreme creative mind—the genius—you are feeling your way along by a study of the manifestations of the average creative mind.

I remember, when about ten years younger, hearing both Mrs. Frances Hodgson Burnett and Mrs. Gertrude Atherton dwell at some length upon the growing importance of the play of the subconscious in their work.

At that time, my attempts at creative writing seemed to me to lie clearly within the bounds of my conscious effort.

I remember in particular my astonishment at a statement from Mrs. Burnett to the effect that she only attempted to write when impelled to do so by feeling a little jerk at her arm, as if someone were tugging at her sleeve to attract attention.

I still feel that to be an extreme expression of the subconscious at work, but each subsequent year of my writing experience is emphasizing how much of my impulse for creative expression takes place in the sub-stratas of my consciousness.

In fact, my last two novels have even suggested to me that I may be rather an extreme example of one who writes with a growing dependence upon the unchartered territories of human consciousness.

Which does not mean that the conscious processes of writings are any the less difficult. In my own case the manner in which the genesis of a theme arrives is identical in almost all cases.

My stories never suggest themselves by incident or character. There usually arises in my mind, apropos of nothing in so far as I am able to directly trace, the beginnings of the idea, some such question as this: Given a combination of certain conditions, how will a given human being react to them? The story then builds itself around this central query.

With one exception, I have never taken an incident, a character, or a situation directly from life.

Indeed, as I continue to write, I find that less and less am I dependent upon concrete examples of human behavior.

In the excruciatingly slow and laborious processes of my writing, I find that combinations of facts present themselves to me from some no-man's land of my consciousness.

I suppose that psychologically these facts actually represent composite sub-conscious impressions that have got themselves caught in my brain-grooves, but there are times when these impressions seem to march themselves out, reluctantly it is true, on to my typewriter roll in a fashion over which I have no particular jurisdiction.

Time and time again I have rebelled against the behavior of a character who would behave no other way.

Time and time again I have found myself writing an incident for which I could find no particular reason at the moment, only to find later in the book that the reason was there awaiting me.

Time and again I have described a concrete place without ever having seen it and then journeyed there afterward to find that my copy needed no change.

Of course none of these incidents is mysterious, but it does mean that the author whose mind works that way is soon to discover that his mental fireless-cooker is going to do a great deal of work for him.

I have written pages, not only in the torment of composition, but in the torment of wondering if that mysterious force in the unchartered areas of my brain was reliable, or was only a madness lurking there.

My only consolation is that apparently the best of my work has been written from those unexplored realms.

It gives one a sense of power and it gives one a terrifying sense of helplessness.

Faithfully yours,

P.S. [handwritten]   *Fannie Hurst*

Dear Mary Austin
I notice that you refer to "The Cartoonist," "The Artist" I would much
prefer, unless to use my name would be a favor to you—that you omit my
name and refer to mine as the experience of "a novelist."

F.H.

Among Mary Austin's friendly adversaries none holds a more distinctive place than Van Wyck Brooks (1886-1963), a dominant figure in the American literary scene from the appearance of his first book, *The Wine of the Puritans* (1909), to the publication of his last, *From the Shadow of the Mountain* (1961). Member of an affluent New York family living in Plainfield, New Jersey, Brooks's environment was always one of art, music, and literature.

Before entering Harvard University, he had traveled in Europe, visited the museums of the great cities, lived in England, and gazed upon such historic figures as the German Kaiser and the English Queen Victoria. He confessed in *Scenes and Portraits* (1954) that at this period of his life Europe was a realm of magic, and the literature, art, and learning of America suffered by comparison. As a matter of course, he chose to live in London after graduation from college in 1907 and to write his first book there. Slowly, however, he began to realize that America interested him more than Europe. Returning to New York, he learned of an opportunity to teach at Stanford University, and in 1911 he arrived in Palo Alto to join the Department of English in that institution. During the next two years, he became acquainted with the Carmel art colony. There he first encountered Mary Austin.

From the Shadow of the Mountain is Brooks's third and final volume of autobiographical memoirs. He tells of a picnic which was held for Austin on the beach at Carmel. Previously she had given him a talisman covered with Indian signs in water color, among them a pair of horns and a pine tree. Having lived with Indians as neighbors, he says, she thought of herself as a medicine woman and resented the fact that her efforts to trace American culture and its literary forms to Indian origins had not been accepted by the New York critics. Brooks describes her as a "lonely disappointed woman with an empress complex." On this particular occasion, however, he states that she was in her element as a storyteller, and was the center of interest as she recounted the legend of Vasquez, a Mexican bandit, whose white horse continued to haunt the highway near Carmel long after its master had been captured and hanged for robbery and other misdeeds.

Letters 52, 53, 54 are three of the nineteen which Brooks wrote to Austin in 1920, 1921, and 1922 when he was associate editor of *The Freeman* magazine. The first letter, sent on June 24, 1920, contains an apology for reporting two personal stories in a critique of her work. He explains that he felt both of them were true and illuminating about her as a public figure, but he admits that he was in error to indulge in such references to a living author. He adds that anecdotes were commonplace in discussing authors of the past. Apparently Mary forgave him, for in *Letter 52*, dated July 1, 1920, Brooks refers to her "gracious letter" written in the previous month.

Successive letters spell out what appears to have been an amiable feud between these two eminent correspondents. *Letters 53* and *54* are addressed to Austin during her second trip to Europe, which lasted from the summer of 1921 until the end of 1922. Her offer to bring him anything he requests and his mention of a pleasant note in which she told of the contacts she had made confirm a cordial relationship at this time. However, only one of the letters greets her as "Dear Mrs. Austin." All the others begin with "My dear Mrs. Austin," and the formal salutation indicates the reserve Brooks felt in their friendship. On January 24,

1921, he expresses regret at missing an opportunity to visit with Willa Cather and Mary in New York, explaining that his residence so far out in the country presented difficulties in the winter as well as compensations in the spring. He makes known his interest in her "Indian poems," which were doubtless those appearing in *The American Rhythm*, a book published in 1923 and revised in 1925. The volume carried a lengthy essay in which she advanced her theory that the ceremonial life and rituals of American Indians illustrated and influenced the structure of American speech and verse.

An undated note from Brooks rejects an invitation to a social occasion with Mary during her residence at the National Arts Club because his family was moving to a location closer to New York City. He was also unable to attend the luncheon in her honor at the Club on January 8, 1922, sending his regrets because a previous engagement with guests would keep him in the country. This occasion was the greatest recognition Mary Austin ever received from a gathering of her literary peers. The event will be fully described in *Letter 64*, in which she humorously confides to A. D. MacDougal a number of details that she omitted in *Earth Horizon*. There is no mention of Van Wyck Brooks in her autobiography. Nevertheless, he pays very generous tribute to her books in his chapter called "The Southwest," written for *The Confident Years, 1885-1915* (1952).

_____ 52

The Freeman
32 West 58th Street, New York
July 1st 1920   (at Mohegan, New York)

My dear Mrs. Austin,
        Your gracious letter has released me from a very unpleasant spell, and I wish to thank you for it most sincerely. And now I may mention, what I can't with will have mentioned before, that this and certain other lucubrations of mine in The Freeman have been preliminary rough sketches, thinking aloud, for a much more carefully considered under-taking later on, that I am, for this and other reasons, anxious to under-stand you, and that I should welcome as a privilege the opportunity to meet and talk with you. Of your books I have read the following: *Lost Borders, The Land of Little Rain, The Arrow Maker, Christ in Italy, A Woman of Genius, Love and the Soul Maker, 26 Jayne Street.* I need not

say that my hasty and superficial survey entirely failed to convey any conclusions about your work save as regards that "sense of the vocation" which seems to me at present the most important quality an American writer can have, which I found in you and which I illustrated in so inept a way. I shall make it a point this summer to read your other books, and to re-read two or three of those I have read, and if, then, you will permit me to call upon you I shall have reason to feel that my "penance" is an opportunity. It will probably be six weeks or two months before I shall be able to do full justice to this undertaking. At the end of that time I shall write to you, in the hope that I may then have the great satisfaction of meeting you.

Sincerely yours,
Van Wyck Brooks

———— 53

THE FREEMAN

116 West 13th Street
New York

July 26: 1921

My dear Mrs. Austin,

I have just come back from my vacation at Martha's Vineyard to find your kind letter, and I do thank you for that very generous offer of yours. Indeed there are so many things that I should like to have and get in England, I should like in a way so much to be there for a while; but there is nothing especially that I want and *can* get, much as I appreciate your having thought of me. As for American literature, the English seem, from all I can gather, to be as "conservative" as ever about it— which doesn't prevent them from coming here, in large numbers, in order to help us make it. New York is overflowing with them this summer.

I can imagine what wonderful times you must be having in spite of the prevailing spiritual apathy you speak of, which appears to have filled everyone who lives in England with a desire to escape from it. And it seems to me that from now on Europe will be for us as much a "luxury" as ever, but very much less of a "necessity." We have so great an opportunity, I feel, here, if we can only seize it.

I gather from your letter that you are working at a new book, which I shall be so curious and delighted to see; and I do hope you'll give me an opportunity to hear of your new experiences when you come back to us again. (I hope by then to be launched in a new book myself.) Meanwhile, my warmest thanks again, dear Mrs. Austin, for your letters, and the very best wishes for the remainder of your journey.

Very sincerely yours,

Van Wyck Brooks

The reference in *Letter 54* to Mary Austin and the English group called "The Fabians" can be interpreted by an article she wrote for *The Bookman* magazine in December of 1921. She called the article "My Fabian Summer," and in it she states that she not only lectured to an audience which included G. B. Shaw, the dramatist, Sidney and Beatrice Webb, social reformers, and Marie Stopes, a feminist who wrote a sensational volume called *Married Love*, but she entertained them all by a humorous burlesque of the American Court of Domestic Relations. The English considered this a legal counterpart of their professional correspondents in divorce cases based on adultery. Mary added that the weather was delightful in Surrey where the conference was held; that she danced a fox trot with Shaw; and at the conclusion of the meeting she encountered Sinclair Lewis and learned that he had sold 300,000 copies of his latest novel *Main Street*.

———— 54

THE FREEMAN

116 West 13th Street
New York

28 August: 1921

My dear Mrs. Austin,

Just a line, which I hope will catch you before you leave England, to thank you for your very pleasant note. It is delightful to hear of your lectures to the Fabians: are you going to publish them, either here or in England? Still the English are ahead of us in *having* such summer schools, in having the desire for them—schools, I mean, at which there is an attempt really to exchange thought.—How much I envy you your meeting with Hardy! But I can see that you are having an extraordinarily interesting summer.

Believe me, dear Mrs. Austin,
Sincerely yours,
Van Wyck Brooks

Among the early contacts Mary Austin made when she began to visit in Santa Fe was her friendship with Alice Corbin Henderson (1881-1949). Henderson, as Alice Corbin, had become known as a poet after she came to Chicago from St. Louis, Missouri, and in 1912 joined Harriet Monroe in the founding of *Poetry, A Magazine of Verse.* Four years later, she came to Santa Fe for her health, and with her artist husband, William Penhallow Henderson, joined the community of painters and writers who had come to New Mexico's capital because of interest in its background of Indian and Spanish cultures. She joined Monroe as coeditor of *The New Poetry, An Anthology* (1917), a publishing event which signaled greater freedom of form and spirit in the writing of verse. Through acquaintance with Vachel Lindsay, Edgar Lee Masters, Bliss Carman, Witter Bynner, Arthur Davison Ficke, Amy Lowell, and Mary Austin (all of whom are represented by letters in this book), she made Santa Fe a hospitable place for short or longer stays. Both English and American poets are included in her collection of New Mexican poetry called *The Turquoise Trail* (1928).

Letter 55 indicates how widespread was the protest against *The Ordeal of Mark Twain* (1920), Van Wyck Brooks's most controversial volume. Henderson's stanzas on Brooks as an amateur psychiatrist practicing on Mark Twain as the victim of his complexes would have found wide applause if she had published them. According to Brooks, Twain was a frustrated author because he had promised his father to succeed as a business man, and his mother expected him to make good on that promise. Therefore, Mark Twain suffered from a "malady of the soul," and in order to make money he ridiculed what he thought the public would find amusing in America's customs and way of life. After surrendering to his mother, he yielded to his wife's desire to improve his taste in language and behavior in accord with her view of gentility. Thus, Twain's creative instincts became suppressed and his soul as an artist was destroyed. Randolph Bourne (1886-1918), who is also mentioned in *Letter 55*, was a contributing editor of *The Dial* magazine, outlet for liberal intellectual and artistic expression. He was the author of *The History of a Literary Radical* (1920), which was edited by his devoted friend Van Wyck Brooks.

The article of New York criticism referred to in *Letter 55* was Mary Austin's review of *Our America* (1919), written by Waldo Frank (1889-1967). This essay type of criticism appeared on July 31, 1920, and it condemned the book because the reviewer believed that Frank did not know the United States well enough to understand the variety of its people and the progress made by minority groups. Frank was a traveled Easterner who had served on the staff of the *New York Evening Post* and the *New York Times*, but in his book he tells of getting on a motor bus at Pueblo, Colorado, to travel through the vast tract which the United States conquered from Mexico in 1848. He reports in a chapter called "The Land of Buried Cultures" that the Indian and Spanish heritages in the Southwest would be blotted out by the iron march of Anglo-American progress. Mary Austin commented that the America Frank knew "was a country centered in New York, with a small New England ell in the rear and a rustic gazebo in Chicago; the rest of it is magnificently predicated from a car window." Time has demonstrated the survival of both Indian and Spanish traditions in American culture.

_____ 55

August 24, 1920

Dear Lady —

Of course, W. P. H. has not had his N. Y. show yet. The page in Vanity Fair was an advance notice. The show is to be at the Kingore Galleries next January. (Including the Indian dance pastels and many fine new canvases.)

About your book, I am sure you know that I want it to add to your reputation. I will send you the mss. with some notes within a few days— am just helping send off a group of pastels to the Buffalo Museum. If you'll send me any new verses you have, I'll be glad to give you the benefit of any suggestions—for what they may be worth!

Have recently finished the balloting for best book of verse for 1919— Poetry Society Prize of $500. My first vote was for Gladys Cromwell's Poems.

I missed your article on N. Y. criticism in The Nation, or perhaps it hasn't come yet. A friend takes it and gives me here, so I don't subscribe.

I mean to subscribe to The Freeman—when I get the price! I'll be glad
to see the Mark Twain book, and will return it as soon as I have read it.

> I want a little complex
> To help me in my work
> So critics can write heavy books
> About each little quirk.

> How lovely is the mating,
> When complex meets complex,
> When lamb and lion both lie down
> Without a thing to vex.

> But then, you see, the lion's *dead*!
> The lamb need have no fear!
> Has Brooks a complex? Why, of course,
> He fears the *pioneer*!

If Twain were alive, he would simply *eat* Brooks, and call it a square
meal!—I've read some of Brooks' other books and Bourne's—and I think
their conception of the pioneer is one of the funniest things I have ever
come across! It's reflected in Waldo Frank's book, also.

My Corona was standing here hitched and saddled, so I just thought
I'd write you at once. I have many things on hand, and have been far
from well all summer, so please excuse haste.

Yours,

A. C. H.

Letter 56, also sent from Alice Corbin Henderson, was written
eight weeks later than Letter 55. However, similar topics arise and references
are made to the same book. Henderson returns *The Ordeal of Mark Twain* which
she had borrowed from Austin. She has read manuscripts sent her by Mary and
explains her delay in holding them. What is more serious is her refutation of a
charge by Mary Austin that in some way a conflict has arisen in their work as
poets. That year Ralph Fletcher Seymour, a Chicago publisher, had issued *Red*

Earth, a collection of Alice Henderson's work which contained her first poems about the Southwestern United States. She states in her "Notes" that the poems about Indians are not just description but are mirrors of nature as a reality which Indians invoke through words and gestures. Such titles as "The Green Corn Dance" and "Prayer Wands" point to a new direction for her poetic interest.

At this time, too, Mary Austin was publishing poems which she called "re-expressions" of Indian thought, and editors of *Harper's, The Dial,* and *Poetry* were accepting verses that later were used in *The American Rhythm* (1923). The exchange of viewpoints in *Letter 56* produced no permanent rift, as a note from Henderson dated December 15, 1920, reports that she has requested her publisher to send Mary a copy of *Red Earth* "for friendship," adding that Mary need feel no obligation to review it.

―――――― 56

Santa Fe, New Mexico
November 20, 1920

Dear Mrs. Austin:—

You certainly understand me very little if you think it would even occur to me to intentionally hold back a mss. of yours for any reason, and least of all in favor of my own work. It had never occurred to me that there was any connection or conflict between my work and yours, and if there had been, I hold that good work can only help good work, and the more of it the better. As a matter of fact, I have always done more to advance the work of others than to push my own, about which I entertain no false idea of superiority.

As it happens, Seymour's offer came very unexpectedly, not very long in fact before I wrote to you. My letter to you was perfectly frank and honest; but if you can't accept me as that, why, certainly there is no possibility of friendship between us, for I can't permit the accusation of ulterior motives, of which I am entirely innocent. Your notion is really perfectly absurd, as I think you may realize on second thought.

I was slow about your mss. because in the first place you said there was no immediate hurry. In the meantime I have been sick and am kept in bed, and what work I do is in spite of restrictions to the contrary.

When I finally did get down to your mss. I wrote you exactly what I thought about them.

I did not realize that you wanted to make any claim as to priority in free verse; but certainly that claim can have no connection with me, as I have never claimed to be a free verse writer—although, like many another, I wrote free verse long before the term was coined or given general currency. But my book makes no claim of any sort, there is no preface, and there are only the poems in it which have not been published already.

If this claim to priority in free verse is your object in publishing, you can perfectly well let your publishers make it for you. On the score of drama, you may be accounted a, or the, pioneer, so far as I know, even though your form is not quite perfectly achieved. But as far as this is concerned, a few months will not make any difference, and at the present rate of publishing, I don't think that high costs will prove any real obstacle. As far as priority in free verse is concerned—apart from drama, Stephen Crane and Whitman antedate the "movement" in this country; and I think the subject of form alone is rather sterile anyhow. However, this is merely my personal opinion, and may be wrong.

I am returning Brooks' book, which I enjoyed reading. Thank you for your good intentions about The Dial. I have subscribed to it, and I get the N. Y. Evening Post.

With best wishes, and deeply regretting your misunderstanding of me, I am

Yours sincerely,
Alice Corbin Henderson

Mary Austin had much in common with the author of *Letter 57*. She was seventeen years older than Sinclair Lewis but, like Lewis, had been born in a Midwestern community, spent her youth there, and found reason to criticize her background as well as pledge loyalty to its virtues and heritage. Neither Lewis nor Austin was endowed with a comely face or figure; both were "loners" in their failure to mix easily with groups of young people; and in maturity each frequently excelled in displays of irritation and discourtesy. Austin remained faithful to her temperance background, whereas Lewis fought the temptations of alcohol about as resolutely as did his friend Jack London.

The letters exchanged between Austin and Lewis faithfully record their mutual esteem and affection.

It is curious that their correspondence, as preserved in the Mary Austin Collection, began so late in their lives. They had known each other since the Carmel days in 1909; he was then 24 years of age and she was 41. *Letter 57,* the first of twelve retained by her, was sent at the time Sinclair and his first wife, Grace Hedegger Lewis, were living in Washington, D. C. This letter was written not quite two months after Lewis's novel *Main Street* had been published on October 23, 1920. The final letter which Lewis wrote was on March 28, 1931, and was sent from Indian Spring, Westport, Connecticut. It is in reply to the letter she had written to him on February 28, 1931. It will be discussed in connection with that letter (see Austin to Lewis, *Letter 60*).

The reader of *Letter 57* will be able to surmise, from Lewis's defense, what Austin had written to him about *Main Street.* First, she had commented upon the chief character's failure to function "spiritually in sex." Lewis replies that he recognized this deficiency, at least in a partial sense, by the chapter (XXV) in which Will Kennicott finds a woman to supply his wife's deficiency. The letter also discloses that Austin had mentioned her own contacts with young women of Carol Kennicott's type. She could even have cited her own successful novel, *A Woman of Genius* (1912), in which she portrays a fictitious character named Olivia Lattimore, who like Carol Kennicott fought the prejudices in small towns and lost her lover because she forced him to choose between accepting her with a career as an actress or as his wife without a career.

Juanita Haydock, mentioned in the letter, is contrasted with Carol in the book as a small town, self-satisfied social type. Miles Bjornstam, the Swedish dairyman, is shown with his family as they become victims of social stratification in Gopher Prairie, which has the Main Street giving title to the book. Others specified in the letter are: the Sam Clarks, generous and friendly folk who own a hardware store; Erik Valborg, a sensitive, somewhat effeminate young tailor, who attracts Carol Kennicott, but leaves town after she encourages his attentions and provokes gossip; and Vida Sherwin, the 39-year-old English teacher, once in love with Will Kennicott, who makes a happy marriage with Raymond Wutherspoon, a clerk in the Gopher Prairie department store.

_____ 57

1639 Nineteenth Street, N.W.
Washington, D.C.,
December 15 [1920?]

Dear Mary Austin:

I'm awfully glad you wrote to me about Main Street and Carol Kennicott, and I want to come back at you hard on one or two things. Can't you see that I *do* know that Carol, to quote your own well-worded prescription, "never functions spiritually in sex"? That is more than indicated in the chapter devoted to Will and his wistful frightened affair with Maud Dyer. The author doesn't say so, and Will, not being at all articulate, cannot say so, but in his confused soliloquy about himself and Carol he indirectly expresses that same idea. . . . You say all the young women you question in these cities are Carols. But don't you see that's exactly why I chose her for the center of this book? I do like her; I think that sometimes she's right, even in her feeblest aspirations for perfection; but I don't for a moment suppose that she's effective or particularly wise—or that she has "good taste" of an order enormously greater than that of the rest of the town. Good Lord, if she were incomparably better than, say, Juanita Haydock, she wouldn't stay in Gopher Prairie at all! But I wanted one who would be (tho I do hope she's an individual and not just a type) akin to all these Carols whom one finds adrift in all these cities. . . . Do you remember the sentence (in the chapters when we first enter war) suggesting that, after talking to Miles Bjornstam, Carol in a flash uncomfortably saw that she patronized even the people she loved? Don't you suppose the author (who, after all, must a little have understood Will and the Clarks, too, to have drawn them) understands that Carol often lacks spiritual perception of these people? Mary Austin, you of all living writers ought not, like our friend Mrs. Dawson of the Globe, to suppose that because I like Carol and am sorry for her, I intend to present her as a model, a standard.

I agree with you about Carol's blind unawakendness to the power of sex, but that was the ill-luck (luck it was—luck of propinquity) of her having married a man without her particular kind of spirituality, splended tho his own power of service and aspiration was.

In one thing I don't believe you are right. You say that on Main Street you'd get more from Mrs. Sam Clark than from Carol. Would you?

You'd damn Carol, you'd praise Mrs. Clark to her, you might even defend Will—but you'd do it in long talks *with Carol*, and actually you'd see mighty little of Mrs. Clark! I've lived in Carmel and, if not on Barrow Street, at least a few blocks away on Charles Street, and you know there's not so awfully many Mrs. Sam's in those places. You'd love, appreciate, honor Mrs. Sam—but you wouldn't go to many of her parties. And you know darn well that if Carol had a Mary Austin, she'd be less desolatingly lonely in Gopher Prairie, she'd turn less queer and frightened.

Some day we'll fight this out vocally, I hope. But mean time don't dast (that's good Main Street) say I don't find any light of the rainbow on Main Street. If I didn't love Main Street would I write of it so hotly? could I write of it so ragingly?

Lord deliver me from complacency of authors, if such a miracle can be performed, but really, Mary, I want you to re-read the chapter Will has to his poor self, and see if perchance I didn't get a *little* under the surface of Carol's lack of sex power and sheer woman, ness. And what did you think I meant in her attraction, simple and fine, to Erik? And didn't you see Vida finding strength and peace in Ray?

Here I haven't thanked you. You know I do thank you, and very heartily.

Sincerely yours,
Sinclair Lewis

Letter 58, written six days later than *Letter 57*, gave Sinclair Lewis an opportunity to expand his defense of his novel *Main Street*. He points to the minor character, a Swedish handman Miles Bjornstam, as the hope for a truly democratic society and states that the chief character, Carol Kennicott, represents condescension in middle class America which challenges Bjornstam to know himself better. Lewis's question about H. G. Wells stresses the influence which Wells had upon members of the early Carmel community: George Sterling, James Hopper, and Jack London, especially. Lewis, too, had been a follower of Wells ever since college days. He named his first child, born on July 26, 1920, Wells Lewis. In *Letter 58*, Lewis writes that the "actual Wells . . . doesn't know that I exist," but Wells congratulated him upon the success of *Main Street* and when *Babbit* was published three years later, Wells called the book "one of the greatest novels I have read in a long time." The two men met on the trip Lewis and his first wife made to England in 1921. They met again when Lewis spent a weekend with Wells on a second trip in 1924. The diagram in *Letter 58*, with which Lewis records his respect for Wells, combines Western mathematical science with Oriental literary philosophy. The chemical formulas are a mishmash of organic substances, and the Greek letters may symbolize interpretations in literature. Lewis equates all of this to the inner meaning of existence.

————— 58

1619 Nineteenth Street, N.W.
Washington, D. C.
December 21—(1920) and a
fine Merry Christmas

Dear Mrs. Austin—only if you were here I'd probably call you Mary, having that Middlewestern way!

Because I think it's going to take so long to shine forth clearly, because I think it's going to shine more quickly if people wake from spiritual sloth, because peculiarly in America our fiction has been smugly contented—that's why, in Main Street, I didn't care to let the rainbow shine forth more obviously. And do you know that in the book, as it is, there is one character who sees the way-out—dimly, anxiously, crudely, but ardently. And that's Miles Bjornstam. For all his crudity, all his soap-box pugnacity, Miles sees the democracy of a trained, taut, eager Common People making themselves worthy to rule and build; sees that Carol is condescending; sees that he must have knowledge himself; sees passion. . . . There was no lack of glorious apotheosizing sex between him and Bea!

Will you see H. G. Wells when he comes to America? I hope some day he will read Main Street. He has long been one of my keenest admirations. I named my son for him—Wells Lewis—now a husky and, I should judge, intelligent person of three and a half. But I have never written to Wells the elder that I named the baby after him—that, I have always thought, I might *perhaps* do when, or if, the younger Wells indicated that he was going somewhat to be worthy of his prototype. Also I have mentioned Wells in each of the six novels I have written. Also once, in an investigation of crooked spiritualist mediums which I did for the Metropolitan Magazine, I got two beautiful messages (one in writing) from Mr. Herbert G. Wells beyond the grave. . . . The actual Wells I have never met—never seen—and I'm quite sure he doesn't know I exist. Yet I would like to have him find some verity and interest in Main Street. . . . He probably never reads anything without diagrams, statistics, and a general air of:-

Sincerely yours,
Sinclair Lewis

$4\,H_{12}C_{22}O_{11}$

$= $ Bhagavad-Gita

        Letter 59 exhibits the warmth of feeling that has grown between Lewis and Austin since the beginning of their correspondence. On December 28, 1920, Lewis thanked Austin for the news she sent about H. G. Wells and expressed his fear that he would miss Wells's lecture in Washington because of a trip he had to make to Ohio. He mentions the possibility that he might hear Wells in Cincinnati. On February 15, 1926, Lewis sent greetings from San Francisco, and reported a plan to drive south to Carmel with George Sterling. A letter sent on May 27 (the year could be 1926) refers to the furor over the Pulitzer Prize (possibly pointing to Lewis's novel *Arrowsmith* which was published the year before). He states that he is planning a "preacher novel," an indication that his *Elmer Gantry* (1927) was in preparation. He sends greeting to Mary Austin and her niece, Mary Hunter, who came to live with her in 1926. He also announces a trip to a cabin in northern Minnesota. Following *Letter 58*, printed here, there are letters from Berlin on January 12 and January 21, 1928; a wedding announcement of Lewis's marriage to Dorothy Thompson, mailed from London on May 15, 1928, a day after the ceremony; and two notes from Monterey, California, on February 19 and March 14, 1930. The first of the Monterey notes mentions returning east with his wife by way of Santa Fe and is signed "Love—ever." The second contains a picture of the Sherman-Rose cottage where Lewis and his wife were staying for two months. However, they did not return as planned but Mrs. Lewis went to New York without her husband. He followed in April. On June 20, 1930, Dorothy Lewis bore Lewis his second child, a son named Michael.

    The heading for *Letter 59* is printed, an indication of semipermanent residence for Lewis at the Grosvenor Hotel. "H. G." (Wells) and "Arnold" (Bennett) are thinkers and stylists uppermost in Lewis's frame of reference among novelists in his day. According to Mark Schorer, whose *Sinclair Lewis, An American Life* (1961) leaves few details for other biographers, Lewis first visited Santa Fe early in February of 1926. Schorer writes that Mary Austin took Lewis to see an Indian buffalo dance, and quotes him as calling the dance "a damned good spectacle."

_____ 59

SINCLAIR LEWIS

The Grosvenor
35 Fifth Avenue
New York

January 31, 1927

Dear Mary:

The very fact that a letter from you is not merely the ordinary pleasant communication from a friend which gives you his address, his present state of unhappiness, is the thing that has kept me from answering, for many months, your last letter. Mary dear, you feel, as I do, the lachrymae rerum; the infinite pity—the infinite glory—of human life. It is something that gets us so completely (and I don't think that it gets H. G. and Arnold that way) that we are always a little bit cramped and a little bit hindered in our work.

The other thing that has kept me from writing to you is that for a year and a quarter now—including even those days when I saw you in Santa Fe—I have given every hour, waking or sleeping, to the new book.

It is called "Elmer Gantry," and I am not at all sure that you will like it. The central character is a scoundrel and a minister of the gospel. But I think that your discerning mind will see how very important are the minor characters, such as Andrew Pengilly, Philip McGarry and Frank Shallard. I think that you shall be discerning enough to know that in the mysticism of Andrew Pengilly and the fine humanitarianism of Phil and Frank there is even more of me than there is in the utter ruthlessness of Elmer Gantry. It is a blast of protest against all organized religion. It is blasphemous, it is in bad taste, it is violent, it is—however humorous it may be in its minor details—in essence unhumorous: it is simply a roar of protest.

Mary dear, I know of no one in all the world who has tried more violently to make some pattern and reason out of this tangled life. I think that I have always understood just what you were trying to do—only in the midst of my wanderings and in the midst of my terrible absorptions in my work, I have not always signified my appreciation.

I am having Harcourt send you a copy of the book as soon as it is published. You will probably get certain things from it which no one else will.

Myself, I am going to have some surcease from the perfectly foolish amount of work I have given the book by sailing for England next Wednesday and tramping for four or five weeks in the southern shires—unless the weather is too terrible, in which case I shall go to southern France.

I appreciate to the full your comparison of myself to Dreiser, that philandering vulgarian, and to Willa Cather, that sweet but unfeeling genius, and I hope only that we may soon again have another of our long talks.

My address in Europe will be Guaranty Trust Company, 50 Pall Mall, London.

Please give to your niece, Mary, my very dear love, and please keep that same dear love for yourself.

Ever yours,
Sinclair Lewis

At the end of the note which Lewis sent on March 14, 1930, expressing his desire to bring his second wife, Dorothy Thompson, to meet Austin, he wrote: "In Santa Fe we can talk about the river." *Letter 60*, from Austin to Lewis, will explain the meaning of this cryptic remark. The reader will learn that Mary was proposing that Lewis collaborate with her in writing a work of fiction centered around "the destiny of one of those rivers which have meant so much to the development of the west." The governor of New Mexico in 1927 nominated Austin as one of the state's representatives to the Second Colorado River Conference, which was to be held in Denver on August 27. The First Conference had met in Santa Fe during 1922 when Mary's friend Herbert Hoover was Secretary of the Interior. Her own background of negotiations about rivers began when she lived in the Owens Valley of California (see *Letters 5 and 6* in this volume).

Before the delegates to the Colorado River Conference was the matter of how to distribute water resources in seven states, an area larger than the territories of the original thirteen colonies of the United States. California and Arizona were concerned about the future of the Lower Basin of the Colorado; Nevada, Utah, Colorado, Wyoming, and New Mexico were involved in the resources of the Upper Basin. Mary Austin's vision of the region was a place filled with small or moderately large communities, prospering through use and respect for natural resources, rather than large industrialized cities concentrating upon wealth and monopolistic power indifferent to the environment. The writing of such a book would call for the imagination of a poet. The economy and the politics of the region would demand an historian and a sociologist. As she said in the sixth paragraph of her letter, the subject was too vast, too complex, and dramatic, to be wholly covered in one book. Ferris Greenslet, to whom she had broached the matter, was on the editorial staff of the Houghton Mifflin Company, her chief publishers. Greenslet wrote to Lewis and Lewis wrote to Austin, as reported on March 28, 1931. In his letter to Greenslet, Lewis seems to have referred to the proposal as "the irrigation matter and its significance," agreeing that he and Mary could work together admirably if he could abandon a number of works already planned for the next few years. Little did Mary realize that her own time for creative activity would be limited to a little more than three years and four months from the time his letter reached her. The Watterson brothers, whom she mentions at the end of *Letter 60*, were bankers whose failure Austin attributed to crimes of the City Water Board of Los Angeles rather than to any faults of their own.

Mark Schorer states that Lewis made his first trip to New Mexico in 1926. He was on a cross continental tour to discover the Southwest. After visits in Kansas, he drove to Santa Fe early in February. Mary arranged for him to see an Indian buffalo dance which Lewis hailed as "a damned good spectacle." Since the weather was cold, he left Santa Fe on February 4 for Los Angeles. His second visit to Santa Fe occurred in March of 1927 when he and his first wife drove there from Phoenix after they had visited with Harold Bell Wright in Tucson. In April of 1933, he made a third visit. He was collecting material for a book about hotels. Helen MacKnight Doyle, who had known Mary Austin during her early California days, states in *Mary Austin, Woman of Genius* (1939) that on one of these visits, Mary gave a dinner party for Lewis, and during the conversation she roundly criticized him, finding fault with his writing and much that he had said and done. Lewis listened meekly, and when she had finished, he jumped up, embraced her, and kissed her, exclaiming, "God damn you, Mary! I love you." The contents of *Letter 60* indicate the rapport that existed between the two Midwesterners and, although some acrimony appeared on the surface, the bond between them was lasting and strong.

_____ 60

February 28th, 1931

Dear Sinclair:

I am here in Florida recovering from influenza and lecturing to pay my way on American Fiction and the pattern of American Life, nine times—and several times yet to come. I have had to explain at length my reasons for thinking Arrowsmith the most important novel so far of the present century.

This is to explain why my mind is turning to you now and to the suggestion to which you seemed to listen not unkindly, that we might pool our separate knowledges in a work of fiction around the destiny of one of those rivers which have meant so much to the development of the west. Just before coming here I had a conference in New York with Ferris Greenslet concerning my new novel Starry Adventure and the autobiography I am writing. When he asked me what I planned next I told him about the River idea, and that I had offered it to you, but if you declined, I might try it alone. To my surprise, he was immensely interested. He said that the really illuminative American novel hadn't been written and might never be except in some such coalition between one whose knowledge of the country like yours was extensive and like mine which is intensive. He thought we might manage it by avoiding the ordinary conventions of such cooperation.

Indeed, I'm not thinking of conventional collaboration. No two people whose styles are as highly individualized as yours and mine could possibly write together, but there is no reason why we shouldn't create together out of our funded knowledge.

This idea of a combination of essential knowledges has been long forming in my mind. I thought of it when I was writing The Ford, and realized that every little while my material disappeared into the intricacies of male life beyond my capacity to follow it. I thought of it when, after an article of mine on the future of the Southwest as established on

the indivisible utility of the River, the head of the Department of Irrigation wrote me that though he had been studying irrigation all his life, I
had given him new ideas. And again when Frederick Kepple—the man
who chiefly disburses the Carnegie funds—came back from a survey of
the Southwest agreeing with me that there is to be the next great rise of
English speaking culture. I think of it every day now as I see Herbert
Hoover drawing nearer through lack of just the sort of knowledge I have
about the Colorado River, to a tragedy of shoddy failure.

I am afraid to think very much in detail how we could work together,
lest I get any sort of fixation about it. As I see it, the subject is too vast,
too complex and dramatic to be wholly comprised in one book. There
might be two or three—. A first book, which I might do almost alone,
covering the period reaching its dramatic climax in the wresting of the
first irrigation system from Indians by the Whites. A middle phase
might deal with the struggle between the ranch lands and the towns.
The third—and this is where your genius would be triumphant, would
illustrate the turning of the indivisible utility of the acequia madre
"mother ditch" with the equally indivisible utility of Power.

I know everything that needs to be known: How the Indians learned
irrigation and taught it to the Whites; how the cities "framed" the
farmers and stole the river for the use of the realtors, all the bitterness
and greed; how three lives and fortunes are sacrificed to every title to
irrigated lands. I was appointed to the Seven States Conference on the
Colorado. I know all about the corruption both commercial and political
that goes to that business. I lived through the Owens River theft and
know why the Watterson brothers still languish in jail. I know why the
San Francisquite Dam went down—I think I know what threatens in
Boulder Dam.

I want to see these things told in imperishable form as you can do it,
and as I can't alone. If you feel we can't do it together, then buy my
knowledge and do the book or books yourself. Nobody knows this as I
do. In twenty more years it will be impossible for anybody to know it
as directly and completely, and in two or three hundred years more
such a book as you could write will be pertinent and readable.

Dear friend, don't turn this aside because of a traditional objection to
collaborating with a woman. I know I'm feminine, damnably feminine,
and not ashamed of it, but I'm not ladyish. You can count on my be-
having like a gentleman.

And in any case, the best of luck to you. Write to me at Sante Fe, where I will be in two weeks more.

Sincerely,
Mary Austin

Of all the New York critics who were well disposed toward Mary Austin and her writing, none was more appreciative than Carl Van Doren (1885-1950). He shared her rural background in Illinois and, as an editor for two magazines that published her work, *The Nation* and *The Century*, he corresponded with her frequently. Between 1918 and 1934, there are eighteen letters, dealing with both editorial and personal matters. Van Doren grew up in Hope, Illinois, a farming community east of Urbana where his family moved when he was attending the University of Illinois. Van Doren's father practiced medicine in both communities. There were many books in the Van Doren home, and his mother taught Van Doren and his four brothers how to read before they entered elementary school. This may have contributed to bookish interests which led both him and his younger brother Mark to select English as major studies and writing as careers. Mark Van Doren (1894-1972), distinguished poet and professor of English at Columbia University and lecturer at St. John's College, Maryland, also has letters in the Mary Austin Collection, in one of which he urges her to "go in for poetry altogether without having to bother with lectures and treatises."

The last twenty years of Carl Van Doren's life were devoted to writing and editing. Among the widely known books he wrote are biographies of Thomas Love Peacock, James Branch Cabell, Jonathan Swift, and Benjamin Franklin; for the last he received a Pulitzer Prize in 1939. The earliest letter in the Carl Van Doren group is dated December 10, 1918. He was then managing editor for *The Cambridge History of American Literature.* In this letter, he invites Mary to contribute a chapter to be called "Aboriginal Non-English Writings," which would offer an account of the literary heritage of the North American Indians, embracing their Creation Myths, legends, folk tales, and poetry. Van Doren had chosen Mary Austin because she had written extensively about ceremonial life among Indians and their poetic expression found in oral song and verse. At this time, she was preparing her own collection of Indian poetry which she called *The American Rhythm* (1923) and to which she contributed collections of her own and those of anthropologists, musicians, and linguists.

When Van Doren published his *Contemporary American Novelists* (1931), he described Austin as writing fiction only after deep reflection and remarked that the effect upon her novels had been to widen their sympathies and lift their style. He added, however, that such depth of thought had complicated their structure and obscured their meaning. He describes her longer narratives as neither glib nor clean cut, and concludes that they lack the "cool, hard discipline of the artist." To confirm or contradict Van Doren's judgment, a reader would have to start with *Isidro* (1905) and proceed through *Santa Lucia* (1908), *Outland* (1910), *A Woman of Genius* (1912), *The Ford* (1917), *No. 26 Jayne Street* (1920), to *Starry Adventure* (1933). Van Doren concludes that no book was like its predecessor and each grew in promise as a work of fiction.

Austin often sent Indian handcraft objects as gifts to her friends. The *tinaja*, mentioned in *Letter 61*, is an earthen jar, probably one produced by a skilled Pueblo Indian artisan. Such pottery was shaped from red or black clay, fired and then decorated with designs in white, black, or gray, and fired again. Another of the personal and cordial letters from Van Doren, including his wife Irita, congratulated Austin on the "glorious" honorary banquet extended to her by friends, from New York and elsewhere, at the National Arts Club on January 8, 1922 (see Austin to D. T. MacDougal, *Letter 64*).

_____ 61

THE CENTURY MAGAZINE	THE CENTURY COMPANY
CARL VAN DOREN,	353 Fourth Avenue
Literary Editor	New York

Dear Mrs. Austin: 23 December 1923

The tinaja you gave me is very beautiful. It came home safely with us Friday evening and is now picking and choosing a place in the house which seems sufficiently honorable for it. I am not yet sure what the place will be, but I am once for all committed to admiration for the gift—and gratitude to the giver. Thank you very much. Merry Christmas!

Sincerely,

Carl Van Doren

In 1921, Carl Van Doren was literary editor of *The Nation*, and Ludwig Lewisohn (1883-1955), the writer of *Letter 62*, was an associate editor in drama for the same magazine. During the next year, Van Doren became literary editor for *The Century* magazine, too, and in December of 1922 he was arranging with Austin for the publication of her book *The Land of Journeys' Ending* (1924). Chapters in this book were to appear in *The Century* during the year the book was published. Lewisohn's first autobiographical volume, *Upstream* (1922), was probably being printed at the time he wrote *Letter 62*. Both *Upstream* and *The Land of Journeys' Ending* are concerned with the cultural development of the United States. Each strives to furnish what Mary Austin called "access to the American mind," a phrase Lewisohn seems to be quoting in *Letter 62* from a letter Mary wrote to him.

Ludwig Lewisohn's "access to the American mind" is described by him as he recounts his family's arrival from Germany in 1890 when he was 7 years old and as he became a successful teacher and writer in later life. The Lewisohns were German Jews, and their first years on American soil were spent in Charleston, South Carolina, where they were guests in the home of an uncle on the mother's side of the family. They lived in a village with a cotton-seed oil mill and a sawmill. Ludwig's father opened a small furniture store and earned a modest living, but he also brought books from Germany to enrich his son's mind and he sent Ludwig to a Methodist Sunday School for social contacts and religious enlightenment. Thus Ludwig's access to the American mind was initially made through Anglo-American society, the Methodist religion, and Southern social consciousness. His name and physiognomy, however, were characteristically Jewish. When he entered a metropolitan university in New York City, expecting to earn a degree in English literature and teach, he encountered discrimination. His applications for teaching positions were rejected because he was Jewish.

After a number of rejections as an English teacher, Lewisohn applied as an instructor in German and was accepted by the University of Wisconsin (which he calls "Monroe University" in *Upstream*). Here he made friends, one of whom was the poet William Ellery Leonard ("Ellard" in the book). Successful in teaching at one university, he moved to a second (Ohio State University under the caption "Central City University") where he taught with growing disillusionment with his students, who seemed to be there for social prestige and economic advancement. *Mid-Channel* (1929), Lewisohn's second autobiographical volume, further criticizes the mechanical progress of materialism in the United States which he considered destructive of higher values. In this book, he portrays the harsh relationships in European culture between Nordic, Latin, and Semitic ethnic groups, and wonders whether any ideal assimilation is possible between such diverse forms of inheritance and attitude.

The Land of Journeys' Ending was published five years before *Mid-Channel*, which is subtitled *An American Chronicle*, but there may be something more than coincidence in the fact that the first chapter of Lewisohn's book is called

"Journeys End." There is no apostrophe; so the reader is left to guess whether Lewisohn is telling only his story or the story of others who were Americans and Jewish like himself. In *Upstream*, he refers a number of times to "Anglo-Americans" and at least once to the "Anglo-Saxon race," a curious ethnic tag in view of the appearance in medieval times of an Anglo-French kingdom with Celtic provinces surviving in an island identified as England, Scotland, and Wales. In Mary Austin's book, her Southwestern frame of reference uses the term "Anglo-American" to designate any citizen of the United States who is not of Indian or Spanish American origin. Thus Lewisohn would have been an Anglo when he toured her "Land of Journeys' Ending."

One more observation is pertinent to the divergent viewpoints reported in *Letter 62*. Austin believed that the land was an ultimate factor in shaping human destiny and determined patterns of speech, thought, action, song, dance, and community life. She idealized these patterns as she saw them in primitive and historic traditions of the Southwest, considering them prophetic of an intimate relation of peoples to environment on American soil. By contrast, Lewisohn writes in Chapter Three of *Mid-Channel*:

Even the pure unhistoried earth of America is not wholly mine. Deeply as I have loved it, I am an alien there too. . . . I come into collision with folk-ways and beliefs and laws as alien to me as the notion that my ancestors poisoned the wells. . . . But Jerusalem is not quaint to me . . . nor Tiberius. . . . The earth is mine.

He inquires of his reader: "How do you live from within outward?" Mary Austin seems to ask: "How does the outer world change you within?"

The asterisk inserted in *Letter 62* is hand written and appears at the bottom of the first page in Lewisohn's typed letter. He supports his comment about unrest in American homes by Joseph Hergesheimer's novel in 1922 which documents a plot dealing with New York suburban country-club life resulting in broken marriages and shattered visions of romance ending in tragedy. Did Lewisohn really believe this to be representative of the fabric of American society? *Letter 62* is printed with the permission of Mrs. Ludwig Lewisohn, 1921 Kalorama Rd., N.W., Washington, D.C., Literary Executrix.

_____ 62

THE NATION

20 Vesey Street
New York

March 11, 1921

Dear Mrs. Austin:

I thank you for your letter, for its frankness, its vividness. There are in this rather dreary world few reactions to be had like that. I do hope we shall talk deeply and at length; I shall be glad to cooperate in every way for an article by you. In the meantime I am much tempted to set down a few observations which may reach you before you go and come up now and then in your thoughts.

That work of yours of which you speak, which has had no recognition here—surely it is not your fiction? That is well known and esteemed. Or is it your work in American ethnology and folk-lore? But that surely is matter for the specialist, and when you speak of me as one who "dismisses" your learning—it cannot be that. So I am curious, in the nobler sense of that misused word.

You offer me access to the American mind. To have access to your mind and opinions I shall count—I speak with the simplest sincerity— a privilege. But access to the American mind I have always had and have now. Life has brought it about that all my closest friends, except a few Germans, have been and are Americans of Anglo-American ancestry and long descent. Take the closest of all, William Ellery Leonard, the poet and professor at Wisconsin. I have talked the nights away with him and with so many others like him. And these friends have not always agreed with me. But they have never attributed either the quality of my experience or the nature of my opinions to my race. Neither do I. And there I come upon the fundamental differences between us of which I should like to have you think.

For instance: No, I have had no "spiritual traffic with God" in my mature years. At least in none but a very tenuous philosophical sense. And that is thoroughly un-Jewish. But it is thoroughly characteristic of those masters whose sense of the quality of experience seems to correspond to mine—Goethe, Nietzsche, Shaw.

"Love as the Anglo-Saxon knows it at its best!" Here, I am afraid, dear Mrs. Austin, you indulge in . . . *German* truth, *German* honor. Well, anyhow, I've often been picked out by men—100 per cent American men, as a receiver of confidences. I have sat at many boards and felt the quality of many American homes. My impressions are those of prevalent sadness, restlessness, dissatisfaction.* I know beautiful relationships, too. But how few they are compared to those that are sustained by nothing but social pressure in its thousand forms. But I don't call that condition American. It is characteristic of Western civilization. You may not agree with me as to its cause—the hideous straight-jacket of Judaeo-Christian, specifically Pauline, moral dualism. But the observation is not a Jewish one. Sherwood Anderson, Edgar Masters, Theodore Dreiser all see eye to eye with me. The Jews, as a matter of fact, show a higher percentage of happy marriages in what I take to be your sense than others. I am not sure that this is a virtue in them—not at all sure!

You challenge me on the basis of my personal life. I may—I cannot yet say I shall—talk about that to you. There are things too difficult, too intricate, too full of pain to others for much speech. But I assure you very earnestly that my experience is *essentially* different from anything you suppose. We shall see.

I'll be glad to speak to Liveright and, later to anyone else you suggest.

Believe me, cordially yours,
Ludwig Lewisohn.

*Hergesheimer's "Cytherea."

Henry Holt (1840-1926), author, publisher, friend, was certainly one of the most amiable and entertaining of Mary Austin's correspondents. He was also the oldest, for on April 11, 1908, when he wrote the first of forty letters to her, he was 68 years old and on the date of his last letter, March 12, 1923, he was 83. Midway in his correspondence, January 23, 1918, he tells Mary that she should stop "mistering him," and call him "Uncle Henry," a role he assumes with all the other "youngsters." As "Uncle Henry," Holt also adopted a colloquial style of spelling, a habit he accepted seriously as member of the Executive Committee of the Simplified Spelling Board. His own performance in this respect casts doubt on his credibility as an advocate of the practice.

After earning an A.B. at Yale in 1862 and a Bachelor of Laws at Columbia two years later, Holt entered the publishing business with G. P. Putnam. In 1873, he established his own company, which he maintained until the time of his death, fifty years later. He began to edit his *Unpartisan Review* in 1914, and published articles by free-speaking liberal contributors until 1921 when he collected them all in a volume called *Garrulities of an Octogenarian Editor, With Other Essays Somewhat Biographical and Autobiographical* (1932). Among the opinions expressed here are that music keeps a person young; the Westminster Catechism bound him by promises made by his sponsors without his knowledge or consent; smoking should never be indulged in by a boy before the age of 6 and only moderately after 60; and though tobacco can be a poison, it is a mighty slow one. He further confides upon matters of diet, exercise, rest, and religion, and pays tribute to many of the distinguished men in his time.

In *Earth Horizon*, Austin tells of her encounters with speakers who appeared at the National Arts Club in New York City. She reports that she usually disagreed with them and that she made her viewpoints known. She mentions a disagreement with Walter Lippman over Bill Haywood's talk about the Industrial Workers of the World. Then, she adds, she disagreed with Henry Holt about his psychic books. In return, she states that he was extraordinarily kind to her about her own work. *Letter 63* offers convincing evidence in this respect. In her autobiography, she does not mention the interview with Sir Oliver Lodge which Holt recommended in his note of introduction.

———— **63**

HENRY HOLT AND COMPANY
Publishers   New York

19 West 44th Street

Dear Mary: June 22, 1921

I am shockt to find that yuurs of May 27th has been so long unanswered but I have been in very much the condition of an exploding bomb, part of the confusion including abandoning our twenty-five year home at 711 Madison Avenue and going into 53 East 66th St. This, however, has been a minor feature of the explosion.

At last I am on the brink of getting out of town tomorrow, after being kept here longer than a man of my age should have been: so I am closing up lots of matters in haste.

The enclosed circular answers a whole lot of questions. I hope you won't like it, but I am old enuf to take it philosophically; and I am glad of the rest.

I enclose the letter yu askt for to Sir Oliver Lodge.

I hope it's not going to be a great while before I'll see yu—next fall—in yuur native land, well and happy.

Faithfully

H H

Mrs. Mary Austin
Lyceum Club, 138 Piccadilly, London, England
ENCLOSURE WITH *LETTER 63*:

HENRY HOLT AND COMPANY
Publishers   New York

19 West 44th Street
June 22, 1921

My dear Sir Oliver:

Mrs. Mary Austin, one of our few American authors—and she is among the fewest of that few, askt me if I could give her a letter to yu, which I am very glad to do. She thinks yu may help her in some philosophical problems. Whether yu do or not, I know yu will have a good time if yu have a talk with her.

With all good wishes, I am, as ever,

Faithfully yours
Henry Holt

Sir Oliver Lodge
Normanton, Lake, Salisbury, England

The dancer Ruth St. Denis (1877-1968) was not only a great performer, but she was also an innovator and leader in the art she practiced. As a contemporary of Isadora Duncan (1878-1927), pioneer program dancer, St. Denis became the teacher of other great dancers, such as Martha Graham, who later achieved fame equal to her own. St. Denis was born and raised on a New Jersey farm by exceptional parents who directed her path toward creative activities. Her mother was one of the first women licensed as a physician in the United States. Her father was an inventor who balanced his activity in a battle with alcohol. Both parents were intellectuals, and Ruth's mother was a follower of François Delsarte (1811-1871), a French musician and scientist, who taught that physical movements were clues to personal psychology. He believed that an individual outlook revealed itself in rhythms of the upper, middle, and lower zones of the human form. Elocutionists, actors, and dancers took up the Delsartian System in order to give appropriate physical expression to emotion and attitude. Such training prompted the earliest efforts of Ruth St. Denis in her acting and dancing, but they were only a beginning.

After an apprenticeship as both a singer and dancer in the years between 1891 and 1899, St. Denis found minor roles in plays directed by the impresario David Belasco, who sent her with stage companies in both the United States and England. She left Belasco in 1906 and toured with her own group which produced dance-dramas. She invented romantic plots for action in eastern world settings, one of which she called *Egypta*. This story involved ancient temple ceremonies to entertain a Pharaoh who carried out a judgment pronounced before the god Osiris. A similar dance interpretation portrayed St. Denis as an East Indian beggar woman and snake charmer. The role allowed her to use her arms as two cobras while her hands displayed glittering rings as the eyes of the snakes. The scene for another ballet was placed in Japan where a great duel was pantomimed and danced by two samurai warriors. In 1913, between tours, St. Denis entertained a group of dancers in New York City. Among her guests was a handsome young Californian who had been dancing in private and public ballrooms. His name was Edwin Myers Shawn, better known as "Ted" Shawn (1891-1972). With the introduction of this young dancer to Ruth St. Denis a new career opened for both of them.

Letter 64 is an introduction to St. Denis after she had been married to Shawn for seven years. He joined her troupe early in 1914, and they were married on August 13 of that year. He was 22 years old and his wife was 37, but she matched his energy and alertness in every way. Shawn lived in Kansas City as a boy; grew up in Denver where he attended the University of Denver planning to become a minister. However, after enrolling in a dancing class taught by a former member of the Metropolitan Opera Company, he progressed to the point that she encouraged him to move to Los Angeles for more study. He held jobs in the City Water Department and an insurance company in order to accept engagements at ballroom dancing, tango teas, and other social entertainments. An opportunity to go to New York City came when the Santa Fe Railroad announced that the line would transport entertainers without charge if they would give performances at various cities for employees of the railroad. Shawn had seen a ballet by St. Denis in Denver, and the impression helped to confirm his choice of a career in dancing. When he joined her as a soloist and partner, they became the best known dance team in the United States.

An exact date cannot be assigned to *Letter 64*. The letter was first addressed to Austin at 138 Piccadilly, London; then readdressed to the National Arts Club in

New York City. The Piccadilly address would have found Mary in July or August of her second trip to England when she spoke to the Fabian Society in 1921. Later in that year, on November 15, her play "Fire" was to be produced at Palm Springs, California. This drama called for scenes on a mountain top where Guardian Spirits danced before a fire cavern. As the plot developed, an Indian steals the Sacred Fire Brand and passes it to another Indian who hands the flaming torch to the tribesmen. Such effects of flame and movement could have been devised with dancing by St. Denis and Ted Shawn most effectively.

Letter 64 is handwritten on two pages, the first of which has an elaborate design filling the entire left hand margin and the bottom of the page. On the left, as the reader gazes at the written contents, a cobra lifts its body with the head touching a shallow base holding a cross-legged Buddha inside a wreath. The face is distinctly feminine. Behind the coil of the snake at the bottom of the page, an incense jar sends smoke upwards to the seated figure. Beneath the coil and to the right, a peacock pulls its feathered tail as it holds one foot high at the edge of the page. The heading on this sheet of letter paper has only the name "Ruth St. Denis." Perhaps there was no letterhead paper for the Denishawn School, but from the time the school was established in 1915 there was rivalry between the cofounders for dominance. Arguments about their careers and their relationships with others led to estrangement. The school ended in 1931 and Shawn founded his own establishment for teaching and performances at Jacob's Pillow in Lee, Massachusetts. Enrollment was limited to male students who constituted a troupe that traveled in the fall and winter and gave a festival every summer from 1953 until after Shawn's death in 1972.

St. Denis appeared occasionally after the closing of Denishawn. She was honored at Bennington College and at other centers of modern dance. In 1964, on the fiftieth anniversary of her marriage to Shawn, they danced together for the last time at Jacob's Pillow. In mood and motion they invoked the spirits of air, St. Denis in classical drapery and Shawn in a short bolero jacket exposed below the chest to his waistline. The white hair of St. Denis was pulled into a chignon, whereas a scarf bound the strands of Shawn. Gestures were adjusted to the age of Shawn at 74 and St. Denis at 87. A suitable comment might be that, despite troubled years, dancing contributed to the longevity of both.

_____ 64

932 So. Grand Ave
Los Angeles
Cal.

RUTH ST. DENIS

Dear Mary Austin—
　　　　Your very interesting letter
reached me in my last incarnation!—
　　　　It offered such a splendid opportunity
to work some of my pet ideas and experience—
but would take some time to prepare
& at the time I was just snowed
under. This is to ask if the work
is going on & if I am altogether
too late to supply what information
I can—Do let me know by return
mail.
　　　　We are now in the midst of a Big
Plan—for Denishawn—a whole University
of Art—& by the time I hear a line
from you I can tell you about it—
　　　　　　　　　　　　Yours sincerely
　　　　　　　　　　　　Ruth St. Denis

　　　　Perhaps the most important honor in Mary Austin's literary career was the dinner held at the National Arts Club to which she devotes only four lines in her autobiography. The date was January 8, 1922, only a short time after she had returned from her second trip to England. She writes that it was "the friendliest possible dinner, with everybody there who should have been there except Herbert Croly, with speeches and recognition and a speech from me." Instead of telling about her friends who *were* there and who gave the "speeches and recognition," she takes a paragraph to complain about Croly, the *New Republic*, and the way the editor and the magazine had neglected her.

Letter 65 fills in data of interest about the occasion and preserves a copy of the program on that occasion. D. T. MacDougal, to whom the letter was written, served as director of the Carnegie Botanical Laboratory in Tucson, Arizona, where he was also a professor at the University of Arizona. There are sixty-three letters from Austin to MacDougal, written from December 31, 1921 to May 27, 1924. In *Earth Horizon*, she credits him with having led her to the study of varieties of cactus and advancing her knowledge of the Papago and Pima Indians in southern Arizona. A much larger group of letters is preserved from Mac-Dougal to Mary Austin, beginning in 1914 when he was associated with the Carnegie Institution in Washington, D. C., and ending on July 21, 1932, when he recommended her for the annual achievement award offered by the *Pictorial Review* magazine.

_____ 65

10 Barrow Street, Jan. 9. '22

Dear Friend:

The party is over, and I am writing to tell you all about it, hoping by that means to get it completely out of my consciousness so I can go properly to work again. It was a very nice party and everybody was immensely pleased with it.

First of all there was I. Since the party was in a sense an admission of the complete subjugation of New York—twelve years it has taken me, but of course there was the war—I felt it obligatory to maintain to the full my attitude of being representative of the larger America, which I think is now entirely conceded. But it meant, to begin with, that I couldn't appear in a conventional Fifth Ave. dress. This means more than a mere man would imagine, for in New York you can never buy anything that is more than two weeks out of vogue. And naturally I wasn't trying to appear out of vogue, simply distinctive.

I began by getting the most magnificent piece of color I could find, which would technically be called rose color, but it was the rose of an Arizona sunset. It had a silver sheen on it, took the light like flame and ran to lilac in the shadows. And since it happened to be the fashion in New York to wear your skirts nearly to your knees, with two flaps on either side, either trailing to the ground or puffed out like the broken wings of a bird, I had mine made—in remembrance of my own southwest—in the fashion which refuted that ancient scandal about the Queen of Spain having two legs, without at the same time concealing the fact that she was very much a woman. This with a Spanish comb and appropriate touches of black and silver, gave to the whole gown the effect of having been made in a candy shop.

Then there was a fan, which bothered me, since to be quite Spanish, a fan must be lacy and spangly, and stand for vivacity. But as I had cut the price in two, in order to buy Mrs. Clarke a blue feather concoction which she wanted quite as much as I wanted her to have it, I had to content myself with plumes also, black of course, which I decided would have to stand for mystery.

But I am persuaded that being born in Illinois and brought up a Methodist is not conducive to the mastery of the fan, for though it went very well when I rehearsed it at home, by the time I arrived at the party, I forgot all about it. In addition to the fan I carried a bouquet, what is known as a "period" bouquet. The middle of it was "Sweet-heart" roses, which I suppose you will scarcely recognize as botanically descriptive, but it means rose and compact and desirable; combined with it were blue forget-me-nots, and some sort of small white flower, smelling like a pleasant memory, tied with long rosy ribbons which by a happy accident just matched my gown.

Now if I have succeeded in making you realize that, so equipped, I was prepared to take the center of the stage even in New York, we will get on to the party. I had invited the young Indian painter to whom I introduced you, to be my guest and he arrived at my house about a quarter of an hour before the performance dressed in quill embroidered buckskin, and wearing the most magnificent black and white and fla-mingo feather head dress I have ever seen. He said he hadn't any evening clothes, and would this do. So I took him in the cab with me, and when the reception committee saw us come in together, I thought they would faint with joy.

Everything went off beautifully. The table decorations were rose and black and silver. There were any number of telegrams besides the one from Carmel, which I appreciated; Joseph Conrad, May Sinclair, H. G. Wells, and the Artist Colony at Santa Fe. My Indian friend let the natural contempt for white men which all Indians at bottom feel, have full play, with astonishing results. One kind lady asked what those teeth were in his necklace. "Alligator," he told her. She said "How horrid!" but hastily and kindly added, "I suppose they are the same to you as my pearls." "Not at all," said my Chickasaw friend, "Any fool can take a pearl away from an oyster."

Some of the painters, thinking to have fun with the savage, took him around to see the exhibition. Said he, "This is the sort of thing that makes me realize that the Americans are not yet a race. You can see that these chaps weren't even peasants." Mrs. Weiss, that's the lady at whose studio we met about the Amerind Foundation, nearly died of delight when she heard it.

There was a lot of speeches made, quite informal and most of them quite genuine. Uncle Henry Holt said that the distinguished guest was the one writer in America who had any vision of the spiritual meaning of America, and would yet be known as the forerunner of the new religion. Mr. Canby said she was the one complete master of the American Environment, making him aware of depths and subtleties of which he was otherwise unconscious. Mr. Van Doren of The Nation said she was the one writer with a tap root, and John Farrar made a charming, blundering tribute on behalf of the younger generation, which was unintentionally so funny that the company was practically in hysterics the whole time he was speaking. The rest was chiefly conventionally complimentary, but at the close of the address, Glen Frank of the Century, acting as toast master, said with unpremeditated earnestness that he had learned more about how an American literary magazine should be edited, than [he had learned] from all other sources together.

Well, I tell you these things not from vanity, but because I know you are interested. And I must not forget that Mary Shaw read the War Thoughts so effectively that it nearly broke up the meeting.

Afterward there was an impromptu expression from those who hadn't been permitted to speak on the regular program, which was both touching and excruciatingly funny. One dear young chap from the New Republic said I took the horror off of middle aged feminity, which is, I suppose really, the secret source of witch hunting. David Edstrom— David is a squarehead sculptor with streaks of absolute genius embedded in an adolescent mentality—gravely admitted that for the first time he had heard a woman speak who impressed him as being co-equal with himself. David is going to do a bust of me as Prophecy.

So by degrees the party broke up and I got home to reflect on the fact which escaped everybody else, that no one who spoke revealed any intimate acquaintance with my books, that two of the speakers seemed to be uncertain just what books I had written, and that every one of them had got what they had got by actual contact.

I am afraid that is very much the case everywhere. Well, I know books are only the evidences of spiritual progress, cast off as we go along. But somehow I can't think mine are so bad as that. What's the use of being praised as a good mother by people who can't even remember the names of your children. However, let's hope that I will be read a little more, if only for curiosity.

By the way, those cards I sent to people at the Highlands, Mrs. Mac-Dougal, the Wilsons and Sphoers, came back. Isn't Highlands a post office?

As ever

Mary Austin

ENCLOSURE IN *LETTER 65:*

A DINNER IN HONOR OF
MARY AUSTIN
will be given at
THE NATIONAL ARTS CLUB
Sunday Evening, January Eighth
Nineteen hundred and twenty-two
at seven o'clock

———

Mr. William Webster Ellsworth
will present the Chairman of the evening
Mr. Glen Frank
Editor of the Century Magazine

———

Mrs. Austin's subject will be "American Literature As An Expression of The American Experience."

Among those who will pay tribute to Mrs. Austin will be: Mr. Henry Holt; Henry Seidel Canby, Editor Literary Review; Edward J. Wheeler, Editor Current Opinion; Carl Van Doren, Literary Editor The Nation; John Farrar, Editor The Bookman; Witter Bynner, President The Poetry Society of America and Dr. Maurice Francis Egan.

Mary Shaw will read "War Thoughts of Women," a poem by Mrs. Austin appearing in The Dial for November 1921.

Guests of honor in addition to those who will speak will be: Mr. John G. Agar; Mr. Ferris Greenslet, Editor Houghton Mifflin Co., Mr. Rutger Blecker Jewett, Editor D. Appleton and Company; Mr. Thomas H. Wells, Editor Harpers Magazine, and Mrs. Wells; Mr. Herbert Croley, Editor The New Republic, and Mrs. Croley; Mr. and Mrs. John Lane of London; Dr. Smythe, Literary Editor The Times, and Mrs. Smythe; Mr. J. S. Watson The Dial, and Mrs. Watson; Mr. Barton Currie, Editor Ladies Home Journal; Mr. Arthur T. Vance, Editor Pictorial Review.

Mr. and Mrs. John R. Gregg; Mr. and Mrs. Ernest Ipsen; Mr. and Mrs. Tunis Bergen; Mr. and Mrs. William Young Westervelt; Mrs. Mary Ripley Weiss; Miss Caroline Parker; Madame Bianchi; Miss Persis Meacham Pomeroy; Mrs. MacDonald Sheridan; Miss Helen Bones; Ida Clyde Clarke; Mr. Edward J. Wheeler, Mr. Hamlin Garland; Mr. George Harris, Jr., Mr. George Martin; Mr. Maxwell Aley; Mr. Alexander Black will compose the reception committee.

Assistants to the reception committee: Miss Julia Hall, Miss Nelle Weathers, Miss Helen Cross, Mr. Frederick W. Woodbridge, Mr. Harry B. Irwin, Mr. Winslow Lyon.

The number of guests must necessarily be limited. Make reservations in writing to "Mary Austin Dinner Committee," National Arts Club. $2.50 per cover.

Letter 66 is the first of four letters written by the poet Amy Lowell (1874-1925) to Austin in 1922 and 1923. The first three of these letters deal with the subject of Lowell's particular poetic style, which was dubbed "polyphonic prose" by the poet John Gould Fletcher, as her letter of May 4, 1922 indicates. In this letter, she confesses that she regrets that term, preferring to call her poetry "contrapuntal verse." In Letter 66, she describes the elements which appear in her colorful writing. Anyone who reads this statement will be impressed by the skill she exhibits in explaining why she considers her medium effective.

Three months before Lowell wrote her letter, she had been a guest of the Henry Seidel Canbys' at a social occasion to which Mary Austin was also invited. At this time, Mary wrote to her "Dear Friend," Dr. MacDougal (see *Letter 65*) that this was the first personal meeting she had ever had with Lowell, although she had heard the poetess speak on several occasions. Austin writes vividly and not unappreciatively of the poet's appearance and attitude:

One looked, of course, for the last of the Lowells . . . imagine a middle aged woman, abnormally stout of body, with a shrewd "clever," kindly face, plainly dressed, without the slightest suggestion of feminine allurement, a thin lipped New England mouth coarsened by the smoking of large black cigars, and a manner which varied from the assurance of the cultivated woman of the world to that of the "hearty" wife of a small town hotel keeper!

Austin's letter continues in a way that becomes an introduction to Lowell's *Letter 66*. She says that Lowell attacked her at the Canbys' because Austin had criticized a poem she wrote called "The Basket Woman," but Austin said that she pleased Lowell by complimenting another of her poems entitled "The Chief's Lament." Then Austin adds that "we thoroughly agreed about poetry in general" and "I liked her very much after the first ten minutes."

Amy Lowell influenced American poetry as much by her leadership and criticism as by her creative efforts. Even though her bibliography includes a total of ten volumes of verse, her critical study called *Tendencies in Modern American Poetry* (1917) and her definitive biography of John Keats (1925) assure her a leading place in the history of poetry and poetry criticism. Amy Lowell was the sister of Harvard University president Abbott Lawrence Lowell and a distant cousin of the New England poet James Russell Lowell. She was born in Brookline, Massachusetts, in 1874. After being tutored in private schools and traveling in Europe, she began to write poetry at the age of 13, achieving fame with her collection called *A Dome of Many-coloured Glass* (1912). On a fourth trip to Europe she met with the ex-patriot American poet Ezra Pound in England and was converted to his theory that authentic poetic impulses came first from images which produced associations developing into words in rhythmic lines. Lowell became the leader of the Imagist School of writing verse. Her own kind of Imagism resulted in such poems as her "Patterns," which appeared in 1916 and opened with the lines:

> I walk down the garden paths,
> And all the daffodils
> Are blowing, and the bright blue squills.
> I walk down the patterned garden paths
> In my stiff, brocaded gown.
> With my powdered hair and jewelled fan

> I too am a rare pattern. As I wander down
> The garden paths.*

The reader discerns more than the images of daffodils and a jewelled fan. The images become ideas, clearly displayed in color and sound. The verse form is nonsyllabic meter based upon the chief accents which create rhythmic cadences that guide the poet's thought. Lowell explains this in an article challenging Ludwig Lewisohn's attack upon the modern free verse poets. (See "The Case of Modern Poetry versus Professor Lewisohn," in *The Bookman*, January, 1919.

*From "Patterns" in *The Complete Poetical Works of Amy Lowell*. Copyright 1955 by Houghton Mifflin Company. Used by permission of the publisher.

———— 66

MISS A. LOWELL
 70 Heath Street
Brookline, Mass.   Brookline, Mass. . . . 28 April . . . 1922

My dear Miss Austin:
      I have been very long in answering your letter of April 5th because it came while I was away, and since I have got home I have been absolutely drowned in things which it was necessary to do at once and my mail has had to wait.
   I think that the best exposition of "polyphonic prose" is in the preface of my "Can Grande's Castle." I have been looking over the places in which I have written about it: an article in the "North American Review," long ago, called "A Consideration of Modern Poetry," my own "Tendencies in Modern American Poetry," and the preface to "Can Grande's Castle," and I think that the latter gives the best account of it. I am quite sure there is nothing at all like it in Amerind verse. It is not a type of technique which a primitive people would think of.
   I do not know exactly what you mean by "instrumented prose." "Polyphonic prose" differs from rhythmical prose by being many-voiced; in other words, it employs assonance, alliteration, metre, cadence, rhyme and return, not regularly, but following the emotion of the poem at the moment. Without this polyphonic structure it ceases to

be "polyphonic prose" and becomes merely rhythmical prose. People are constantly confusing rhythmical prose with "polyphonic prose," and comparing me to various great writers of the former—for instance De Quincy, etc.—and asking wherein they do not write as good "polyphonic prose" as I do. As a matter of fact, they never wrote "polyphonic prose" at all, but rhythmical prose, which is an entirely different thing. I should be very glad to know exactly what you call "instrumented prose," as I do not quite understand what that can be.

I see perfectly what you mean by my giving an entirely wrong interpretation to the basket dance, in that little group of Indian poems which came out in the "Dial" some years ago. I realized my blunder after talking to you, and particularly since reading this beautiful rendering of the original of one of the songs in the basket dance which you have sent me. You say that it may not be your final rendering; I can only tell you that I cannot conceive how you can make a better one, and I am going to take the liberty, with your permission, of keeping this copy for my own pleasure. Of course, I had no original to work from; I got my idea of the basket dance (I have never seen it) from a description in a book, the name of which I have now forgotten, and I do not know whether it was the Oraibi dance or some other. You see I really *know* almost nothing about the matter, having been forced to gain all my knowledge through books and not through observation. There was a minute description of the dance in the book I followed, but no interpretation whatever of its meaning, and when the women threw the baskets at the men and were pursued by the men, splashed with mud, thrown down, etc., I took it, I think not unnaturally, as fecundity symbolized by human intercourse. I can see perfectly that this was not exactly what the Indians intended, but I am still a little in doubt as to what throwing the women down and spattering them with mud can have meant if not this. Perhaps you can elucidate the mystery.

I thank you very much indeed for letting me see this poem of yours and for telling me where I went wrong in mine. Please let me know when your collection is coming out, for I must certainly get it. I enjoyed so much seeing you for those few brief minutes at the Canbys' and only wish I might have the opportunity again.

Very sincerely yours,
Amy Lowell

Kate Douglas Wiggin (1856-1921), the second oldest correspondent in the Mary Austin correspondence group, earned a cycle of literary immortality with her *Rebecca of Sunnybrook Farm*, first published in 1903, then republished in German and Dutch in 1905, in Polish in 1912, and in English again in 1908. The Shirley Temple Edition appeared in 1959, after the successful moving picture was made with Temple as the heroine in the story. The book was portrayed by different illustrators in printings of 1962 and 1965.

Wiggin became Mrs. George C. Riggs on March 30, 1895, but continued to use her maiden name for such books as *Penelope's Progress* (1898) and *The Diary of a Goose Girl* (1902). She tells her personal story in *My Garden of Memory* (1923), which begins with life in Hollis, a rural village in Maine. When living with her sister there, she traveled to Portland, Maine, to hear Charles Dickens give a reading from his works, and even sat beside him on the train that went toward Boston on the morning afterward. Although she was only 12 years old, she had read his *David Copperfield* and other books; and she astonished Dickens by discussing them with their author.

Kate Wiggin suggests that this began her literary professional career, leading not only to the writing of books for young readers, such as *The Birds' Christmas Carol* (1888), but to the interpreting of her stories (as did Dickens) by public readings in both England and America. Under her own name or in collaboration with her sister, she authored twenty-six volumes and edited eight more, of both verse and prose, plus five plays, one of which was a dramatization of *Rebecca of Sunnybrook Farm*. To a modern reader, the plot of the latter story seems unexciting. Rebecca has lost her father, who left her mother with seven children and a mortgage on the farm. She is sent to live with two maiden aunts, upsetting their routine by a campaign to sell soap and to rescue some earnest missionaries. Her friend is the stagecoach driver, who becomes like an uncle to her in a number of situations. Finally, her energy and concern for others win the affection of her aunts, and stir the interest of the schoolmaster, who discovers Rebecca's talent for poetry and story writing. Upon the death of the older aunt, Rebecca is rewarded by inheriting the home and land to care for her mother, the remaining aunt, and the rest of her family.

In *Earth Horizon*, Mary Austin mentions the occasion on which she met Kate Douglas Wiggin at the home of a society leader in Los Angeles, an aspect of Mrs. Riggs's life which is stressed by her contacts at home and abroad with eminent people. She tells of meetings with Ralph Waldo Emerson, William Ellery Channing, James Whitcomb Riley in America, and Lady Gregory, Edward Dowden, Lord Aberdeen, and the actress Ellen Terry in the British Isles. Kate Douglas Wiggin was active in establishing Free Kindergartens, Babies Hospitals, Homes for Crippled Children, and Improved Tenements. She frequently read for high schools and was welcomed everywhere. In 1907, she published *New Chronicles of Rebecca*, the sequel to *Rebecca of Sunnybrook Farm*.

The poem which is mentioned in the letter has been added here to enable the reader to share the pleasure of the sisters who commented on it.

_____ 67

August 28, 1922

Quillcote
Hollis Centre
Maine

Dear Mary Austin,

Anybody could and would read with delight and appreciation your poem "Going West," in the Bookman, but only those who have lived in California twenty years or more can love it sufficiently.

I have nearly swooned with joy over every heavenly line, and remembrances poured over me in waves, till I could hardly bear to be here, not there. My sister Nora is in the same state of delight, but I must send my letter by itself.

Yours most heartily,
Kate Douglas Wiggin

GOING WEST

Some day I shall go West,
Having won all time to love it in, at last
Too still to boast.
But when I smell the sage,
When the long, marching landscape line
Melts into wreathing mountains,
And the dust cones dance
Something in me that is of them shall stir.

Happy, if I come home
When the musk-scented, moon-white gilia blows.

When all the hills are blue, remembering
The sea from which they rose.
Happy again
When blunt-faced bees carouse
In red flagons of the incense shrub
Or apricots have lacquered boughs,
And trails are dim with rain.

Lay me where some contented oak can prove
How much of me is nurture for a tree;
Sage thoughts of mine
Be acorn clusters for the deer to browse.
My loving whimsies—will you chide again
When they come up as lantern flowers?

I shall be small and happy as the grass,
Proud if my tip
Stays white, webby moons the spider weaves,
Or down my bleaching stalks shall slip
The light, imprisoning dew,
Where once you trod
I shall be bluets in the April sod.

Or if the wheel should run too fast,
Run up and rest
As a sequoia for a thousand years.*

*Permission to print this poem has been given by the Henry E. Huntington Library, San Marino, California.

In the boxes containing the correspondence written by Mary Austin to various friends, there are two undated letters sent from the National Arts Club to B. H. Clark at Briarcliff Manor, New York. In the first, she states that she had not read James Branch Cabell's novel *Jurgen* (1919), nor had she heard of an Emergency Committee in New York, because she had been away from the city for two years. The second letter, also undated, contains the following sentence: "Count me as opposed to the methods of the Society for the Suppression of Vice, in general. But do not commit me to any particular book which I may not have read." The "emergency" referred to may be explained by *Letter 68* in which Gelett Burgess requests Mary to speak at a luncheon to be held by the Authors' League Fellowship at the Hotel Martinique on October 6, 1922. At that time, John Saxton Sumner, secretary of the New York Society for the Suppression of Vice, would address the group, and Burgess asks Mary Austin to lead the discussion following the lecture. Among those also discussing the lecture were Heywood Broun, F. Scott Fitzgerald, and the publisher Horace Liveright.

Gelett Burgess (1866-1951) was a Bostonian who earned fame as editor, humorist, author, and lecturer, One of his earliest books added the word "goop" to the English language, at least that language as practiced in the United States during his lifetime. A "goop," according to Burgess, was an unmannerly child which he first defines in the book entitled *Goops and How to Be Them* (1900). He carried on his definitions with pictures and verses of bad infantile behavior through five more books: *More Goops* (1903), *Blue Goops and Red* (1907), *The Goop Directory* (1913), *The Goop Encyclopedia* (1915), and *New Goops and How to Know Them* (1951). Equally popular were his titles *Are You a Bromide?* (1906) and *The Maxims of Methusalah* (1907). Burgess first earned his living as a draftsman with the Southern Pacific Railway, but then turned his skill to illustrating the "goop" books with drawings of children in antisocial attitudes at the dinner table, school, and at play. While editor of *The Lark* magazine, 1895-1897, he printed his quatrain entitled "The Purple Cow":

> I never saw a Purple Cow,
>   I never hope to see one;
> But I can tell you, anyhow,
>   I'd rather see than be one.

The protagonist at the Martinique Hotel who spoke for certain types of censorship was John Saxton Sumner (1876-1955), the son of an admiral in the United States Navy who became a banker in New York City. In addition, he was a lawyer and had become secretary of the New York Society for the Suppression of Vice, an organization which devoted energies to maintaining decency in publication, on the screen, and on the stage. He had been in active military service during World War I, and later served as a leader in political and social movements in New York and Florida where he retired. Further discussion will follow the reading of the letter from Gelett Burgess to Mary Austin whom he addresses as "Miss" but cites as "Mrs." in the printed invitation to hear her speak at the "first Luncheon of the Season" to be held by the Authors' League Fellowship.

_____ **68**

Gelett Burgess
250 West 94th Street
New York City
Tel. Riverside 9388

Sept. 15th, 1922

My dear Miss Austin;

Cannot I depend upon you to speak for five or ten minutes at a luncheon of the Authors' League Fellowship, on Oct. 6th?

We are to hear the ineffable John S. Sumner, of the Society for the Suppression of Vice, (and good books) who is to state his views. It is of the utmost importance that he should be answered, or, rather, that the author's side of the question of suppression should be presented ably—and I know of no author better able to do it than you.

I have asked Mr. Hergesheimer to come, and also Mr. Cabell. But it is doubtful if either can be there. If they are, however, it will only limit the length of your remarks. Heywood Broun also consented to speak, and Mr. Liveright, the publisher.

I know this is no great pleasure I am offering you, but I am in hopes that you may conceive it in some sense a pious duty toward literature, or even toward liberty in general.

May I hope to have a reply from you at your earliest convenience? It will help me so much.

Yours very sincerely,
Gelett Burgess

CARD ACCOMPANYING *LETTER 68*:

Note the Change of Meeting Place!

THE AUTHORS' LEAGUE FELLOWSHIP
Will hold its first Luncheon of the Season at the
HOTEL MARTINIQUE, Broadway and 32nd St.
on Friday, October 6th, at 12.30 p.m. sharp

There will be a Friendly Discourse by Mr. John Sumner, Secretary
of the New York Society for the Suppression of Vice.

To be followed by a Discussion by Mrs. Mary Austin, Mr. Heywood
Broun, Mr. Horace B. Liveright, Mr. F. Scott Fitzgerald and others

---

Note: During the Season of 1922-23 the following Meetings will be
held. Luncheons at $1.50, on Oct. 6th, Dec. 1st, Feb. 2nd, April 6th
and June 1st. Dinners at $3.50, on Nov. 12th, Jan. 7th, March 4th
and May 6th, subject to change.

Gelett Burgess, *President*   Maravene Thompson, *Secretary*

On the day following the "Friendly Discourse" announced by
the Authors' League Fellowship, Mary Austin wrote to her acquaintance Dr.
MacDougal (see *Letter 65*) telling him how she had spoken in favor of freedom
of the press and claiming that she had defeated "the smug New England puri-
tanism" held by Sumner. She restated her position seven years later when the
Honorable Bronson Cutting, of New Mexico, introduced in the United States
Senate a bill to amend the Tariff Act of 1890 which authorized officials in the
United States Bureau of Customs to exclude books and pamphlets which they
considered to be obscene.

The particular book Senator Cutting had in mind when he proposed a change
in the Tariff Act was James Joyce's *Ulysses* (1922), first printed by an English
publisher in Paris. Following the action of the Senate in 1930, Judge John M.
Woolsey, of the Southern District Court of New York, issued a decree on
December 6, 1933, that permitted the book to be admitted into the United
States. He declared that *Ulysses* was not written to exploit obscenity, but to use
a new technique of narrative showing how middle class people in a certain Irish
city thought and acted on a given day in early June. Judge Woolsey compared
the stream of consciousness style to the multiple exposure possible on a cinema
film. In developing this technique, Joyce found that he needed to use old Anglo-
Saxon words criticized as dirty but familiar to almost all men and known to
many women. The words were used like a bit of mosaic in the picture Joyce
was constructing for his readers. As a result of Judge Woolsey's decision, *Ulysses*

received its first authorized American printing in 1934. Morris L. Ernst, an attorney who was spokesman for the New York publishing house that brought the case before the court, wrote in a Foreword to the book:

Under the *Ulysses* case it should henceforth be impossible for the censors legally to sustain an attack against any book of artistic integrity, no matter how frank and forthright it might be. We have travelled a long way from the days of Bowdler and Mrs. Grundy and Comstock. We may well rejoice over the result.

A magazine called *The Laughing Horse*, published by Willard H. (Spud) Johnson, of Taos, New Mexico, in February 1930, devoted the entire issue (No. 17) to "A Symposium of Criticism, Comment and Opinion on the Subject of Censorship." Among the twenty-nine contributors, with the designations supplied by Johnson, were: Carl Sandburg (poet), Will Irwin (publicist), John Dewey (professor of philosophy, Columbia University), Arthur Davison Ficke (poet), Sherwood Anderson (novelist), William Allen White (editor, "The Emporia Gazette"), Witter Bynner (poet), Ellery Sedgwick (editor, "The Atlantic Monthly"), Alfred A. Knopf (New York publisher), Mabel Dodge Luhan (writer), Upton Sinclair (social reformer), Lincoln Steffens (ex-liberal), Harriet Monroe (editor, "Poetry, A Magazine of Verse"), Henry Goddard Leach (editor, "The Forum"), and Mary Austin (feminist). This group and the other fourteen contributors were unanimous in supporting Senator Cuttings's amendment, and congratulated him upon his success when the United States Senate approved it by the narrow margin of 38 to 36. A copy of *Laughing Horse* was distributed to every member of the Senate.

An excerpt from Mary Austin's statement in the magazine doubtless coincides with the remarks she made at the request of Gelett Burgess in *Letter 67*:

Without doubt, every one of the people who undertake to forbid the expression of ideas on sex or politics differing from their own, could be shown as entertaining ideas on sex or politics or education or economics, which have already been pronounced "bad" by experts in those fields. . . . I often ask myself whether organizations devoted to the suppression of opinion are not in their nature unconstitutional to the degree that would warrant their abolition. Or at least, could we not demand of them a pledge that every member hold himself willing, on being convicted of incorrect thinking on any other subject, to suffer the same fines and penalties prescribed for the thinkers they hope to suppress?

EARLY SANTA FE INTERESTS

V

One of the most unusual autobiographies in American literature was written by Mabel Dodge Luhan (1879-1962) in what she called her *Intimate Memories*, and developed in four volumes: the first was *Intimate Memories, Background* (1933); the others were *European Experiences* (1935), *Movers and Shakers* (1936), and *Edge of Taos Desert* (1937). These reminiscences required a total of 1,658 pages. Then they were supplemented by two other books which added 588 pages and supplied more details about the people she knew and what they meant to her. The two supplementary books were *Lorenzo in Taos* (1932) and *Winter in Taos* (1935). *Lorenzo in Taos* may be the most important of all the volumes, for it is addressed to Robinson Jeffers, the California poet (see *Letters 109, 110,* and *111*), and deals with the lengthy stay in Taos of the English novelist D. H. Lawrence, who lived with his wife, Frieda, at Kowa Ranch after it was given to them by Luhan in exchange for the manuscript of Lawrence's *Sons and Lovers* (1911), perhaps his most successful work of fiction. Following their visit at the ranch, during intervals between September of 1922 until September of 1925, the Lawrences traveled to Sportono, Italy, near Genoa, where they were sent pages of Luhan's *Memoirs* for comments and criticism. On April 12, 1926, Lawrence wrote urging her to change all the names of persons written about in the autobiography. Lawrence called Luhan's disclosure "the most serious 'confession' that ever came out of America, and perhaps the most heart-destroying revelation of the American life-process that ever has or ever will be produced."

Since portions of the first and third volumes and practically all of volume two were devoted to the period from 1902 until 1914, the years Luhan spent in Europe with her second husband, Edwin Dodge, the *Memoirs* describe a life-process as much European as American. The Dodges renovated a villa near Florence, Italy, which became a social center for visitors from England, France, Italy, and the United States. Such distinguished guests were entertained as the English actor and designer, Edward Gordon Craig; the Italian actress Eleanora Duse; the French novelist Andre Gide; the American experimenter in language and narrative, Gertrude Stein, and her companion Alice B. Toklas; along with such other well known Americans as George de Forest Brush, artist; Carl Van Vechten, novelist; John Reed, poet and revolutionary; and Robert Edmond Jones, producer and designer of plays. The Villa Curonia was a center for gifted intellectuals and introduced Mabel Ganson Evans Dodge as a patroness for creative activities. Upon her return to America, she continued such patronage at 23 Fifth Avenue, where her apartment was described by Van Wyck Brooks as the focus of Greenwich Village. In *Movers and Shakers*, Luhan tells of an evening during the winter of 1913 when a group of socialists, trade-unionists, anarchists, and others gathered there. It was a time of labor unrest, and Bill Haywood, Emma Goldman, Lincoln Steffens, Max Eastman, Elizabeth Gurley Flynn, Margaret Sanger, and Mary Austin were present. Mary Austin was not at home with the bolder radicals. However, as a reformer in programs for social betterment, she stood with the foremost. Walter Lippman was among the "dangerous characters" in attendance, as was Hutchins Hapgood, another journalist and author. Luhan describes Austin as "sitting with her lips thrust out and her eyelids heavy, her gray hair coiled high, portentous in prairie-colored satin."

In his autobiography, Lincoln Steffens calls Mabel Luhan "the one hostess in the world who could entertain 200 writers, artists, and musicians and keep all of them pleased and amused." However, something more than amusement developed on one occasion when a small group of her guests experienced effects from eating peyote buds which produced hallucinations, antics, and sickness for nearly all of them. A number of the members in her New York circle followed her to New Mexico in the 1920s or earlier, either as permanent members of the art colonies in Santa Fe and Taos or as frequent visitors: the poets were Witter Bynner, Arthur Davison Ficke, Vachel Lindsay, and John Gould Fletcher, and the artists were Andrew Dasburg and Marsden Hartley; plus her third husband, the painter-sculptor, Maurice Sterne, whom she married in September of 1917.

John Evans, Luhan's son by her marriage in 1900 to Karl Evans of Buffalo, had spent the summer of 1917 on a Wyoming ranch, and his reports of the West were joined by letters from New Mexico urging Sterne to visit the picturesque Indian pueblos and old Spanish towns. Sterne wrote to his wife from Santa Fe on November 30 asking her to come there: "Do you want an object in life? Save the Indians, their art—culture—reveal it to the world!" With this in mind, Mrs. Sterne took the train and arrived in New Mexico's capital city via the Atchison, Topeka, and Santa Fe Railroad spur at Lamy. She was greeted by her husband and boarded a stagecoach that rolled into Santa Fe through an empty plaza and up a narrow, hilly street to a flat-roofed adobe house with three white-washed rooms and one small fireplace. Despite the perfume of aromatic piñon logs in the fireplace and the friendly surroundings, she did not remain in Santa Fe, but chose Taos seventy miles farther north where she built a large house and stayed the remainder of her life.

Her book *Winter in Taos* makes the Spanish village and the Indian pueblo stages on which scenes are presented against the backdrop of the sacred Taos Mountain, and the forest where Blue Lake lies becomes a shrine of religious mysticism. Mabel Ganson Evans Dodge Sterne found the communal life of the Pueblo Indians a new form of reality, a group spirit which served to shape her individual will to harmony with nature and the tribe. In April of 1923, she married Antonio Luhan, a Taos Indian, after he agreed to abandon the use of peyote as a ceremonial ritual. She preferred the assurance of his way of life to the insecurity of her own (see also *Letters 72* and *73* from Sherwood Anderson and *Letter 80* from Robert Edmond Jones). Mary Austin was a friend and often a guest in Taos as revealed by the forty-three letters, dating from 1921 to 1933, found in the Austin Collection. In the pamphlet entitled *Mary Austin, A Memorial*, published by the Laboratory of Anthropology, Santa Fe, September 1944, Luhan calls Mary "one of the best companions in the world in a house or on a trip." Then she adds:

She loved to put on a big apron and go into our big old kitchen and toss a couple of pumpkin pies together. She loved to hob-nob, to sit and spin out reasons for strange happenings, to hear and tell about all the daily occurrences in both our lives. She was a romantic and loved the romance of the mystical and the occult and often induced in herself peculiar symptoms. She could see and hear and truly experience more than the rest of us, so when she least knew it she really became fascinatingly delphic and sibylline.

Letter 69 bears only the day, Sunday, as a designation in time, but internal evidence suggests the month of December and the year 1922. *Letters 55, 56* and *97* and *98* convey additional information on Alice Corbin and Witter Bynner. Francis Wilson was a Santa Fe attorney who was associated with Austin in support of Indian legal charters and who served as attorney for the trustees of her estate. Ralph Emerson Twitchell (1859-1925) was born in Ann Arbor, Michigan, and educated at Midwestern universities, but after serving as assistant solicitor for the Atchison, Topeka, and Santa Fe Railway Company, he became president of the New Mexico Bar Association, settled in Santa Fe, and devoted his life to research in New Mexico history. In 1914, by authority of the state, he compiled *The Spanish Archives of New Mexico* in two volumes. Albert Bacon Fall (1861-1944) was a Kentuckian and a lawyer who became a rancher in New Mexico. After serving as a justice of the State Supreme Court and as a United States Senator, he became secretary of the interior in the cabinet of President Harding, but was forced to resign in 1923 when he was convicted of defrauding the government in connection with oil leases. John Collier (1884-1968) was a reformer who directed the People's Institute, Fifth Avenue and 13th Street, New York City, and later the National Training School for Community Centers, 1915 to 1919. He was also secretary of the Indian Defense Association, and in 1933 President Franklin D. Roosevelt appointed him Commissioner of Indian Affairs. *Letter 69* has much underlining for emphasis (see reference to the Bursum Bill in the discussion following Lou Henry Hoover's *Letter 43*). The article Luhan announces for *The Dial* appeared in February 1923, and was entitled "Indians and an Englishman." Her book *Lorenzo in Taos* contains excerpts from the original manuscript which were omitted in the magazine. Another article by D. H. Lawrence, entitled "Taos," was published in *The Dial* for March of the same year (see Robinson and Una Jeffers, *Letters 109, 110, 111*).

_____ 69

Taos, Sunday.   [December, 1922?]

Dear Mary.

The volume of newspaper publicity—magazine things—personal letters from significant people etc—resolutions—*all kinds* of stuff that has arisen in response to that Indian meeting in Santo Domingo [pueblo] and the Petition they sent out is very remarkable. It shows that there was *a latent sympathy*, almost fierce, for the Indian, in "These States." The country almost has seemed to *go indian*. There hasn't been a single denial or refusal. *Universal* response. Is it possible that the little drop of indian *in* every one awakened and answered the call?

Any way—what was *latent* is now awake and conscious and must be kept awake and nourished until vigorous and undeniable. We want *interest* and *appreciation* of the indian life and culture to become a part of our *conscious* racial mind. We want *as a nation* to value the indian as we value our selves. We want to *consciously* love the wholeness and harmony of indian life, and to *consciously* protect it. This publicity is invaluable. That it began in politics does not prevent its being channelled into aesthetics. Please get busy and write—write. *No one* but Alice Corbin and Bynner is writing in Santa Fe. All the other work there is secretarial.

Keep the indian *in* the public eye and soon he will be an integral part of the public welfare.

Francis Wilson—one time U.S. attorney for the indians—is working almost gratuitously for them at this period—and is watching Twitchell *most* carefully as we all are. Renehan—Twitchell—receiving thousands a year to act as attorney *for* the indians *drew up* most of the Bursum Bill depriving the indians of their lands and water! He has now gone to Washington but so has John Collier—and soon Francis Wilson will follow.

Do not be disheartened over your work. Don't you *want* to write about indians? Any magazine will publish things about them now and this must be followed up. About D. H. L. He is a very sweet person on some sides and terribly neurotic at the same time. Terribly overcome and oppressed by indians who he thought disliked him (though indians are not personal and rarely like or dislike people)—he stood it here about 3 months and now has gone up the mountain away from here about 20 miles—on to the Hawk's ranch where he never sees an indian.

Too much indian affect both before coming and *after* coming. You will see signs of this in, I believe, January *Dial* or Century's.

Please get busy. Be interviewed of World or Globe or something.

Love from Mabel.

Letters written at a later date by Mabel Luhan tell of "making up with D. H. Lawrence"; receiving Mary Austin's *Land of Journeys' Ending* and praising it; reporting that the Lawrences have left for Mexico in October of 1924; telling of her plan to make her house a center for artists and writers and rejecting a proposal to use it as a dude ranch; proposing that Austin speak at a lecture forum in Taos; and informing Austin that a group of her friends were using prayer and exercises of the will to pull Mary through a period of depression. *Letter 70* refers to this effort to transfer healing by means of group concentration. The "Bobby" mentioned in the letter was Robert Edmond Jones, a New York producer of plays whose *Letter 80* will provide more information concerning his acquaintance with Mabel Dodge Luhan both in New York City and Taos.

_____ 70

Taos, Wednesday
May 28   [1923?]

Dear Mary—Your letter dated 22nd arrived yestereen the 27th—
So you see what posts are. Maybe this will never catch you in San Juan.—
It is too far to drive to in one day.

We work for you *every night* and I am certain all you are going thro' is
a recapitulation—a cleaning up period—preceding the benefits envisaged
for you. We all feel so certain of *things happening* to you—and wonderful
new waves vibrating towards you that we only rejoice in your present
temporary sense of obscurity, for it is the natural state of one who leaves
all the old ways of thought, belief, and action before the adaptation to
newer, *other* ones.

You are going thro' a metamorphosis—a kind of rebirth. Once *through*—
other values will manifestly appeal to you than the ones to which you
are so used.

And in the period nearing you—you will have more of the things we
all want than you have ever had before—more of love and money—and
external beauty but I will foretell one thing to you—you won't care
much about them for you will be fixed transfixed by other images.

Things always come to us as we pass on from them. And you are
essentially one who passes on. It is beautiful here now. My instinct is
that you would do well to come and sink down here to work as much as
you can. There is loads of material. Everything is sweetly peaceful now.
The building goes on. I have a big log work room studio nearly completed. Bobby is supposed to be coming. I constantly hear that he is.
I wish something could be done with indians in the drama—music world.
We will see.

I hope this will catch up with you somewhere.

Best love
Mabel

_____

When General John Alexander Logan died in 1886, after
serving in the United States Senate as a Republican from Illinois during 1871-
1877 and 1879-1886, Mary Austin wrote a high school poem praising him as a
hero in the hearts of his fellow citizens. Her family, evidently, was Republican

in its politics even though the poem was printed in the Carlinville *Democrat* on January 6, 1887. Furthermore, her support of Herbert Hoover, as detailed in *Letters 38, 39, 40,* and *41* plus the support lent her programs by Bronson Cutting, the Republican Senator from New Mexico from 1929 to 1935, indicate that she was conservatively Republican despite her emotional leanings toward social causes more often supported by the Democratic party. Women were a minority group which, as a feminist, she supported in any political party. Therefore, her friendship with the author of *Letter 71* was the logical outgrowth between two like-minded women. Frances Perkins (1882-1965) was the first woman ever to hold a position in the cabinet of an American President. There are only two letters from Perkins in the Mary Austin Collection, but both indicate agreement between the two women as to many of their aims and much of their motivation.

Letter 71 was written when Perkins was a member of the New York State Industrial Board, and the second (which carried an invitation to dinner on January 12, 1928) was mailed when Perkins was chairman of the same board. From 1929 until 1933, she was Industrial Commissioner for New York State, and when Franklin D. Roosevelt became president he appointed her secretary of labor. This was on March 4, 1933, and the appointment was opposed by the American Federation of Labor, which expected a choice from someone in its own ranks as had been the case in all previous holders of the office. Perkins explained the background of her selection in a book she wrote called *The Roosevelt I Knew* (1948). She tells not only of Roosevelt's concern for the codes, wages, and hours of labor but also of how she observed his progress as a person and a leader. Her story begins with Roosevelt's entry into politics in 1913 and proceeds to the term he spent as governor of New York, 1929-1933, and the era of his presidency, 1933-1945. She called him a very complicated man, whose insight and imagination into the most varied human experiences enabled him to lead the nation toward greater social justice and higher standards in the corporate life of the country.

Letter 71 is one of the last that Austin received while a resident at the National Arts Club in 1923. In April of that year, she left New York for Arizona where she embarked on a writing and sketching trip with the artist Gerald Cassidy and his wife, Ina, of Santa Fe. The writing and drawings resulted in Austin's book *The Land of Journeys' Ending* (1924). After weeks in the Indian country of Arizona and New Mexico, she visited in Santa Fe and Taos, returning to New York in February of 1924. Later in that year she settled in Santa Fe. Perkins calls the ideas in *The American Rhythm* (1923) "stupendous," a judgment with which many readers would agree. However, the subject matter in the book became very controversial, as will be shown by Witter Bynner's *Letter 98*, in which he challenges Austin's theory that climate, topography, landscape, and the physical environment determine racial tempo and rhythm.

_____ 71

Official Seal of	State of New York
New York State	Department of Labor
Frances Perkins	Industrial Board
MEMBER	124 East 28th St., New York City
	March 5th, 1923

Miss Mary Austin,
National Arts Club,
15 Gramercy Park
New York City

Dear Mary Austin:

This is just a note to say that I have just read "American Rhythm" and it is by all odds the most stupendous and moving thing that I have read in years. I did not suppose anybody could do such a thing just now when the world is in doldrums and my dear, I think you are probably the only person who could. Bless you for being alive and doing it.

Sincerely yours,
Frances Perkins

FP-IA

Sherwood Anderson (1876-1941) first appeared on the American literary scene in 1913 when one of his short stories was accepted for publication by *Harper's Magazine.* In the previous year, he had abruptly ended his career as a businessman by walking out of an office where he managed a paint factory in Elyria, Ohio. Returning to Chicago, he took up where he had left off as a copy writer in an advertising firm. He was then 36 years old. In addition to his decision to use words and imagination to sell commercial goods, he began to employ his wide reading and capacity for recalling experiences to qualify him for a professional career as an author. He possessed genius for observing and understanding people, those he met in the small towns of Ohio where he grew up and those he met in Chicago where he worked as an unskilled laborer. Details about his family on a chicken farm, his father as an actor and as a salesman, his own work in a bicycle factory and a storage warehouse were to appear in his fiction chiefly because he met people and felt close to them. In his *Memoirs*

(1942), he states that from early childhood he experienced a "penetration into other people's lives." His fiction reveals the crude as well as the refined, the selfish as well as the generous aspects of human behavior. His short stories, novels, even the little book of so-called poems, called *A New Testament* (1927), are just narratives for the sake of portraying people in joy and sadness, happiness and distress, and serenity as well as confusion. All are disclosed in his stream of Midwestern life.

Sherwood Anderson shows that he is proud of his background, proud to consider environment as a testing place for literary art. He makes this clear in his two autobiographical books, *A Story-Teller's Story* (1924) and *Sherwood Anderson's Memoirs* (1942), a volume published a year after his death. He knew that such Midwestern writers as Theodore Dreiser, Carl Sandburg, Edgar Lee Masters, Sinclair Lewis, Ben Hecht, George Ade, Arthur Davison Ficke, Harriet Monroe, Maxwell Bodenheim, Floyd Dell, and others were representative of its culture. His own books, *Winesburg, Ohio* (1919), *Poor White* (1920), *The Triumph of the Egg* (1921), *Many Marriages* (1923), and *Dark Laughter* (1925) have been compared with the work of Turgenev and Balzac. It is pertinent to *Letters 72* and *73* that they were sent to Mary Austin in 1923 when Anderson was living in Reno, Nevada, preparing to divorce his second wife, Tennessee Mitchell, a music teacher he had married in 1916. The sentiments Anderson expresses in *Letter 73* indicate that he would have included Mary in any list of Midwestern cultural protagonists if she had remained long enough in Illinois to become a member of the "Chicago circle" with whom he allied himself.

_____ 72

My Dear Mary Austin,   [Summer, 1923]
    I have been here several months at the edge of the deserts and have found your books. They have been such a relief to me after all the other books of the western country I have read. What Twain and Harte missed you have found and set down with such fine understanding.
    The books have been a real joy to me.

Sincerely
Sherwood Anderson

Mail address,
c/o Max Radin
2597 Buena Vista Way
Berkeley, Calif.

Letter 73, like Letter 72, is undated but the Huntington Library collection of Austin's correspondence has an envelope for the letter which was directed to the Houghton Mifflin Company, Cambridge, Massachusetts, and redirected to 132 East 19th Street, New York, N. Y., then to Santa Fe, New Mexico, and finally to Taos, N. M. where it eventually found Mary Austin. Anderson writes that he may see her before he leaves the West and thanks both Mary and Mabel Luhan for their invitation to visit them in New Mexico. "The Field" he mentions is doubtless the chapter entitled "My Neighbor's Field" in Austin's *The Land of Little Rain*. *Letter 73* was printed in the edition of Anderson's *Letters* (1953), which was annotated by Howard Mumford Jones assisted by Walter B. Rideout. These editors report that Jacques Copeau (1879-1949) was the French actor and producer who brought Vieux Columbier Theatre to New York City in 1917-1918 and, after announcing his retirement in 1924, returned in 1926 to begin producing plays again. In the *Memoirs*, Anderson describes how Copeau came to live in a small bedroom at the back of Anderson's ground floor apartment. They were to collaborate in dramatizing the stories from *Winesburg, Ohio*. Copeau did not buckle down to the task, and before they had made any real progress, robbers removed everything Copeau possessed by opening a window that looked into the alleyway behind the apartment. At a later time, Anderson did consult some Hollywood directors about filming his stories, but he never wrote a script for screen or stage. The idea gradually faded from his mind. He even burned a manuscript which might have been suitable for either purpose.

_____ 73

Dear Mary Austin—   August 9, 1923

Perhaps I had to be for a time out in the west before I could know the people and things you write about. I shall look up the *American Rhythm* the next time I am in some place where the book may be had. I may see you before I leave the west—but when that may be I do not know.

I like particularly your own writing about wandering people and there was one thing of yours called "The Field" I loved very much.

Do not be annoyed that I have been so long finding you out—will you? I am such a long time finding anything out.

Jacques Copeau and several others have tried to get me interested in writing drama, but wherever I go to the theater I shudder at the notion. I've a fancy myself that anything I have to give can be given as a tale teller as well as any other way. God knows I have yet enough to learn about that.

I am sorry you have been ill. Have been myself recovering from nerves. They go along more steadily now. You may be sure I shall write you when I have got my hands on *The American Rhythm.*

May I thank both Mabel Luhan and yourself for the invitation to come in and see you. I may, one of these days, be wandering past.

Sincerely,

Sherwood Anderson. ⋆

⋆From *Letters of Sherwood Anderson,* ed. by Howard Mumford Jones and Walter B. Rideout. Copyright 1953 by Eleanor Anderson. By permission of Little, Brown and Company.

Willard H. (Spud) Johnson (1897-1968) was a member of the Taos colony that welcomed the D. H. Lawrences in September of 1922. He was secretary and confidant of Mabel Luhan, and a poet in his own right beside serving as editor, printer, publisher, and promoter of his unusual magazine called the *Laughing Horse.* Johnson was born in southern Illinois, but became a "Westerner" at the age of 9 when his family moved to Colorado where, at a later age, he attended institutions of higher learning before transferring to the University of California at Berkeley. *Laughing Horse* first appeared there as a student publication in 1921. Issue No. 4 featured excerpts from *The Goose Step* by Upton Sinclair plus a letter by D. H. Lawrence. Sinclair's book attacked the structure of higher education, and Roy E. Chansor, the student editor, was suspended by university authorities. It was in this number that Spud Johnson became a member of the editorial staff and a friend of the Lawrences. He, too, was suspended from the university. With the help of Witter Bynner, at that time an instructor in the university, Johnson moved the magazine to Santa Fe in 1923, and shortly afterwards *Laughing Horse* found a home in Taos. From this time until December of 1939, the magazine appeared at irregular dates with poems, articles, and stories printed by a hand and foot operated press in Spud's workshop. The press "run" produced only 200 copies. Consequently, copies of the *Laughing Horse* are today collectors' items.

In 1926 and 1927, Johnson was on the staff of the *New Yorker* magazine. Returning to Taos, he became a columnist for both the *Taos Valley News* and the *Santa Fe New Mexican.* In 1935, Writers' Editions, a cooperative group in Santa Fe, published his book of poetry entitled *Horizontal Yellow,* which contained original poems and reprinted selections from other journals.

Letter 74 includes the names of a number of Johnson's friends in Santa Fe, Taos, and New York: John Sloan, artist, who taught and painted in both New York City and Santa Fe, and was an innovator as an exponent of stark realism; Victor Higgins, one of the pioneers in the Taos art colony, who won awards for murals in the Missouri State Capitol and other public buildings; Gustave Baumann, Santa Fe craftsman in the art of colored block prints; Alice Corbin (see *Letters 55, 56*); Elsie (Elizabeth Shepley) Sergeant, social worker and author in Boston and New York, who lived for a time at Tesuque, near Santa Fe (see paraphrase of *Letter 86*).

———— 74

November 19, 1923

Dear Mrs. Austin,

Thank you for sending me the beginning of *The Land of Journeys' Ending*. It came special delivery this afternoon. I was afraid that you had not been well since your return to New York; and I was hesitating about writing you again—wanting very badly to have something from you, but not wanting to annoy you!

Of course the pages came in plenty of time. I was a little impatient because I wanted to be sure of what I could depend upon. So now the only promises I am doubtful about are those of John Sloan in New York, Victor Higgins in Taos, and D. H. Lawrence in Mexico. They may all come across yet, but meantime I am impatient.

Gus Baumann, Alice Corbin and I have been in conference recently and may make some sort of compromise of cooperation. I may turn the Horse over to them for a special number to be called The Turquoise Horse, or we may consolidate as one body—myself as managing editor, a group of the artists and writers as a board of advisors.

But this is a hurried note of thanks; I will tell you later if anything is definitely planned. Many more thanks; and with the hope that you will be enjoying better health soon, I remain

Yours sincerely,

Willard Johnson.

P.S.   If you see Elsie Sergeant can't you persuade her to send me some sort of New Mexico sketch immediately? I will copy the two pages you sent and return your copy soon.

There are fifteen letters from Johnson to Austin, dating from 1921 to 1930. The earliest are addressed to "Mrs. Austin" and the latest to "Aunt Mary." The subject matter discussed deals with his magazine, his doubts about Mary's theories on Indian poetry, and his contemplated trip to Mexico with the D. H. Lawrences. In the letter dated January 23, 1930, he announces that No. 17 of *Laughing Horse* will be a symposium concerning the subject of censorship (see *Letter 68* in this volume). *Letter 75* is written on correspondence paper which has a drawing of Mabel Luhan's house with an outline of Taos Mountain in the background. The cabin from which he writes is a guest house once occupied by Tony Luhan. The D. H. Lawrences had not yet moved to the Kiowa Ranch which became their home later in the year 1922. Frieda Lawrence and Johnson were good friends. In *Frieda Lawrence, The Memoirs and Correspondence*, edited by E. W. Tedlock, Jr. (1964), she addresses him as "The Spoodle," an affectionate translation of the sound "Spud" into something corresponding to it in German.

———— 75

Dear Mary Austin—   "Visiting Mabel"
I have thought of you so often during my week here. You must have left something of yourself when last you were here. Or perhaps you have merely been sending your thoughts to us frequently during your illness. We speak of you, Mabel and I, often. No one else is here except the D. H. Lawrences who have the house across the alfalfa field.

I am in the cabin, which is my favorite room here, and I always sit a long time before the fireplace each night after the others have gone to bed. . . . Making Medicine.

And I hope it has helped, for some of it has been for you.
Sincerely yours
Willard Johnson.
P.S.   The pickled peaches we had for dinner this evening were so excellently done by you, Mabel informs us. Our compliments!

When *Letter 76* was mailed in the summer of 1924, George Bird Grinnell (1849-1939) was 75 years old and had been writing about nature and the native American Indians for more than thirty years. Perhaps the fact that he attended a private New York City school which was directed by the widow of John James Audubon, a famous naturalist, turned Grinnell's observation to natural history and the unexplored areas of the United States. After completing studies at a military school and earning his baccalaureate degree at Yale, Grinnell in 1870 joined a research expedition to collect fossils and describe wild life in the Black Hills of South Dakota. Five years later, he engaged in a similar expedition to areas of Yellowstone National Park. His reports on birds, animals, and wonders of nature led to appointment as natural history editor for *Forest and Stream* in 1876. Then he became editor-in-chief for this magazine and its principal owner. Grinnell was influential in passage of a number of conservation laws. He was also founder of the Audubon Society, devoted to conservation, and as trustee of the New York Zoological Society, helped to draw up plans for its famous Zoological Park.

During the trips Grinnell made to the West, he filled his notebooks with details and pictures of the Indian tribes he encountered, notably the Pawnees, Blackfeet, and Cheyenne groups. With the help of interpreters, he was able to record folklore and accounts of tribal history. These personal contacts brought participation in tribal councils. He even represented the Indians on a number of occasions when they were negotiating with the United States government about treaty rights and privileges. Grinnell wrote more than forty books, the most important of which are: *Blackfoot Lodge Tales* (1892); *The Last of the Buffalo* (1892); *The Story of the Indian* (1896); *American Big Game and Its Haunts* (1904); *American Game Bird Shooting* (1910); *The Cheyenne Indians, Their History and Ways of Life* (1924); and *Beyond the Old Frontier* (1930).

Mary Austin's review of *The Cheyenne Indians, Their History and Ways of Life*, referred to in *Letter 76*, praises the book because she says that Grinnell adds illuminating details to the facts of history. She reports that he humanizes the Indian so that the effect of reality is heightened: "He comes into the Tepee as a streak of light, revealing more than would otherwise be seen." *Letter 76* exhibits the qualities which made George Bird Grinnell not only famous but admirable as a person. He was modest about his own achievement, concerned with the well-being of others, and cordial friend to a reviewer who shared his interests.

_____ 76

Geo. Bird Grinnell
    238 East 15th Street   August 18, 1924
    New York, N. Y.

My dear Mrs. Austin,
    I am taking the liberty of writing to you not to thank you for your very flattering review of my Cheyenne book in the last *Saturday Review,* but to express my gratification that you comprehend my point of view about Indians.

I have been writing about these people for a good many years, and always trying to tell of them so that the white people would realize that they were real "folks," just about like ourselves.

It is only once in awhile that I find some one who seems to understand that this is true, and those who do understand it are always of those who have known Indians intimately, and, of course, sympathetically. You are one of those, as an author and a book reviewer—as I have been for so many years—you know better than most people how unusual it is for one who writes a book to find anyone whom he has been able to make see just what he tried to put in the book. The author who finds such a reader feels as if he had been presented with a jewelled crown.

"I shake hands with you."

                        Yours sincerely,
                        Geo. Bird Grinnell

Mrs. Mary Austin
    National Arts Club
      20th St.
        New York

Marianne Moore (1887-1972), school teacher, librarian, and spinster, published her first book, entitled simply *Poems*, when she was 34 years old. The volume appeared in England, and contained only twenty-four items, but they attracted such attention that fourteen years later her *Selected Poems* earned an introduction by the noted poet-critic T. S. Eliot, who stated that her work contributed to "the small body of durable poetry written in our time." A graduate of Bryn Mawr in 1909, Moore taught at Carlisle (Pennsylvania) U. S.

Indian School, then became an assistant in the New York Public Library, and in 1925 assumed the post of acting editor of *The Dial* magazine. It was at this time that Mary Austin requested a contribution to her book *Everyman's Genius* (1925). This project developed from a talk Austin gave to a class in creative writing at New York University. The class was conducted by John Farrar, who was editor of *The Bookman* (see *Letter 116*). He suggested that her ideas were of such interest that he would publish them as a series of articles. They first agreed upon three essays, but the response was so enthusiastic that the series was increased to ten and finally became fifteen chapters in the book. An appendix was added containing "Notes of Personal Methods" used by creative workers active in their respective fields. Two of these "Notes" appear with letters in this book, those written by Fannie Hurst and Marianne Moore (see also introduction to *Letter 80* by Robert Edmond Jones).

Austin's central idea in *Everyman's Genius* was that the word "genius" does not identify an isolated quality but a creative power possessed to a degree by everyone. She calls genius the capacity to make use of inherited aptitudes held in the subconscious storehouse of the average as well as the exceptional individual. Personal activities enrich this storehouse, but the latent basis for genius is the most natural thing in the world. Whether the quality is released in an operatic aria or a folk song, in a mural painting or in the embroidery of a pillow case, the skill flows from an inheritance of racial gifts, and everyone can release such an aptitude with a timely opportunity and the right stimulus. Austin makes clear her meaning by defining such terms as *psyche, genius, talent, immediate-self, deep-self, subconscious, invention, creation, intuition, contemplation,* and *autosuggestion.*

The reader or writer of poetry will find Moore's "Note" on how she composed her poetry of great interest. She discloses that a thought suggested by her reading or in conversation keeps recurring to her. Words that occurred to her may have changed the concept or helped to shape imagery called to mind. She illustrates the process by viewing a piece of armor that reminds her of a mammal encased in bony plates or of a wall of interlocking shields used in battle. Other aspects of conflict occur to be succeeded by aspects of beauty in the figures seen as the poem evolves. From her comments, the reader learns that Moore's mind is ideological rather than emotional. Only such a creative person could produce such lines as those found in her poem "England": with its baby rivers and little towns, each with its abbey or cathedral"; Greece "with its goat and its gourds, the nest of modified illusions"; and France, "the 'chrysalis of the nocturnal butterfly.' "

_____ 77

14 St. Luke's Place,
New York City,
February 9, 1925.

Dear Mrs. Austin:

Miss Gregory, of The Dial, has forwarded to me, your letter of February 2nd in which you invite me to give you a slight synopsis of my method of work. I hope I have not completely misunderstood you in writing the reply which I enclose.

I am returning to you, the enclosure—Mr. Jones's synopsis—which you sent to Miss Gregory. Had you not intended it to be returned, will you not allow me to keep it as I should very much enjoy having it? I enclose an addressed envelope.

Sincerely yours,
Marianne Moore

Mrs. Mary Austin,
The National Arts Club
15 Gramercy Park
New York City

ENCLOSURE WITH *LETTER 77*

"Note on personal Method"
by Marianne Moore

An attitude, physical or mental—a thought suggested by reading or in conversation—recurs with insistence. A few words coincident with the initial suggestion, suggests other words. Upon scrutiny, these words seem to have distorted the concept. The effort to effect a unit—in this case a poem—is perhaps abandoned. If the original, propelling sentiment reasserts itself with sufficient liveliness, a truer progress almost invariably accompanies it; and associated detail, adding impact to the concept, precipitates an acceptable development. To illustrate: a piece of armor is impressively poetic. The moveable plates suggest the wearer; one is reminded of the armadillo and recalls the beauty of the ancient testudo. The idea of conflict, however, counteracts that of romance, and the subject is abandoned. However, the image lingers. Presently one encounters the iguana and is startled by the paradox of its docility. The concept has been revived—of an armor in which beauty outweighs the thought of painful self-protectiveness. The emended theme compels development.

Letter 78 acknowledges receipt of the book in which Moore's "Note" joined those of fifteen other "creative workers," including Robert Edmond Jones, Ryan Walker, Fannie Hurst, and Bill Robinson, each of whom is represented by a letter in this book.

_____ 78

14 St. Luke's Place
New York City
June 21, 1925

Dear Mrs. Austin:

I am enriched in having the copy of *Everyman's Genius,* received from you some time ago. If you knew my habit in the matter of prompt replies and acknowledgments, you would only commiserate me upon the handicaps and burdens of the past few months, rather than suppose that I could be so careless in receiving so valuable a gift. I remember reading with interest, in The Bookman, the article Making the Most of your Genius. You must feel the labor of formulating and compiling this volume to be richly rewarded.

Sincerely yours,
Marianne Moore

The link between Percy MacKaye and Mary Austin was certainly in their mutual concern for drama about "native" peoples and their localities. MacKaye used the term "native" in his Foreword to *Tall Tales of the Kentucky Mountains* (1926), a book he says grew from his "lucky sojourn" among friendly people with memories of "dim Irish hills, Scottish heaths, and English moorlands." He speaks of himself as an "up-country neighbor" from a north hill-creek in New Hampshire. *Letter 79* was mailed from Windsor, Vermont, which was the post office for a colony of writers at Cornish, New Hampshire. However, MacKaye kept an official New York address at the National Arts Club as did Mary Austin for a number of years. Thirteen letters from MacKaye are in the Austin file, beginning on February 21, 1911, when he thanked her for seats to a performance of *The Arrow Maker*. On July 30, 1911, he criticized the attitude of The New Theater toward plays by American playwrights (see the introduction to *Letter 16* in this volume). Other letters between 1913 and 1916 arrange for meetings in New York and contain comments on current plays. On March 29, 1929, MacKaye sent a note concerning a visit by his daughter, Christy, to Santa Fe. He expressed hope that she might meet some of the young people there.

Percy MacKaye (1875-1956) was among the most distinguished American dramatists. He also lectured widely on the history of the stage and America's contribution to its development. He was appointed to the board of governors for the Cambridge School of Drama at Harvard in 1930 and became a prominent member of the Dramatist Guild of the Authors League of America. MacKaye's contribution to the stage included plays, masques, and operas. Some of the most notable of the plays and operas were: *The Canterbury Pilgrims* (1903), *Yankee Fantasies* (1912), *Jeanne D'Arc* (1914), *Rip Van Winkle* (1919), and *The Mystery of Hamlet*, a tetralogy (1950). The community masques included: *Caliban, Saint Louis, The Evergreen Tree* (A Christmas Masque), and *The Roll Call* (A Masque of the Red Cross). Among his poems were *Lincoln, A Centenary Ode,* and *The Present Hour, Poems of War and Peace.*

_____ 79

Percy MacKaye
Windsor, Vermont
22 May, 1925

Mrs. Mary Austin
Santa Fe
New Mexico

Dear Mary:

The National Arts Club has been very slow in forwarding to me the copy of your new book "Every Man's Genius," which you were so friendly as to send me.

Marion has already begun to devour it, and as soon as I can get rid of a mass of accumulated work, I look forward to reading it with her. Of course, I am sure that I shall find it rich with your own experience and meditation.

Please feel assured that I appreciate very sincerely the good talks which I had with you last winter. I only wish that we were nearer neighbors, so that we might more often exchange our thoughts in conversation.

It is splendid to learn from your letter that you are feeling better in health. So are Marion and I. We are all of us, thank God, away from the noise and confusion of that New York maelstrom.

With love to you from us both,

Faithfully yours,

Percy MacKaye

I hope you got my letter acknowledging your beautiful poetry to me at the time of my birthday.

Letter 80 brings a reader of these letters again into the circle united by friendship for Mabel Dodge Luhan. It also joins a literary community in New York City to those in Taos and Santa Fe, New Mexico. No greater contrast could be imagined than the walled environments of Fifth Avenue and Washington Square in America's largest city and the open world of the mountain settlements in the American Southwest. But space and clouds shifting in sunlight against a backdrop of dark mesas and angular peaks called for paint brush and molding clay. The sketch pad of Robert Edmond Jones (1887-1954) was more accustomed to designs for the stage than for an easel or a sculptor's stand. He was famed for a new type of stagecraft, a fluid and dramatic use of light, shadows, color, elevated platforms, and dimensional levels of facade and positioning which abandoned the old realism and brought new dimensions to acting and scenery. David Belasco (see *Letter 13*) called Jones "the most influential artist-designer in the modern American theater." When he became an instructor in the Fine Arts Department at Harvard University, he learned of the designs by Gordon Craig, whose school of theatrical art brought Jones to Europe at the time Edwin and Mabel Dodge were remodelling their Renaissance villa near Florence, Italy. Returning to New York, Jones roomed in the Ninth Street apartment house where Mabel Dodge inaugurated her famous salon. They became friends for a period that lasted through their lifetimes, as detailed in Luhan's *Movers and Shakers* and her *Edge of Taos Desert*. In the latter book, she states that some of the semiabstract stage settings designed by

Jones after a visit to New Mexico reflected the irregular outlines of adobe architecture in Taos.

Letter 80 is of interest not only to a reader who follows the career of Robert Edmond Jones, but also to students of the plays written by Eugene O'Neill and their presentation in the Provincetown Playhouse as well as in New York City. After first being associated with the producer Arthur Hopkins in New York from 1915 to 1920, Jones designed a set for O'Neill's *The Hairy Ape*. This play was produced by Hopkins, and it was followed by more of O'Neill's plays, all designed by "Bobby" Jones, as Mabel Dodge Luhan refers to him. *Desire Under the Elms*, discussed in *Letter 80*, was produced in 1924. A year earlier, Jones had become an associate director of the Provincetown Playhouse, joining Kenneth MacGowan and O'Neill in this role.

Of the six letters from R. E. Jones in Austin's file, only two have dates. *Letter 80* would appear to have been written not long after the staging of *Desire Under the Elms*, possibly in 1924 or 1925. On February 25, 1928, he wrote from 142 West 79th Street to say that he hoped to come west later in the spring. He offers to see that Arthur Hopkins reads a play script by Mary, adding that he is sorry he had missed her in New York. The allusion to "your book" and "courses in Inspiration 2b" may be related to Austin's *Everyman's Genius*, which was published in 1925.

————— 80

HOTEL LAFAYETTE
University Place
Cable Address: Lafayette
NEW YORK

Dear Mrs. Austin—

Don't take too seriously any reports of what I may have said about your letter—even Mabel's. As a matter of fact I liked it extremely. I feel that in the case of *Desire* the fault is more mine than O'Neill's, because I could never get the actors to express the transfiguration at the end of the play. And with better lighting equipment the sky should be a symphony of color over and beyond the action, ending with a strange new dawn. I am trying always for better people and better technical facilities but that these great dreams should fall short of complete realization for any reason whatever is a heartbreak to the wise. I am not sure yet whether I shall go on with the Provincetown. This last year nearly finished me physically.

Thank you very much for your book. I suppose the Universities will presently be offering courses in Inspiration 2b!

Always yours
Bobby Jones

Mary Austin's interest in the stage, as previously illustrated by correspondence from Elmer Harris, Winthrop Ames, Percy MacKaye, and Robert Edmond Jones, was broadened to include vaudeville and tap dancing as proved by *Letter 81* sent from the famed entertainer Bill Robinson (1878-1949). Reviews of his performance referred to him as both dancer and actor, but his fame rested chiefly upon his skill in buck and wing dancing, which was a solo tap dance with much leg-springing and heel-clicking. He raised this terpsichorean art to a high level of dexterity. He was the first performer to use a flight of stairs as a stage, and his combination of shuffle and tap stepping anticipated the more polished accomplishments of Fred Astaire and Gene Kelly. Mary Austin reports in *Earth Horizon* that she took her friends Tony and Mabel Luhan to a Keith vaudeville show in order for them to see Robinson in his tap dancing routine. Later she interviewed Robinson and wrote up the interview for *The Nation* magazine. She also persuaded Robinson to contribute a "Note" about his creativity so that she could publish it in *Everyman's Genius*. He said in this article that he never had a dancing lesson, but just danced "out of his head," a theory which supported her belief that traits came from inheritance and required only exposure to develop. Robinson announced that his music had to be exactly right and not just anything in ragtime would serve: "I can't dance to jazz," he said, "but I have danced to some high class music, like 'The Brazilian Dance,' and I go up the stairs to the 'Melody in F.'" Austin added a footnote to the effect that some folklorists had identified buck and wing dancing as a religious invocation for the increase of spiritual power. She volunteered that this interpretation of the movements reverted to racial sources in the deepself, and she considered that dancing up the steps had spiritual significance.

Bill Robinson was born in Richmond, Virginia, where he went to the public schools and upon finishing their educational touches began to dance on vaudeville circuits. His accomplishments earned him stage appearances in "Blackbirds of 1927" and the motion pictures entitled *In Old Kentucky, Big Broadcast of 1935,* and *Rebecca of Sunnybrook Farm.* He was voted honorary "Mayor of Harlem" by the League of Locality Mayors in 1934, and accorded honorary membership in the Dancing Masters Association and the New Jersey State Police.

On July 12, 1925, Robinson wrote again and mailed a clipping from the *Morning Telegraph*, Sunday, July 5, 1925, headed "The Perennial Hoofer." The subject matter deals with Bill Robinson and Eddie Leonard, both of whom were blackface minstrel entertainers, but as the article explains: "Eddie acquires his color for every performance, while Bill was born with his makeup on." Robinson is described as a man of endless vitality who, at 47 years of age, has the spontaneity and endurance of youth. His rules for the preservation of youth are to avoid tobacco, drink liquor infrequently, go to bed early, and take plenty of exercise in addition to your dancing. The only bad habit he admitted was an inordinate appetite for ice cream.

_____ 81

New York, N. Y.
June 14 - 1925.

My dear Mrs. Austin:

I received "Everyman's Genius" with your compliments some time ago, and have tried all this time to locate you to tell you how much I thank you, and how I appreciate the honor of being in the contents of your wonderful book. I wrote the Bobbs-Merrill Co and they told me where I could locate you. I would like to know where "Everyman's Genius" can be obtained as I have a host of friends who would like to have one. Again I thank you and wish that I could find words to express my sincere appreciations to you.

I am,
Most sincerely,
Bill Robinson

Thomas B. Wells (1875-1944), author of *Letter 82*, was an editor for *Harper's Magazine* from 1919 to 1931. His letter was written in answer to a request by Mary Austin for *Harper's* to publish her comments on an article by Katherine Fullerton Gerould, which she called "New Mexico and the Backwash of Spain." This essay had been published by the magazine in

June of 1925. Its author was not only a journalist, but she had earned a reputation for short story and novel writing, plus her success in the teaching field at
Radcliffe and Bryn Mawr colleges. Her husband was Gordon Hall Gerould, an
eminent professor of English at Princeton University, the community where
they made their home. Before arriving in Albuquerque and Santa Fe, in order to
write about these Southwestern cities, Katharine Gerould had visited and
written about Tacoma, Seattle, Portland, San Francisco, Reno, and other places
in the West. What she said in her article about New Mexico aroused such controversy as to keep both readers and editors in an uproar for a period of several
months. When the articles appeared later in a book called *The Aristocratic West*
(1925), the furor had somewhat abated. A reader today can rest his opinion on
judgment, rather than emotion. Gerould found New Mexico a wild and uncivil-
ized state; so she says. But she also writes that New Mexico records the oldest
continuous human habitation in the United States and has a landscape of
absorbing beauty.

In his letter, Wells defends her article by pointing out that Gerould had
written about other cities without receiving such an outcry as came from New
Mexico. A reader of the articles on Seattle and Tacoma will find that she poked
fun at their wrangling about totem poles, claiming that they had either been
faked or stolen. She stated that Indians squatted on the curbstone in abject
poverty in one of the cities, and described the downtown section of the other as
old fashioned and ugly. As for Santa Fe and Albuquerque, she preferred Albuquerque because it was larger and on the main line of the railroad. However, she
called the American part of Albuquerque "altogether hideous," but preferred
it to Santa Fe which she dismissed as "a much disfigured museum piece." She
spoke critically of New Mexico's politics, and developed at length her opposition
to what she called the "Hopi" architecture she observed in both Santa Fe and
Albuquerque. Just why she chose to identify the buildings as "Hopi" is strange,
for the designation locally applied is "Pueblo" or "Spanish Colonial." Both
terms describe an adaptation of native styles of construction using adobe mud or
other materials to preserve building outlines appropriate to mesas and patios
with colonnades called *portales*. Not satisfied with choosing the adjective "Hopi"
to indicate that the architecture was suitable only to one isolated group of
Indians, Gerould selected such adjectives as "grotesque," "insane," "impossible," and "disillusioning" to condemn the "architectural facade" she found in
view. That individual builders and architects had chosen the style for its comfort
and charm did not deter her intemperate disapproval. No one could blame
Austin and others for registering their protest, but the editor of *Harper's* was not
justified in giving space to letters attacking Gerould. She had every right to
express her opinion however objectionable it may have been.

Gerould made an effort to balance her criticism of New Mexico's people and their performance by reporting that the drive from Albuquerque to Santa Fe was one of the most beautiful and exciting trips in the country. At this time the highway ascended a precipitous elevation called La Bajada Hill. Both courage and skill were required to guide a vehicle around the curves and slanting stretches of gravel and dirt on the highway. She was mistaken when she predicted the end of Indian and Spanish cultures or the economic decline of the state. Her article reflects the judgment of a highly sophisticated personality whose background in New England and the Atlantic seaboard lacked the flexibility to interpret the alien traditions she encountered. However, she appreciated the historical continuity in New Mexico and praised its scenic beauty. Throughout the articles she wrote on the West, she praises the democratic and progressive spirit she encountered and even goes so far as to say that she mght like to live in certain parts of the region. It is clear from her articles that, if she carried out her decision, her preference would be for a home somewhere on the Pacific Coast between San Francisco and Seattle.

The allusion by Wells to the Bursum Bill may be associated with the letter written by Lou Henry Hoover to Mary Austin on December 17, 1922, in which Mrs. Hoover agrees with Katherine Gerould that the intention of the bill was to unsnarl claims to title rather than to steal the Indian lands. Wells's defense of Gerould's report that Indians in an "obscure" pueblo sacrificed "a living baby every year to the snake-god" provokes an inquiry as to *Harper's* standards of credibility.

_____ 82

Seal	HARPER & BROTHERS
Established	Publishers
1817	New York and London

49 East 33d Street, New York, N. Y.
July 10, 1925

Mrs. Mary Austin,
Santa Fe,
New Mexico.

Dear Mrs. Austin,

Thank you very much for your letter of July 6th. It seems to me, however, that if any letter such as I suggested you write has to be submitted to the Chamber of Commerce and has to be made to suit their fancy, it would probably not be the sort of letter that we should care to publish.

Looking at this whole matter in a dispassionate way it seems to me that the good people of Santa Fe are making a mountain out of a mole hill. It is characteristic of the small town American in every part of this country to resent any criticism of his habitat and to lose completely his sense of humor when anybody makes a venture in this direction. I have read over Mrs. Gerould's article since your first letter reached me. Anybody who can take serious offense at that article or can take seriously Mrs. Gerould's humor is not likely to be a person on whose support we could ever count. We have published articles about Chicago and Boston which offered equal opportunities to the citizens of those two cities, and no such rumpus was ever raised. The Chamber of Commerce could engage itself in far better projects than making objection to magazine articles printed about their city, and the idea of any such trivial event giving cause for a community meeting can hardly be without humor to such a cosmopolite as yourself.

I am afraid I can hardly agree to the conditions you impose as to the quid pro quo of our enlisting your aid in persuading the citizens of Santa Fe to let us alone. I'd like to see that article that you have in mind very much, but I would not venture to give you a definite commission for it. So we must let the good people of Santa Fe rave on, though we shall try to publish some of their letters stating their point of view.

You missed one point in the article where I think a mistake was made. That is where Mrs. Gerould touches on the Bursum Bill and does not touch on subsequent legislation and on the bill which was finally put through and resulted in a commission now sitting in New Mexico. I have brought this point to her attention because it seems to be important.

I can't attach the slightest importance to the feeling of anybody in regard to her very obvious joke in regard to the business man of Santa Fe, nor can I see any reason why she should not have told what she was told in regard to the Indian baby matter. Too many people are born in this world who lack a sense of humor. You used to have a very good one, so I am sure you will agree with me that a great deal of all this disturbance that has been created is absolute rubbish. In any event, you may be sure that I should not be justified in printing any such comments on Mrs. Gerould's authority and competency as are embodied in your letter.

Very sincerely yours,
Thomas B. Wells

TBW/RD   *[In pen and ink script.]*
              Please don't think that I am angry and haughty. I'm not in the least. A letter has just come from a citizen of New Mexico who thinks Mrs. Gerould has put everything too mildly.

There are twenty short, single page letters from H. L. Mencken (1880-1956) in the Austin correspondence. The letters were written between 1925 and 1931, during his term as editor of *The American Mercury.* Many of these letters are headed only by the day they were sent. Perhaps this pattern was all that was demanded by the circumstances required for communication. *Letter 83* is typical of the editor's need to express his pleasure in Austin's gift for storytelling. It also indicates Mencken's preference for realistic rather than mystical plots, and his cordial as well as businesslike attitude toward contributors to the *Mercury.* In *Earth Horizon,* Austin expresses her gratitude to Mencken for publishing a half dozen of her folktales, which were brief tellings of experience in a style popularized by Honore de Balzac and Leo Tolstoy. Their stories had European backgrounds, whereas Austin wove her plots against Indian and Mexican settings. The Austin stories, however, like their French or Russian counterparts, have themes of universal appeal. Both the narratives accepted in Mencken's letter were reprinted in *One-Smoke Stories* (1934), her last book. A brief synopsis of each story will make clear why the editor accepted them.

"The Man Who Was Loved by Women" satirizes the vanity of a handsome Navajo whose height and features earned notable rewards from the women in his tribe. Even the women in neighboring tribes, both married and unmarried, contributed to Tsaysiki's satisfaction. When brought before the council, he complained that their attentions were not his fault. But hostility from the men finally drove Tsaysiki to seek refuge in a small tribe dominated by a woman. He was forced to marry her and accept her terms which permitted her as much freedom in marriage as he had known before marriage. Tsaysiki discovered that he was assigned to second place or even third place in the household, and ridicule replaced the previous prestige he had known. "Hosteen Hatsanai Recants" offers a contrast between the teaching at a Mission School and the realities of paganism as practiced by Navajos. After many years of following the Jesus-way at the Mission, the wife of a Navajo is blinded by cataracts. He brings a young woman to assist his wife, who looks upon the girl as a sister. When her "sister" becomes pregnant, the old wife urges her husband to marry the girl. The missionaries refuse to perform the ceremony and condemn the Indians severely. The Navajos return to their pagan faith, but they look back with sorrow to Jesus whom they still love as an elder brother.

Mencken's preoccupation with the advancement of humanity through the sciences led him to seek articles for the *Mercury* from leaders in biology, medicine, and social studies. His attitude toward expanding literary horizons gave encouragement to Mary Austin's short fiction pieces. Author of more than seventy-five books dealing with subjects from wine to politics, Mencken may be remembered best for his epoch-marking volume entitled *The American Language* (1919). He asserted that the English spoken by people in the United States was in no way inferior to the speech heard in the British Isles, and he furnished adequate data to support his assertion. His evidence was supported by such authorities as William Archer, the Scottish playwright and critic, who wrote; "New words are begotten by new conditions. . . . America has enormously enriched the English language."

On March 4, 1926, Mencken returned "with great reluctance" an Austin folktale because it was written in dialect, and then on March 18, he rejected an article on marriage "perhaps because my own interest in the subject is so feeble." On December 26, he hesitated to print her article on George Sterling because he was in San Francisco when Sterling killed himself and the rumor was to the effect that "Sterling had done so following an argument with me." Mencken denied this. He suggested revisions and the article appeared in *The Mercury* for May of 1927.

——————— 83

H. L. Mencken . *Editor* . ALFRED A. KNOPF . *Publisher* .
SAMUEL KNOPF . *Business Manager*

THE AMERICAN MERCURY
730 Fifth Avenue
NEW YORK

Cables: Knopf . New York   *Telephones*: Circle 7670 . 7675

September 13th [1925]

Dear Mrs. Austin:

Thanks very much. I'll be very glad to do more of the stories. But
I believe that it would be well to take out those dealing with the super-
natural, and so keep them realistic in general tone. I am, in fact, inclined
to think that even "The Woman Who Was Never Satisfied" lies rather
outside the series. Would you consent to the use of the other two: "The
Man Who Was Loved by Women" and "Hosteen Hatsanai Recants"?
Somehow, the ghost of the Navajo's wife, in "The Woman Who Was
Never Satisfied," seems to take that story out of the series.

Sincerely yours,

H. L. Mencken

———

Although twenty-nine letters from Henry Seidel Canby (1878-
1961) were retained by Mary Austin as well as two she wrote to him, she does
not mention him in her *Earth Horizon* nor does he include her name among the
acquaintances recorded in his *American Memoir* (1947). A letter she sent to
Canby on April 1, 1930, names him as her "literary executor." He must have
accepted this appointment, but there is no evidence that he acted upon it at the
time of her death four years later.

Letter 84 is a genuine expression of Canby's pleasure at the honor extended to
Mary Austin by Mills College for her achievement in fiction, poetry, and social
thought. The office stationery he uses carries the heading of the *Saturday Review
of Literature*, a magazine he founded in 1924 and for which he served as editor
until 1936. After that year, he became chairman of the editorial board until

1958. The *Saturday Review* (a short name) was the most influential American periodical devoted entirely to book reviews, poetry, and articles discussing literature and the arts. From 1928 until 1931, the magazine published five articles and three poems by Mary Austin. She was included in the twenty-six writers who were invited to celebrate the tenth anniversary of the *Saturday Review* on October 6 of 1934. Mary Austin died on August 11, and had not written her tribute. The issue of September 8 carried an appreciation of her achievement written by Elizabeth Shepley Sergeant, who had known Austin both in New York and in Santa Fe.

Henry Seidel Canby was born into a Quaker family who lived in Wilmington, Delaware. In his *American Memoir* (1947), his schooling there and at Yale is detailed as a history of late Victorian conventionality. The town, society, sobriety, and minimal cultural interests within well-bred security are portrayed before his life at Yale was followed by faculty appointments there and elsewhere. In the chapters entitled "An Arsenal for Literature" and "The Literary Zoo," Canby related his life with publishers in New York City preliminary to the eminence he achieved through his own books and the contacts made with authors who were acclaimed in the *Saturday Review*.

Letter 84 underlines contacts Canby maintained with his alma mater and its Department of Drama, when it was directed by George Pierce Baker. Baker invited Austin to lecture at Yale in February of 1929 and again in the spring of 1930. His assistant, Alexander Dean, staged several New Mexican religious folk dramas during the time of her second visit. She kept correspondence from both men. Letters from H. S. Canby express his agreement with Austin on her article "New York, Dictator of American Criticism," in *The Nation*, July 31, 1920; congratulates her upon the address she gave to the National Arts Club on July 23, 1924; withholds a hostile review of *Everyman's Genius* unless she consents to answer it; and endorses her intention to write an autobiography.

At a memorial meeting on September 1, 1944, the testimonials which were published by the Laboratory of Anthropology, Santa Fe, contained the following words written by Canby:

My association with Mary Austin began late in her career, but were close and animated. I felt that she was potentially one of the great American women of letters of our time and that she had won her right to a prominent place in American literature. . . . She was a great woman—also, thank Heavens, a great eccentric. For one of the roads to greatness is undoubtedly eccentricity when accompanied by such character and such imagination as hers.

In *Letter 84*, Canby refers to "another novel." The Austin manuscripts show that at this date she was at work on a novel to be entitled *Love Is Not Enough*. By the time she had cut and revised the text in accord with suggestions from her publisher, she had chosen another title, *Starry Adventure*, the heading under which the novel was published in 1931. A reader of the book will discover that the original title has meaning for the plot in which she stressed love as a platonic rather than a passionate emotion for the central character.

_____ 84

THE SATURDAY REVIEW
of Literature
25 West 45th Street, New York City
Henry Seidel Canby, *Editor*
Amy Loveman, *Associate Editor*
William Rose Benet, *Associate Editor*
Christopher Morley, *Contributing Editor*
Mrs. Mary Austin,
Santa Fe,
New Mexico.   June 28, 1928

My dear Mary Austin:
        I am delighted that Mills College gave you a degree. The president was a fellow student of mine in the Graduate College at Yale and I have always thought very highly of the institution. I have hardly been in New Haven for the last three or four weeks, that is, at the college or in town, and I have seen Baker at a performance of a play where I could not get to him. Of course the last month has been his busy time but I still hope we'll be able to get you to New Haven. Under the circumstances I had to work through him. I am so glad you are writing another novel and glad, too, you are considering an article for us.

With best wishes, I am
Yours very truly,
H. S. Canby
Henry S. Canby
*Editor—*THE SATURDAY REVIEW.

Mark Van Doren has been presented as a critic and a poet in the introduction to *Letter 61*, written by his brother Carl. Since Mark was literary editor of *The Nation* magazine and in 1924 had written his first book of poetry,

Spring Thunder and Other Poems, Mary Austin doubtless appreciated his praise of her own verse. However, the chief purpose Mark Van Doren had to perform in *Letter 85* was to assuage her injured pride in not winning the prize in *The Nation's* fifth annual poetry contest conducted between Thanksgiving and New Year's Day of 1925. The manuscripts were to be submitted between December 1 and December 31, and the winning poem was to be published in the Midwinter Literary Supplement on February 11, 1925. The judges were the editors of *The Nation.*

Mary Austin's poem not only failed to win the prize, but it was not even awarded an Honorable Mention. Six poets were named in this category. Since Mark Van Doren specifically mentions "The Aged Poet" as her entry, he must be identifying the poem printed by the *Saturday Review* on August 29, 1931, with the title "The Aged Poet Discourses." Austin had aged by six years then, and she may have changed more than the title. However, she may have just been shifting a poem turned down by one magazine to another. The winning prize poem in 1925 was printed in *The Nation* on February 11, 1925. The author was Eli Siegel, who was born in Dvinsk, Russia, and came to America when he was 3 years old. At the time he submitted his poem, he was 22 years old and working as a printer in Baltimore. He attended high school in that city, and had not published a poem until his prize winning work appeared. He called his poem "Hot Afternoons Have Been in Montana." The poem consisted of 101 sentences, some of which ran from five to eight lines of type. The central theme, heat in the afternoon, covered time from the Indians of pre-historic America to the monks in Europe's Middle Ages, including as well poets of all times from everywhere. The poem is kaleidoscopic in imagery and telescopic in point of view, but the author is entirely literate in allusion, drawing references from world literature. He makes use of freely cadenced lines as illustrated by the ending of the poem which is as follows:

> Afternoons have to do with the whole world;
> And the beauty of mind, feeling knowingly the world!
> The world of girls' beautiful faces, bodies and clothes, quiet
>   afternoons, graceful birds, great words, tearful music,
>   mind-joying poetry, beautiful livings, loved things,
>   known things; a to-be-used and known and pleasure-
>   to-be-giving world.*

Four thousand manuscripts were submitted to the judges. The response of readers to their choice was mixed. Upton Sinclair, not a poet, wrote in denunci-

---

*This excerpt from the poem is printed with appreciation to Mr. Siegel and permission from the Nation Associates, 333 Sixth Avenue, New York, N.Y. 10014.

ation, stating "from first to last there is not one line of poetry in it." He then wrote another letter eight days later in which he apologized for his harsh words and congratulated *The Nation* for holding the contest whatever the outcome. A prospective subscriber to the magazine questioned the sanity of the writer and the mental condition of the judges. The poet Maxwell Bodenheim announced that he would never again send a poem to the magazine even if his work had been previously accepted. Ludwig Lewisohn called the poem a "mass of ill-organized prose." But there were also readers who wrote that they were "thrilled by it," "welcomed a new poet," and congratulated the editors "on the happy choice of choosing a poem that sang with the color of life."

The same issue of *The Nation* carries an article by Mary Austin which she entitled "Artist Life in the United States." Mark Van Doren may have this article in mind when, in *Letter 85*, he chides her for criticizing poetry contests and then entering one. Van Doren was a loyal friend of Mary Austin, as his twenty-four letters to her attest. In addition to his work in journalism, he was a member of the faculty at Columbia University for more than thirty years. Between 1924 and 1972, he produced seventeen books of poetry plus anthologies of verse, studies of John Dryden, Henry David Thoreau, Nathaniel Hawthorne, E. A. Robinson, and Carl Sandburg. He wrote on liberal education and literature in general. In 1942, he conducted a radio program called "Invitation to Learning," assisted by educators in many fields of writing and study.

———— 85

THE NATION
20 Vesey Street
New York

February 5, 1926

Dear Mrs. Austin:

Don't think I was not interested in the Aged Poet. We all were, but just then we were in the throes of deciding upon the winner among those actually on the ground, and so back went both of your pieces.

I have never had any doubt about your poetry, and I hope you will feel like sending us some. Only let me say that the shorter things will be easiest to use. You probably have noticed that we almost never go in for length except in connection with the prize. What, by the way, of the glancing blow you struck at poetry contests in your article a year or so ago? I agreed with you then, and do now, and I am sorry for that reason also that you could not take the cake this year. It would have been a nice piece of irony—an editor who does not believe in contests giving the prize to a contestant who does not.

I shall like to hear any time of an article on Indians or Indian poetry that you feel disposed to write.

Sincerely yours,
Mark Van Doren

Mrs. Mary Austin,
Santa Fe, N. M.

During her career as a novelist, the pendulum swung for Willa Cather (1873-1947) from East to West in her native land. Her taste and sensitivity were a family heritage in a Southern town named Gore, her birthplace, in Virginia not far from Winchester. The scenes and stories for her fiction grew from Eastern cities, Midwestern prairie towns, and Southwestern Indian pueblos neighbor to Spanish villages. Elizabeth Shepley Sergeant, who knew Willa Cather when Cather was an editor for *McClure's Magazine* and afterward, wrote that the scenes in Cather's novels were "psychic homelands" for the love and adventure she eagerly sought and embraced almost as "fragments of her soul." Sergeant compared Cather with William Faulkner, who wrote entirely of a region in the South, and with Sarah Orne Jewett, whose stories dealt only with New England. By contrast, Cather seemed almost a wanderer, led by her search for beauty in admirable characters associated with places of legendary romance.

In 1912, the year Cather retired from the *McClure* post, she visited her brother, Douglas, in Winslow, Arizona, where he was working for a construction company with the Atchison, Topeka, and Santa Fe Railroad. During the daylight hours when he was away, she found time to explore the country around the town, where sandy stretches of desert joined green bands of forest and wild flowers. She saw Indian pueblos where Spanish missionaries built churches in the sixteenth century. In the evenings, she attended dances in the Spanish villages and heard the mariachi guitar music while men in bolero jackets and black trousers whirled women in fiesta dresses in a fast polka or courtly varsoviana rhythm on the dance floor. A new world of interest opened to her, an interest that extended to the cities, such as Albuquerque, a railroad center, which she said had a "Spanish feeling," and was in a setting of mountains and space as beautiful as any place she had ever seen.

Letter 86 may not be reproduced because Cather dictated in her will that none of her correspondence should be printed. However, there are thirteen of her letters in the Austin file and all of them may be viewed by readers at the Huntington Library. Paraphrases of these letters are presented here and violate no proscription against their printing, as written. Cather's earliest letter to Mary

Austin was mailed on January 8, 1921, from her residence at No. 5 Bank Street, in Greenwich Village, New York City. She had lived there since 1913, in a brick house with white trimming. Sergeant described the second floor apartment as very attractive with a row of front windows which caught the sunlight and brightened the interior. A marble fireplace adorned the living room where the mantelpiece was filled with flowers at every season. The furnishings were not ornate, but a number of bookcases, some colorful pictures, a small writing table with her typewriter, and comfortable chairs made Cather's guests feel at home. Most of the Austin letters were written from this address. Their tone is personal and affectionate, extending over a period of ten years, from January 8, 1921, to October 22, 1931.

The earliest letter from Willa Cather thanked Mary Austin for remembering her at Christmas and stated that she had just returned from France a few weeks ago. She invited Mary to come see her soon. Three days later, Willa expressed regret that she was unable to call upon Mary because she had sprained her ankle badly: she concluded by saying that she hoped they were going to be neighbors. Mary moved to No. 10 Barrow Street about this time, and the address was a quarter of a mile south of No. 5 Bank Street. They did become neighbors as Cather had hoped they would. A letter sent on a Sunday, without a date, invites Mary to have tea with William Archer, whom Cather calls a pleasant person to know. Austin did know Archer (1856-1924), for ten years earlier he had encouraged her to produce her play *The Arrow Maker* in New York, and subsequently shared her disappointment in its failure to achieve success. Other invitations to tea are recorded in the next three months, one of which announces that Friday afternoons from 4 until 7 o'clock were social occasions at No. 5 Bank Street.

During 1922, Cather sent further invitations to tea, canceling one in March because of illness and another in April for a similar reason. On March 20, 1925, Cather expressed both curiosity and envy over Mary's plan to build a house in Santa Fe. She stated that she had just been to visit her family's home in Nebraska, and expressed the hope that she might see Mary's Santa Fe house some day. A year later this became possible, as witnessed by *Letter 86*, which will be paraphrased in order to fulfill the stipulations of Cather's will and yet preserve the intention of this book to present mary Austin's correspondence with a broad spectrum of acquaintances in a variety of fields.

_____ 86

This letter was mailed from La Fonda in Santa Fe using the hotel stationery, which showed the Pueblo style inn with a Mexican driving a burro loaded with kindling wood. Another blanket-wrapped figure walks toward the hotel. *Letter 86* was addressed to Austin at the Missouri Baptist Hospital in St. Louis. The date in the right hand corner is written as "June 26" giving no year, but the year may be fixed by post office cancellation on the envelope as "June 27, 1926." Cather first states in the letter that she went from the hotel up to Austin's house a week ago in order to determine whether she could write there. Since that first visit, she has gone to the house every morning. She calls the house a most peaceful and harmonious place to work. She chose the library instead of Mary's study, because she liked the open space around her as she sat in a small blue chair and used her knee to hold the writing pad. She opened a screened part of the big window to allow the breeze to come in and everything was comfortable.

Cather reports that the young woman appointed to care for the flowers and the house was faithful to her job. She called Mary very generous to permit her to make use of the house. This solved a real problem for her. She had planned to go to Taos after her brother and his family left Santa Fe, but Tony [Luhan], who had been sick during their visit there, grew worse and, even though ill, he and Mabel [Sterne] eloped to Albuquerque, where they were married. The Luhans planned to remain in Albuquerque for ten days or a couple of weeks, because Tony was still running a temperature. Mabel reported that she had never seen Tony ill before. She pled with Cather to return to Taos, but Cather thought the situation would not be pleasant. She added that Mary Foote would arrive in Taos on July 3rd and she planned to join Foote and Luhan soon afterward. She expressed her friendship for Miss Foote.

It was fortunate, Cather said, that after leaving the big, empty house of Mabel Luhan in Taos, Mrs. Huey should bring Cather the key to Mary's house in Santa Fe. She writes that waiting for an operation is worse than having it, as she knows from experience, and she hopes that Mary's doctor will move as fast as possible to perform the necessary surgery. Cather ends the letter by sending her love and best wishes along with her gratitude for the pleasant hours she has enjoyed in Mary's library. The letter is signed "Faithfully yours" with Cather's full name.

Death Comes for the Archbishop was copyrighted in 1926 and published in the following year. Willa Cather may have written the last part of the book in Mary Austin's house. Among the books in Austin's library was an autographed copy with the following inscription from Cather:

For Mary Austin, in whose lovely study I wrote the last chapters of this book. She will be my sternest critic—and she has the right to be. I will always take a calling-down from my betters.

In *Earth Horizon*, Mary remarked that Cather used her house to write in, and she expressed distress that Cather had given her full allegiance to the French blood of Archbishop Lamy and his desire to build a French cathedral in a Spanish town. In her book, Sergeant reported that Cather denied writing any part of the novel in Austin's house, saying that she left the manuscript for her novel in a New York vault, and walked up to Austin's library in the afternoon only to write a few letters.

Following *Letter 86*, there were only four more communications from Willa Cather, one of which refers to the demolition of her apartment in order to build a subway station; another explains that the editors at Houghton Mifflin publishing company were trying to persuade her to write a biography of Amy Lowell, which she said would have been for her an ordeal of incomparable difficulty; a final letter on October 22, 1931, reported the illness of her mother in Pasadena and added the hope that she might be able to stop off in New Mexico sometime during the year when she returned to New York. She also mentioned the hardships of the depression and expressed concern that Mary Austin's eyes had been giving her trouble. She urged dark glasses against the glare of New Mexico's sunlight and stated that she always protected her eyes when she was in the state.

Vachel Lindsay (1879-1931) wrote *Letter 87* late in his career as an artist and a letter writer. The word "artist" is chosen with accuracy because, after finishing high school in Springfield, Illinois, and three years at Hiram College, Ohio, Lindsay registered for classes at the Chicago Art Institute where he enrolled in magazine illustration. He supported himself from 1900 until 1903 as an employee in the toy department of Marshall Field and Company. Then he transferred to the Chase School of Art in New York City where the famous artist Robert Henri not only surveyed his drawings but heard his poetry and helped Lindsay decide that his poetry was more important than his art.

While Lindsay was in New York, he found a position teaching art classes at the Y.M.C.A. He was now 24 years old and realized that he should support himself. Beside teaching art, he tried to sell his drawings and his poetry in bakeries, drug stores, delicatessens, and saloons. In the biography *Vachel Lindsay* (1935), Edgar Lee Masters writes that the poet enjoyed only moderate success as a salesman. According to the poet's diary, Lindsay found lunch rooms and drug stores better markets for poetry than candy shops and delicatessens. Furthermore, as a salesman, he learned not to sell poetry when customers were examining other types of merchandise. Undiscouraged, Lindsay decided to carry his salesmanship on a tour through the South, and in March of 1906 he and a friend boarded a ship in new York for Jacksonville, Florida, where the two of them planned to walk back to New York City. They disembarked south of Jacksonville, then proceeded to a college campus where Lindsay obtained permission to give a lecture. He also persuaded the secretary of the Y.M.C.A. to allow him to speak there. Thus the two travelers obtained board and lodging for the night. Abandoned by his friend, Lindsay repeated this pattern of minimal subsistence until May, having walked through Florida, Georgia, North Carolina, Tennessee, Kentucky, and Indiana. When he arrived at Orange, Indiana, he was welcomed by his grandmother, Frances Austen Frazee, with whom he had corresponded since childhood. Here he received an invitation from his father, a physician in Springfield, to join his parents for a trip to Europe, and further thoughts of peddling art and poetry vanished until he returned to New York several months later.

In 1912, the open road again beckoned to Lindsay, and he started from Springfield on the longest hike of his life, one that led him across Illinois, Missouri, Kansas, Colorado, and part of New Mexico toward the destination in California. The book he entitled *Adventures While Preaching the Gospel of Beauty* (1914) tells the story of this uncompleted and at times hazardous journey. While traveling, he wore corduroys, a fancy sombrero, and a brightly colored shirt and necktie. He carried a worn oilcloth knapsack in which he had copies of his booklet called *Rhymes to be Traded for Bread*. The letters he wrote home told of picking stems from gooseberries for his lodging with the inhabitants of a boxcar in Illinois; crossing the Hannibal, Missouri, toll bridge on charity from the gateman; and watching the sunset in Kansas from a hayloft bed. He was forced to abandon his trip in New Mexico, because he was not physically equipped to surmount the hardships of lonely western highways. He telegraphed for money to take the train to Los Angeles. Back in Springfield, he spent the next two years preparing his books of poetry for publication: *General William Booth Enters into Heaven and Other Poems* (1913) and *The Congo and Other Poems* (1914). In the fall of 1919, Lindsay came to Santa Fe to lecture under the auspices of Mary Austin and Alice Corbin Henderson, both of whom regarded him as a leading figure in American poetry.

Fame as a poet and prominence as a speaker enabled Lindsay to write and recite throughout the United States. In 1920, he was invited to England where circles in London and the universities of Cambridge and Oxford greeted him with applause. In the belief that college life might satisfy him, he accepted appointment as poet in residence during 1923 and 1924 at Gulf Park College in Gulfport, Mississippi. However, the narrow range of interests exhibited by faculty and students disappointed him. He left Gulf Park for Spokane, Washington, upon the urging of a group that persuaded him to believe that his lectures and writing would create cultural activity in the community. Percy Grainger, a distinguished pianist, and Elizabeth Conner, a writer whom he had met at Mills College during a lecture tour, were members of the artist colony in Spokane. Conner became Mrs. Lindsay on May 19, 1925. Both his *Letter 87* and her *Letter 88* express the happiness the Lindsays knew in their first years together in Spokane.

Letter 87 was sent to Austin at the Missouri Baptist Sanatorium in St. Louis. Printed at the bottom of each page in the letter is a series of hieroglyphic symbols which, according to Edgar Lee Masters, Lindsay found in an *Egyptian Grammar* (1920) by Guenther Roeder. These symbols, as shown from left to right, represent such concepts as the sun and the horizon, the human heart, good judgment, writing, the deity, and the soul. The final symbol may indicate the voice and speech, in which case the entire group becomes a signature for the life and activities of Vachel Lindsay. The reference in *Letter 87* to appearing before Chautauqua groups supports a campaign being waged at this time by Mary Austin and others in Santa Fe to stop an organization of women from establishing a summer colony on the outskirts of the city for Chautauqua programs. The commercial interests in Santa Fe supported this enterprise, but it failed because of the opposition of influential artists and writers, among whom Mary Austin was prominent. Her article, "Town that Doesn't Want a Chautauqua," appeared in the *New Republic* for July 7, 1926. The postscript to *Letter 87* recalls that Colonel A. W. Doniphan, a Kentucky lawyer and statesman, who became a brigadier general in the Mexican War of 1846, succeeded General Kearney as military governor of New Mexico. He later moved his forces south to assist General Wool in Mexico. Lindsay's daughter, however, was named for her grandmother, Susan Doniphan Frazee.

———— 87

514 1/2 West 15th . Spokane
July 9, 1926

Dear Mary Austin:

Great good wishes to you. I used to proclaim in London in the fall of 1920 that Santa Fe was the spiritual capital of America, and your ringing article in the New Republic proves it all over again. Please tell all my friends in Santa Fe that care to know that I am with you heart and soul. With very few exceptions I have never spoken willingly for a Woman's Club or a Chautauqua. I have spoken, since I was a beggar, almost exclusively for the English departments of various schools and universities, and then, generally because I received no money from my publisher, and had to keep the wolf from the door. But I have seldom been poor enough to speak for Woman's Clubs. I am glad the issue is joined so clearly, and I hope every artist and writer in Santa Fe makes himself heard.

I have just been preparing a screed on the subject of the necessity of every artist in America starting his own series of Pamphlets, (like the fathers of the Revolution, from Tom Paine to Alexander Hamilton). Because we do not own skyscrapers the owners of skyscrapers think they can bully and misrepresent us till time out of mind, and the time has come for every artist to have his own position stated clearly on his own private press if it takes his last cent. The "smothering" process, the affected flattery of the Woman's Clubs is all a part of the same mood as the over-assured oily blurbs on the jackets of the books. Writers and artists are simply smothered in blurbs and reviews by people who have not once looked at their stuff. My cure is—pamphlets—and more pamphlets and then again more pamphlets, and the sassier the better. Let us raise Jimmy Whistler from the dead! The time has come for all artists to live on bread and water and use their own local printing press and foot the bill *first* instead of last.

God bless you, dear Mary Austin. Your article put an enormous amount of needed courage and exhiliration into me, and you may be sure I will re-read it many times.

With great good wishes,
Nicholas Vachel Lindsay

Please congratulate me and my dear wife Elizabeth on the arrival of Susan Doniphan on Sunday (our first). Doniphan ought to mean something in Santa Fe.

A second letter in Austin's file from Vachel Lindsay is dated July 7, 1930, and is written on a Springfield letterhead paper. In the letter, he asks for news of Santa Fe and sends some enclosures which have not been kept. *Letter 88* from Elizabeth Conner Lindsay is one of the six she wrote between December 10, 1926, and January 15, 1934. They span the period between Lindsay's departure from Spokane in the spring of 1929 and his death in Springfield on December 5, 1931. She states in her letter that she had assumed secretarial as well as household duties for her husband. Doubtless she shared his literary life as well, for she had graduated in English at Mills College. Her reference to "the pamphlets" may include a new series of *War Bulletins*, like those composed by Lindsay in earlier times, when he championed lost causes and forgotten campaigns in prose and verse, such as free speech, freedom from social and religious bigotry, poverty, drunkenness, money-greed, and selfishness in general.

_____ 88

2318 West Pacific
Spokane
December 10, 1926

Dear Mary Austin,

It is really too bad of Vachel not to have answered your letter "in person," long ere this. However, he has been, for him, phenomenally busy studying and dictating, and correcting, and revising articles, in a noble attempt to substitute the written for the spoken word, and still support his flourishing family; and all his mail has been left to me, as a result. And, since I help him with these same articles, and see to young Susan, and have only recently acquired a housekeeper, cook, and nurse, combined, I have been a very poor proxy, indeed.

Vachel is wanting to write an article on Santa Fe before long, if the opportunity in any way offers; his loyalty to the group there goes deep with him, and he longs to return in spirit, and in the flesh, as soon as may be.

There is little other news with us. There are no other books under way. THE CANDLE IN THE CABIN, just out, is the last verse writing Vachel has done; this year has mostly been devoted, I fear, to domesticity and paternity; but we hope for more deeply creative moments to come.

When the pamphlets get under way, you shall be the first to know. They are ever present, I think, in our poet's mind; and the harder he tries to "conform" outwardly, the more they haunt him, and demand utterance. I am in most hearty agreement with Vachel's theories on the subject. There is seemingly no way to grow wealthy while writing; so one might as well chuck the idea, I think, and be free and outspoken, and untrammelled by any considerations except those of beauty and truth as they seem to one's own mind and heart. No power, human or inhuman, has a right to put a trade mark on that.

We send you greetings of the season, and our earnest good wishes. Love from the three.

Yours most sincerely,
Elizabeth Lindsay

P.S.

My mother, Claribel Sims Conner, tells me that she knew you, ages ago, in Carlinville, Illinois, when you were a Senior at Blackburn, and she was an entering Freshman.

E. C. L.

On November 11, 1929, from the family residence at 603 South Fifth Street, Springfield, Mrs. Lindsay wrote to express her husband's delight in visiting with Mary Austin in Santa Fe as he returned from a lecture tour. She and Vachel Lindsay joined in hoping that Mary could return this visit when she made her next trip to Illinois. *Letter 89* gives some of the details of the last days in Lindsay's life. Upon his return to Springfield, the poet suffered recurrent spells of depression. There were financial problems which fees from his lecture did not solve. Fantasies possessed him about his lost youth. He viewed his marriage as a block to the chastity demanded for union with visionary religious powers. Failure to reshape Springfield into a place of beauty and enlightenment led to despair about his mission as a poet. After a week of illness, he attended an afternoon tea with friends, came home weakened from the excitement, and experienced hallucinations of persecution and rejection. Pretending to go to his room for rest, he went instead to the kitchen where he drank from a bottle of Lysol. A doctor was summoned, but when he arrived, Lindsay was dead.

On January 15, 1934, Elizabeth Lindsay wrote her last letter to Mary Austin. It was sent from Mills College where she held a position as teaching fellow in the English Department while studying for a Master of Arts Degree. She told of her struggle to rebuild a world in which she and her children could be happy. Her son Nicky, age 6, was in the first grade of school, and Susan, 8, was in the third grade. She reported that Austin's *Earth Horizon* was part of the "law and gospel" in the English Department at Mills. Friends there spoke of Mary often with admiration and affection, and asked to be remembered.

——————— 89

210 S 7th, Annex A
Springfield, Illinois
February 17, 1932

Dear Mary Austin,

I am terribly sorry to learn that you have been ill, and so dangerously. I hope that you are better now—that you can go quietly, and make a sure recovery. And I appreciate deeply your goodness, in taking your strength to write me words of love and sympathy which give me strength to go on.

I do, indeed, believe that Vachel lives now—perhaps for the first time, as he always wanted. He was always keyed not only to his own time and place, and its traditions, so deeply that the song of it he left us can but grow greater and truer with the years; but also and almost agonizingly to a realm of pure beauty and joy, unrealizable here except in rare and isolated moments; and now one can be very sure that he is the eternal inheritor of all he dreamed and saw—and far, far more. I think he is there, and not here—though the two meet in a dimension which as yet we vaguely apprehend—and I think, just now, that he is resting. He was terribly tired; life held for him shadows, burdens, and pain, due to increase; and he needed such luminous quiet as was our last sight of him. I am almost afraid to think of him very much, lest it trouble his sleep—as one fears to look at a sleeping child, whatever love may desire, for fear there may be an awakening in darkness, with a cry before the full hour of morning. And yet, how think of anything else?

Love to you and every good wish: I am still hoping some day to see you, to know you better.

Yours faithfully,
Elizabeth Conner Lindsay

———————————————————————————————

Bliss Carman (1861-1939) was, in his day, the best known poet of Canada, although he spent most of his life in the United States. In fact, he is often considered to have been an American because of his life and work in this country. He was born in Fredericton, New Brunswick, and became a graduate of the university in this province of Canada. His manuscripts of poetry and essays are now held in the Bliss Carman Collection at the University of New Brunswick, and are printed with the permission of the Trustees of this repository.

Carman's ancestors were early settlers of the United States. On his father's side, the Carmans lived on Long Island in 1631, and his mother's people were descended from an early New England preacher, the Reverend Daniel Bliss, who was the great grandfather of Ralph Waldo Emerson. With this background, perhaps the outlook of optimism and faith in nature expressed by Carman can be understood. Both his life and writings show what Padraic Colum called the "gayety and color of his mind" and the "frugal dignity" of his style and behavior.

Bliss Carman attended the graduate school at Harvard University from 1886 until 1888, and he found a friendship with Richard Hovey who joined him in the writing of *Songs of Vagabondia* (1894). This book was reprinted in seventeen editions during the next twenty years, and it established Carman and his companion among the most popular writers of the period. "Vagabondia" was a world of friendship in the out-of-doors where field and stream, forest and hill offered joy and song free from care and drudgery. *More Songs from Vagabondia*, printed two years later, went through twelve editions. The message was the same, and the younger of the poetic wanderers writes of the open road in France where, along the riverside, castle ruins and bird songs in the moonlight allure the free spirit. Carman is the more serious poet, using such sober themes as the passing of youth, the loss of loved ones, the allure of poetry, and the permanence of friendship.

While serving as a literary journalist in Boston and New York, Carman contributed additional volumes of "Vagabondia" in 1900 and 1912, a dozen more books of poetry, and essays on the study of nature and the development of personality. He edited ten volumes in *The World's Best Poetry* series published in 1904; then prepared *The Oxford Book of Canadian Verse* in 1913 and *The Oxford Book of American Verse* in 1927. In the summer when the latter anthology appeared, Bliss Carman visited Santa Fe and met some of the poets whose work he had selected for the book. Shown in a photograph kept in the Mary Austin Collection are Alice Corbin Henderson, Witter Bynner, Arthur Davison Ficke with his wife Gladys, Bliss Carman, and Mary Austin. Several other Santa Feans are lined up with the group standing before a sunlit wall. *Letter 90* mentions the cordial reception given to Bliss Carman by this group and their associates upon the occasion of his visit. A second letter Carman wrote to Austin on April 25, 1928, invites her to submit several of her Indian poems for a new edition of *The Oxford Book of American Verse*. Carman died on June 8, 1929, before finishing this editorial task. Another editor assumed the job. Neither Austin nor the other Santa Fe poets appeared in the revised edition which was published in 1950. The "gift book" referred to in *Letter 90* was Austin's *The American Rhythm* (1923). It contained the Indian poems which appealed to him.

───── 90

B. C.
New Canaan, Connecticut

25 June, 1927

Dear Mary Austin:

Please accept the very small book of verse which goes to you to-day as a reminder of my glowing appreciation of our happy meeting. It was so very kind of you all to admit a wayfarer to the very precious circle of Santa Fe poets. I shall never forget the real pleasure, and must thank you again.

Your gift book was a help on the homeward journey—and needed. For as you know one doesn't easily come down from the mountains, and I was so glad to have anything genuine and reminiscent with me.

I enjoyed the poems and the essay thoroughly, and am promising myself another careful reading of the little volume this summer. Your ideas on rhythm are very suggestive and deep. I was tremendously taken with the ceremony at San Felipe, and am eager for real instruction such as you have so abundantly.

Maybe if I am very good I shall be allowed to revisit your high city even in this life. I hope so.

When you get the little book please read the last three poems, will you?

Ever so truly yours,
*Bliss Carman**

────────────────────────────────────

In two of her books, Mary Austin criticized the universities in America by calling them "temples of Imitation" (*The American Rhythm*, p. 7) and "vast caravansaries of book learning" (*Earth Horizon*, p. 169). However, she numbered among her friends many college professors who offered support for her ideas. One of them was Lew Sarett (1888-1954), an English professor and specialist in oratory and debate, who was also a distinguished poet. He shared Austin's feeling for nature and her understanding of Indians, their mythology, and their gift for storytelling. As a boy, Sarett had learned to love

*Reprinted by special permission of the Bliss Carman Trust, The University of New Brunswick, Fredericton, N. B., Canada.

the woodland surrounding his home in Marquette, Michigan. After a period when his mother took him to Chicago, he returned to the lake country of the upper Midwest. There he progressed through high school and Beloit College, which he followed with a post-graduate year at Harvard University. He earned a law degree at the University of Illinois, where he taught English to support his studies. Instead of practicing law, he became a guide in the Canadian woods, and worked as a forest ranger in the Rocky Mountain states. He remained in the academic world, however, writing a number of books on speech communication. He first began to write poetry while teaching English and studying for his degree in law, but he never abandoned expeditions to the out-of-doors, which may have become an antidote to the disciplines of rhetoric and the search for legal precedents in the casebooks of law.

Slow Smoke (1925) was published when Sarett was teaching in the School of Speech at Northwestern University. The poems are reprinted from the *Atlantic Monthly*, *Century Magazine*, the *Bookman*, *Poetry*, *A Magazine of Verse*, and other outstanding journals. The Poetry Society of America voted the book the prize winning volume for poetry published that year in America. Titles like "To a Wild Goose Over Decoys," "Colloquy with a Coyote," "Crazy Medicine," "Tamarack Blue," and "Deep Wet Moss" indicate what Harriet Monroe, founder of *Poetry, A Magazine of Verse*, called Sarett's love "for the primitive forest and its wild beasts and birds." Carl Sandburg wrote the Foreword to *The Collected Poems of Lew Sarett* (1944), in which he praised the poems because they contained "the loam and the lingo, the sand and the syllables of North America." *Letter 91* indicates how much Sarett shared Austin's outlook for the enrichment of American literature and art through the beauty and significance of native resources. In his second letter, written on February 28, 1929, he thanks Mary for the gift of a copy of *The Children Sing in the Far West*, which he calls "a sheer delight" containing as "varied beauty for adults as for children." He also refers to a "friendly chat" he enjoyed with her at a time they met in Chicago. This may have been the outcome of his suggestion at the end of *Letter 91*.

_____ 91

LEW SARETT

Laona
Forest County
Wisconsin

December 29, 1928

My dear Miss Austin:

For many years I've wished to meet you, to know you, and to chat with you. Circumstances have shot our trails to different regions; you to your beautiful Southwest, me to the mountains of Montana, the forests of Minnesota, Wisconsin, and Canada. I don't know you even through correspondence; I am rather reticent about making friendly overtures, and, too, something of a solitary, a lobo. This shouldn't go on forever, it seems to me. Here are you, a most eminent authority on Indian matters, one who has devoted much of her life to the business of capturing the soul of primitive America; and here am I, gambling my life in the enterprise of capturing the beauty and significance of the Indian and of the wilderness of America. We have so much in common: our knowledge of and our interest in Indian matters, in the social and political problems of the Amerindian as well as in his potentially rich literary legacy. We both know, too, that work in this field is a hard, thankless work, with no returns except the consciousness of work honestly and perhaps well done; and there are times when one would like so much to talk with a kindred spirit—and there are so few people with whom one wishes to talk or can talk to on common ground. Under the circumstances I feel very deeply that we should know one another, at any rate that I should not let go by an opportunity to meet you and to know you.

Last year you spoke in Evanston, my stamping-ground. I regretted so keenly my missing you. You see, I do not live now in Evanston; for the past three years I've been living in northern Wisconsin among the Pottowatomies. I never get out of my woods and away from my writing except in January and February, when I go on a cross-country platform tour, and in March, April, May when I hold a Professorship at Northwestern. The rest of the year—June to January—I never leave these woods. So I missed you.

When I received my friend Edson's invitation to a tea for you I determined to make a great effort to get down in time for it. And I shall be there, delighted at the opportunity of grasping your hand. I should like so much, however, to see more of you if I could. If you could—and were disposed to—pry out an hour or two on Saturday January 5 or Sunday, January 6 for a good visit and a good talk on Indian matters and literary matters, I should be very grateful. I am very sure that those hours will be, for me, very rich hours. One goes it alone and silently so much of the time, that when an opportunity comes to talk with a kindred spirit whose judgment and achievements one respects very deeply, naturally he is avid for those hours of companionship.

Would you be disposed to visit for a little time on those days? If you would care to, I shall be at your command.

I plan to drive down the 325 miles from my home—if the snow isn't too deep, otherwise train. On January 4 and 5 I shall be registered at the Hotel La Salle, Chicago, Illinois. A note to me at this address—or a telephone message—will be transmitted to me.

With my most cordial wishes, I am,

Sincerely yours,
*Lew Sarett**

*This letter is printed with the permission of the writer's wife, Alma J. Sarett, Department of Communications, University of South Florida, Tampa.

THE LAST YEARS

VI

As Mary Austin tells her story in *Earth Horizon*, she crowds the last ten years of her life into just fourteen pages. In 1924, when this cycle begins, she decided to build a house in Santa Fe. An adviser in this venture was Frank Applegate (1882-1931), a painter and sculptor who had moved his family from New Jersey to the Southwest in 1921. The Applegates were originally from Illinois, a tie to Austin who was also an emigrant from that state. The Applegates became her neighbors after she built her house. Frank and Alta had remodeled a large, two-story adobe home on a lane near the building site chosen by Mary on the Camino del Monte Sol. Applegate designed his house with a balcony facing a patio enclosed by two wings of the house and a wall across the front of the patio. A collector of Spanish American antiques, Applegate furnished the home with handcrafted chairs, tables, cabinets, and hand woven rugs and tapestries. The walls held hammered tin frames and sconces beside painted *retablos* or plaques with the painted images of Christian saints as copied from similar subjects brought in from Mexico and Spain. Applegate was the author of two books drawn from the story world indigenous to the Southwest: *Indian Stories from the Pueblos* (1929) and *Native Tales of New Mexico* (1932).

Ansel Adams (1902-   ), the author of *Letter 92*, is a musician from San Francisco, who turned from performing as a pianist and teaching music to the practice of photography. In 1929, he drove to Taos in order to produce pictures of the pueblo for a book to be published by the Grabhorn Press of San Francisco. This is the volume referred to in the letter, for which the Foreword was written by Mary Austin. Her fourteen pages are an eloquent and documentary description of the scenic world in which the pueblo is situated. *Taos* (1930), *Photographed by Ansel Adams and Described by Mary Austin*, was a large folio, handsomely bound with ornamental end papers and illuminated initial lettering. In the following year, Adams was the guest of the Applegates when they began a manuscript on the history of Southwestern Spanish arts and crafts. Adams supplied nearly 100 photographs for this study. The original manuscript has disappeared, but copies are now in Special Collections at the Zimmerman Library in University of New Mexico, Albuquerque.

Taos was the beginning of a distinguished career for Adams as the interpreter of dramatic aspects of scenes in the natural environment of the United States. He later produced portfolios and books of photography, including *This is the American Earth* (with Nancy Newhall), *Death Valley and Yosemite Valley* (1960). In 1929, Adams married Virginia Best. They make their home in Carmel, California.

_____ 92

ANSEL EASTON ADAMS

San Francisco

December 22nd
1930

Dear Mary Austin,

Your delightful Christmas book came yesterday, and Virginia and I are indeed pleased. Thank you so much. I had hoped to be able to send you some prints, but just could not find a moment to make them—sent some little things for the house instead, from us both.

At last—TAOS is out! or will be out Monday. Your copy goes off on that day, and I am indeed relieved. It has been a fearful job all through, but the results justify every effort. I do not know why, but there is always a delay in books of this sort. I had my prints on time, and the binder has "done noble" but the printers were most distressingly slow. However, TAOS is out, and I am sure will go well. I have disposed of about half to date.

I will write later on in more detail and will tell you all about the birth pangs of TAOS. Affectionately yours—greetings from us both.

Ansel and Virginia

Stafford Wallace Austin (1860-1932) became the husband of Mary Hunter on May 18, 1891. His occupation was that of vineyardist or grape-grower, farming irrigated land in the Owens Valley near Lone Pine,

Inyo County, California. He was also manager of the water association in the valley and found time as well to teach at Lone Pine. Pictures of Austin show a slender, sandy-haired man of above average height, with sharp features adorned by a mustache. Wallace Austin was born in Hawaii, where his family had been early settlers, owning a sugarcane plantation and educating their children in leisure and refinement. Mary Hunter met him while she was teaching school at Mountain View southwest of Bakersfield. The neighbors spoke of him as "Professor Austin" because of his school teaching. At this time, Mary was living in the home of Mr. and Mrs. D. M. Pyle, who were also schoolteachers and whose children were in her classes. The wedding of Mary to Wallace was presided over by her mother, Susanna Hunter, who arranged both the ceremony and the sociability. Music and refreshments entertained a large crowd of guests. According to Helen MacKnight Doyle, in her book *Mary Austin, Woman of Genius* (1939), some of the guests came from as far as Bakersfield and were conveyed to the house in a large stage drawn by four horses.

After the wedding, the Austins moved to Wallace's orchard near the Pyle ranch. When his efforts at vine growing became unprofitable, Austin returned to teaching school. A few years later, both of the Austins were teaching at Bishop, farther north in the valley. Since Wallace continued as an employee of the irrigation company, his activities took him into San Francisco where the headquarters of the company were located. There his wife met people in literary circles, such as Ina Coolbrith, poet and librarian; the young Jack London, who was to become a radical and an author; George Sterling, poet; and the journalist and critic Ambrose Bierce. She states in her autobiography that at the outset of their married life, her husband accompanied her on trips to the mountains and desert where she found stories of people and places.

Gradually, however, their paths led in different directions, and in 1906 she sold the house at Independence and built another residence at Carmel. On October 21, 1914, Stafford Wallace Austin alleged in a complaint for divorce filed at San Bernardino, California, that during the month of October 1907 he had been "deserted and abandoned" by his wife, and ever since that time had continued to live separate from her. He was then working for the Potash Company of America at Trona, west of Bakersfield near the area of Death Valley. A business center in this small community was named Austin Square with stores under a kind of overhang.

Wallace Austin's contacts with his former wife did not end with the final judgment of the divorce on November 19, 1915. There are nine letters in the Mary Austin Collection which show he kept in touch with her almost until the time of his death on September 12, 1932. It was in this year that Mrs. Austin's autobiography was published. Letters from the publisher show that pages of *Earth Horizon* were being reset in November of 1932 because of a protest registered by H. G. Wells who objected to Mary's reporting of a conversation with him in the spring of 1909 (see Mary Austin to H. G. Wells, *Letter 107*). It might be that Wallace Austin would also have registered a protest if he had read his ex-wife's account of their life together. The pages devoted to Wallace Austin are largely derogatory since they report Mary's opinion that he failed in his business and as a teacher. She stressed his "lack of direction" in life and complained that he did not cooperate in advancing her career. The impression left with the reader is that his life was a failure. Nine letters, however, are retained in her family archives. These show that Austin remained on friendly terms and that he went on to responsible and rewarding service with the company he worked for since the early days at Trona.

The earliest letter, dated February 4, 1904, was written by Wallace Austin in reply to a request from the *Mt. Whitney Club Journal* for an article by Mary. He stated that she was in San Francisco, but he felt certain that she would write the article, and he enclosed a clipping from the San Francisco *Bulletin* which described *The Land of Little Rain* as a "classic of California" and a "study of nature in her least known moods." The eight letters which follow were written by Austin between December 21, 1920, and May 13, 1930, including *Letter 93* which is printed in this book. In summary, they report to Mary that she is named the beneficiary of an insurance policy specified in his will; announce sending her Christmas gifts and a birthday present; outline early events in their family life to assist her in writing the autobiography; offer to come to Santa Fe to help in this project; send an itinerary for a trip he is taking around the world; and relay his plan to mail her a cashmere shawl he purchased for her in India.

Most of Wallace Austin's letters end with the conventional "Sincerely" or "Sincerely yours," but in one letter he includes "With very best wishes" and to another he adds "With love." The death certificate for Stafford Wallace Austin was signed by Dr. George Hunter, Mary's younger brother, who practiced medicine in Los Angeles. The certificate states that Stafford Wallace Austin died of angina pectoris; that he was born in Hawaii on May 16, 1860, and had lived in California for fifty-three years, sixteen of them at 601 North Possmore; that he was a retired sales agent for the American Potash Chemical Company; that he was divorced; and that the name of his wife was unknown.

_____ **93**

San Francisco Limited
CHICAGO & NORTH WESTERN RY
UNION PACIFIC SYSTEM
SOUTHERN PACIFIC LINES

September 22, 1929 (?)

Dear Mary,

I think I wrote you that I am making the trip around the World. My niece Margaret, Herbert's youngest daughter, is in New York and she will go on with me from there to Honolulu. The inclosed indicates about the route we will take but we are not obliged to stick to it.

After visiting Egypt we plan to go through Palestine to Damascus and then by auto over the desert to Bagdad where I want to spend a few days as it is one of the few old Mohammedan cities out of easy reach of the tourists. From there we will take the train to the Persian Gulf via Babylon and the country of Abraham. We will take the usual route thru India, Burmah, and Siam, and then a side trip into the jungles to look at the ancient city of Angkor. From Singapore we will visit Java where I have friends among the Standard Oil people. From there on to Manila where I have a cousin, Harry White, and Margaret has many friends among the young people. I would like to spend more time in Europe, but the delay will bring us into the tropics at the wrong season. Also I must take it easy and not overdo, as I cannot stand roughing it as I used to.

If there is anything you are particularly interested in from Asia let me know en route and I will try to bring it back—providing it is not too heavy.

Hope you are well. Please remember me to Mary Hunter when you write to her.

With very best wishes,
Wallace

Ernest Thompson Seton (1860-1946), one of the most famous authors in modern American literature, was born in South Shields, Durham, England. His family was of the Scottish nobility, but according to the account in *By a Thousand Fires* (1967), written by Julia Moss Seton, his second wife, the name "Seton" was abandoned by Ernest's grandfather when he escaped with outnumbered and defeated Scots at the battle of Culloden in 1746. The grandfather assumed the surname of "Thompson," which was well known in the English community. At a later time, members of the family employed the hyphenated name "Seton-Thompson," but there were two reasons for Ernest to choose "Seton." One was family pride in the clan name, and the other was dislike for his father, whose tyranny alienated Ernest and some of the other sons.

Beatings and a domineering manner were involved, as was an incident when Seton reached the age of 21: at that time his father presented him with an itemized bill of every expenditure he had made during his son's boyhood and youth. He asked Ernest to repay the amount of $537.50 with interest thenceforward at 6 percent. Seton took care of the debt in two years but with lingering resentment. However, not until his mother's death in 1897 did the young author petition for a legal change in his name. In 1901, he received a decision from the New York Supreme Court to affirm "Thompson Seton" as his legitimate publishing name. Unfortunately, articles and a book had been published under the earlier name and confusion continued for a number of years between the two names.

Seton's father, Joseph Logan Thompson, had been a prosperous ship owner until misfortune struck as one ship ran aground in the Bristol Channel, another sank in the Indian Ocean, and a third was plundered off the Gold Coast of Africa. He sold his property in 1866 and moved the Thompson family to Canada where they first lived at Lindsay, Ontario, and then, ten years later, moved to Toronto in the same province. After study in the public schools, Ernest went to England to continue the work in art for which he had been awarded a Gold Medal at the Ontario Art School. When he had completed two years at the Royal Academy in London, he was forced by illness to return to Canada. Seton decided to come to the United States in 1883 after he learned that the *Century Magazine* in New York City made use of the type of drawings which were his special skill. He displayed a portfolio of such sketches to the art manager of the monthly periodical and came away with a contract to make bird and mammal drawings at $5.00 apiece to be used in the forthcoming *Century Dictionary*. In 1893, he came to New Mexico and began to write his most famous book, *Wild Animals I Have Known* (1898). The first story, "Lobo, King of Currumpaw," tells of a giant gray wolf that is the leader of a pack which has been ravaging cattle and sheep in the valley for a good many years. The tale is a masterpiece of description and plot, ending with the downfall of Lobo, coming only after the capture and destruction of Blanca, his mate. She was less skillful at evading man than he was. Seton illustrated almost every page of the book with the outline of an animal, a rope, a trap, or a trail to enliven the story that accompanied the design.

Sixteen letters and a telegram sent by Ernest Thompson Seton are catalogued in the Mary Austin Collection. The dates range from May 11, 1915, to March 3, 1932. The mailing places are Greenwich, Connecticut; New York City; Los Angeles; and Santa Fe, New Mexico. One additional letter, on April 14, 1915, was written by Seton's first wife, Grace Gallatin Seton, a lecturer, book designer, and author, who married him on June 1, 1896, and was divorced from him in 1935. This letter arranged a luncheon for Mary Austin on Sunday, April 25, 1915, in Greenwich, Connecticut. Mary was then living in New York City, and a letter from Seton a year later gives a New York address for him at 512

Fifth Avenue. He supplies the information that this is a part-time habitation because he is "running around the country" giving lectures "with occasional visits to Greenwich." His home in Connecticut was called "The Fincherie," and he says the house was three miles from the Greenwich station and two miles from the trolley at the head of the street. On April 26, 1917, Seton's letter was written on Woodcraft League of America stationery. The letterhead names forty-eight people on the National Council of the organization and gives the founding date as 1902. Later correspondence on Woodcraft League paper comes from 405 South Hill Street, Los Angeles.

On January 13, 1919, Seton reminded Austin that her membership in the Woodcraft League had lapsed and he urged her to renew it. A letter on September 15, 1927, was written on stationery headed "Little Pequot, Greenwich, Conn." and referred to his residence as "my joint on the lake." He spoke of his "kind, bright memories of the good people in Santa Fe" and reported that a recent stay in that city accompanied by Julia M. Buttree might be more than just a pleasant visit: "It looked like the opening of a new epoch." This expectation was confirmed by *Letter 94*, in which Seton told of his plan to purchase a tract of land on an old Spanish Land Grant six miles southeast of Santa Fe. On November 27, 1930, he sent Mary Austin *Letter 96* from Seton Village where he had established a community for nature studies and the training of youths and their leaders in such organizations as the Boy Scouts, the Campfire Girls, and the Woodcraft League.

The site consisted of 2,500 acres of foothill land dotted with sage and cedars in the midst of which the Setons built a large house called "The Castle." Surrounding this main building were numerous units of smaller lodgings and museum halls for exhibits of stuffed birds and animals along with Indian artifacts. "The Castle" held more than 3,000 of Seton's paintings and a library of 70,000 books. When he died in 1946, his cremated ashes were scattered over Cone Mountain, a peak at the edge of the village. On July 10 of the following year Seton Village became a National Historic Landmark administered by the Park Service of the Department of the Interior. Julia M. Seton offered the collection and library to the Philmont Scout Ranch at Cimarron, New Mexico, and on August 13, 1965, the offer became a gift. Later a handsome permanent structure was built to hold the exhibits as a memorial to Seton as founder of the Boy Scout Movement in America and a leader in the preservation of outdoor life in his adopted country. Seton was chief scout of the Boy Scout organization from 1910 until 1915, and in 1942 was awarded the John Burroughs Medal for his research and publications on wild life and natural history of North America.

The correspondence between Seton and Austin was both professional and personal. His lengthy letter on December 6, 1927, gave advice about her projected lecture tour and was based upon his own experiences with Women's

Clubs and Lecture Bureaus. A letter in the following year gave an opinion on what he calls "White Indian music" by Cadman, Lieurance, Troyer and "Red music," meaning the music by Indians themselves. All of Seton's letters end not only with his signature, but also with little hand-drawn designs of animal footprints, which keep the receiver mindful that he is a nature lover. Forty-six titles make up a bibliography of his published works. Aside from *Wild Animals I Have Known*, which was often reprinted, and the widely used handcraft and camping manuals, the most popular are: *The Biography of a Grizzly* (1900); *Lives of the Hunted* (1901); *Two Little Savages* (1903); *Rolf in the Woods* (1911); *Gospel of the Red Man* (1936); *Trail and Campfire Stories* (1944); and his autobiography, *The Trail of an Artist-Naturalist* (1940).

_____ 94

Greenwich, Conn.,
Sept. 26, 1929

Mrs. Mary Austin,
Santa Fe, N. M.

Dear Mary:

I am after you again. This question of moving to New Mexico is quite serious with me; in fact, my mind is made up to move. But, whether I go to the De Vargas Grant, the Lamy Grant, or the Sandoval tract depends on the terms I get. All are ready to deal.

I enclose a map of the De Vargas tract as at present. Will you indicate on this, as nearly as possible, where the two wells and the five springs are to be found; also the two Indian pueblos. If you know of any wells on adjoining territory outside the limits, I should be glad to know of their whereabouts.

I expect to arrive on October 26th, to complete the investigation, and close a contract with somebody, if my terms are accepted.

* * *

You were looking for a door knocker when last I saw you. A friend of mine brought from Cuba, after the close of the Spanish war, a typical knocker which I am sending you. It is a hand grasping a ball. I never cared much about it, and it may not appeal to you. If you like it, use it; if not, hold it till I come.

Ever cordially,
Ernest Thompson Seton

_____ 95

Nov. 29, 1929
Woodcraft League of America
405 South Hill Street
Los Angeles, Calif.

Mrs. Mary Austin,
Santa Fe, N. M.

Dear Mary:

I have a dim remembrance that you were going East about the time we went West from Santa Fe. Maybe by this time, you are back. Anyhow, I shall take a chance on it.

I have been working on my Message of the Redman. Would you be willing to read over the chapter of it which deals with his religion? It is only three pages; but I should be glad to have it endorsed or corrected by you.

The papers here have all the rest of the country under snow, with zero weather, California being the only land of sunshine. I suppose it is a little cold in Santa Fe. But I often wish I were there instead of in this rackety, automobile-crazy town.

Dorman has a couple of properties that he wants me to look at. His descriptions sound all right, and may result in my coming back soon for a personal inspection.

Mrs. Buttree joins in kind regards,

Yours cordially,
Ernest Thompson Seton

In *Earth Horizon*, Mary Austin wrote that she first met Ernest Thompson Seton after she had sold *The Land of Little Rain* and had begun to work on "The Basket Maker," which presumably is the school edition of *The Basket Woman, A Book of Fanciful Tales for Children* (1904). She stated that Seton was lecturing in Bakersfield, and they were taken forth to see the town and succeeded in seeing each other and "in exchanging wayfarers' news of the trail." Since Seton states in *Letter 96* that he "has it down" as to the month and year, the probability is that his dating is more accurate than hers. His last two letters were dated on April 15, 1931, and March 31, 1932. In the first, signed from the College of Indian Wisdom at Seton Village, he thanks Mary for her offer to donate some plants to the Village and invites her to come to a lecture he will give at the Museum of New Mexico. In the second, he informs her that Brentano's plans to reprint her story "Arrumpa the Mastodon" in a book he is preparing and will forward a check to her publisher. Seton and Austin were writers who appreciated each other because both were naturists in related but different ways.

_____ 96

Ernest Thompson Seton
Seton Village
Santa Fe, New Mexico

Nov. 27, 1930

Mrs. Mary Austin
Santa Fe, New Mexico

Dear Mary:

I am busy just now taking out my final papers as a citizen of the United States. It is necessary that I give two references, persons of good standing who have known me as a reputable citizen and member of the same community.

I have taken the liberty of giving you as one of my Santa Fe vouchers. I hope it is all right, and that you will be able to say something good when questioned.

Our first meeting, by the way, I have down as Bakersfield, California, October, 1899.

Cordially ever,
Ernest Thompson Seton

Many healthseekers came to the Southwest in the early years of the twentieth century in order to benefit from the sunshine and clear, dry air. Among them was the poet Witter Bynner (1881-1968), who before moving to New Mexico had been an assistant editor of *McClure's Magazine,* an advisory editor to another publisher in New York City, a lecturer on poetry throughout the United States, and a faculty member at the University of California at Berkeley. Following his early years in Brooklyn, New York, he acquired an A.B. cum laude at Harvard in 1902, and celebrated the event five years later when he published verses in a book entitled *Young Harvard.* He wrote five more volumes of verse and two plays in New Hampshire and elsewhere before coming to New Mexico in 1921. The dramatic works were collected with two others in *A Book of Plays* (1922). The poetry books were represented in *The Selected Poems* (1936), edited by his companion Robert Hunt with an appreciative introduction by the novelist Paul Horgan.

After the *Selected Poems,* Bynner published four more books of verse; also a small volume called *The Way of Life According to Laotzu* (1944); and a biographical memoir reporting his friendship with the D. H. Lawrences, entitled *Journey with Genius* (1951). The essay on Laotzu, plus the sayings of this noted philosopher, emphasized the influence of Chinese thought as one of two exotic cultures upon Bynner's thinking and his writing of poetry. A trip to the Orient and study with Chinese scholars produced *The Jade Mountain,* a collection of 300 poems of the Tang dynasty from 618 to 906 A.D. Interest in the book required two printings before publication in October of 1929 and a fifth printing in January of 1939.

The other influence which was outside the stream of English and American poetry was the native Indian world he encountered along the Rio Grande and in other parts of the Southwest. The poems in his volume *Indian Earth* (1929) offer new impressions and interpretations of the first Americans. "A Dance for Rain at Cochiti," with the vivid picture of Indians dancing in a line, "their elbows green with growth of pine," is probably Bynner's most famous poem.

During a long life in Santa Fe, Bynner was a patron of music (he was himself a pianist), art, and literature. He was known to his friends by the nickname "Hal," a shortened form of his first name "Harold." He was genial with friends, a hospitable host, and a community figure, believing as did the Chinese poets that he should devote his early years to some form of public service. Consequently he served on the council that arranged the annual fiesta celebration after Labor Day; he even ran for the state legislature on the Democratic ticket a few years after he arrived in Santa Fe.

Critics have disagreed about his achievement as a poet. Harriet Monroe, founder of *Poetry Magazine*, pointed out that Bynner broke away from his Harvard-New England tradition and made the Southwestern "wonderland his permanent home, not only in terms of real estate and residence, but in the loyalties and wistful ardors of his spirit." However, she never forgave him for a literary hoax he perpetrated, with the help of Arthur Ficke, in the autumn of 1916. William Jay Smith, in *The Spectra Hoax* (1961), gives details of this outrageous satire on the new schools of poetry that included Monroe, Amy Lowell, John Gould Fletcher, Ezra Pound, and many others. Bynner and Ficke, as conspirators, chose the pseudonyms of "Emanuel Morgan" and "Anne Knish," then wrote a volume of poetic caricatures using these artificial names. They entitled their book *Spectra, A Book of Poetic Experiments*, and sent the manuscript to Mitchell Kennerley, who had previously published books for each of them under their own names. He agreed to keep their secret.

Emanuel Morgan and Anne Knish claimed Pittsburgh to be their home, using the address of a lady friend to cover their disguise. They not only published their Spectrist book, but they sent Spectrist poems to magazines and, as Witter Bynner and Arthur Ficke, wrote reviews of the book and discussed their imaginary selves as actual poets. Some of the best known poets and editors were deceived. Edgar Lee Masters praised Spectrism as "the very core" of poetry and "imagism" as only "the surface." Harriet Monroe, however, resented the entire effort even though she had accepted contributions from the hoaxers. Amy Lowell called the two poetic impersonators "charlatans." A final balance was achieved when Bynner and Ficke were exposed. There was general agreement among friends and foes that the hoax had been laughable, and that some of the Spectrist creations were not only amusing but impressive, as demonstrated by what Emanuel Morgan names his "Opus 101":

> He not only plays
> One note
> But holds another note
> Away from it—
> As a lover
> Lifts a waft of hair
> From loved eyes.

The piano shivers
When he touches it,
And the leg shines.*

Nineteen letters and a card from Bynner are to be found in the Mary Austin Collection, beginning on September 3, 1925, and ending on March 11, 1934, three months before her death. The first letter was sent from Chapala, Mexico, and Bynner joins in condemning Katherine Fullerton Gerould's article on the architecture and cultural activities of Santa Fe. He supports the letter of protest Austin wrote to the newspaper and offers to write to Thomas B. Wells, the editor of *Harper's* (see Wells's *Letter 82* with commentary). Bynner tells of the work he has been doing with Chinese translations as these were to appear in *The Jade Anthology*. The pain he has been suffering with an infected jaw has caused him delay; nevertheless, he has written a great number of lyrics. He expects to be home in six weeks and invites Mary to dine with him.

A letter in November of 1926 sends Mary some Spanish poems she requested, and another in September of 1929 thanks her for a sympathetic review of *Indian Earth*, his latest book of poems. *Letter 97* was written in appreciation for comments Austin must have made on *The Jade Anthology*. His reference to her "generosity with goodies" certainly acknowledged a gift of jelly or some other product from her kitchen. Mary Austin's skill and generosity in this respect were well known to all her friends.

_____ 97

WITTER BYNNER
342 BUENA VISTA ROAD
SANTA FE, NEW MEXICO

December 5, 1929

Dear Mary,

The difficulty and despair of some of those eleven years fall away into nothing when I receive such a letter as yours. It was especially gracious of you when you have already spoken vocal words to take time from your busy life and set them down in a note.

I like your word "feeling knowledge." I had not heard it before.

I wonder if you will let me quote your sentiments—"I am sure no Chinese poet could ever, in another tongue, do any better by the poetic genius of his people," or possibly, "I have nowhere seen, among English translations, anything that gives so satisfactory a feeling of the happy serenity, the serene and unembittered acceptance of hard fortune which is characteristic of the Chinese people whom I have personally known."

In our flurry the other afternoon, I did not half thank you for your generosity with goodies. I am beginning to think of you, not only because of your friendliness to me, but because of other things, I hear, as the angel of the hill.

Affectionately yours,
Hal

Letter 98 was written just after a new and enlarged edition of *The American Rhythm* had been issued and brings forward Mary Austin's central thesis that life on the American continents, plus associations with native peoples, had produced changes in the speech and activities of newcomers which resulted in rhythmic variations of vocal sounds and body movements. These changes, she maintained, appeared in both verse and prose forms as they adjusted to the environment of nature and climate on the plains, deserts, and woodlands, even to the patterns in crowded centers of population. She traced the measures of European verse to their wine presses, market places, outdoor stages, and altar rituals. The ceremonies of Indian kivas and village squares of the New World were much freer and encouraged freer forms of movement and expression.

Austin interpreted the versification of Walt Whitman, Robert Frost, and Carl Sandburg as responsive to the rhythms of American life. The most memorable illustration of a rhythm she called native to America was the prose of Abraham Lincoln's Gettysburg Address. She excerpts passages which she says represent the stride of a man walking a woodland path with an ax upon his shoulder:

> The world will little note nor long remember
> What we say here:
> But it can never forget what they did here.

And as Lincoln approached the end of his speech, he spoke with the upswing and downstroke of the ax on a chopping log:

> That government of the people
> For the people
> By the people
> Shall not perish from the earth.

In her lectures, Austin was accustomed to lift and lower her arms as she delivered this passage and, by contrast, to have paced the rhythms in an ode by Shelley or Keats as strophes derived from the Greek and Latin poets. The statement in the letter that Arthur Ficke, too, was unconvinced by Austin's thesis is confirmed by his *Letter 102*. On March 31, 1930, Bynner mentioned a proposal made by Mary that they select adjacent burial lots in a Santa Fe cemetery. The final line in *Letter 98* may have been an allusion to this suggestion, which was never acted upon.

_____ **98**

WITTER BYNNER
342 BUENA VISTA ROAD
SANTA GE, NEW MEXICO

May 26, 1930

Dear Mary:

At last I have read the *American Rhythm* and I am gladder than ever that you gave it to me. I'm sure you will not dislike my honesty in telling you that the second half of the book is what I best admired and enjoyed. I am with Arthur in doubting your success as to establishing an Indian rhythm as basically important to the rhythm of American art. I consider it immensely important relative to American life,—the quick stepping rhythm of our national existence, the masks that cover our faces, the pathetic mistake that we are leading an animal life, the architecture behind our rhythms, the bright lights we wear on the streets of our bodies, the whole strange tom-tom of our existence—yes, that is the American rhythm.

But I think you could relate it much better to Broadway, to haberdashery advertisements, to electric signs, to Ziegfeld ballets, to night clubs, and even to clairvoyant parlors up and down Manhattan island, than to the quintessence of our life as exhibited, however badly, in Sandburg, or you or myself. Your main error seems to me to be in trying to connect what you call the American rhythm with the English rhythm of your translations of an original Indian rhythm. You could never convince me that your rhythms in the translations have anything to do with the American soil in the sense that the original Indian rhythms belong to it. Your rhythm, like mine, is Elizabethan, Victorian, Georgian, Rooseveltian, Wilsonian. Our rhythms are inextricably mixed with those of the little island which hardly knows the difference between the Indians of the West and of the East.

As a matter of fact, I should say that there is more influence from Queen Elizabeth down through Gershwin on Hopi Indian songs than on so-called American rhythm from any Amerindian whatever. Some night in New York we shall put our heads together, literally, and debate this fine subject. Meantime I bless you. Meantime I lie with you in peace.

Yours ever,
Hal

Ezra Pound (1895-1972), one of the most controversial figures in American intellectual history, has only one letter in Austin's file, but this letter exemplifies two of the qualities for which he was famous: personal integrity and social irascibility. *Letter 99* requires an introduction both to the author and to his career. Ezra Loomis Pound began life in Hailey, Idaho, where his father, Homer Pound, had opened a Government Land Office to register mining claims. After four years in Idaho, Pound moved his family to Philadelphia, where he became assistant assayer in the United States Mint. Ezra grew up in a Philadelphia suburb and, except for a trip to Europe in the company of an aunt, he experienced the normal home life and schooling of other American youths. He attended the University of Pennsylvania for two years, and then transferred to Hamilton College where he earned his baccalaureate degree in 1905. As a fellow in Romance Languages, he completed a Master's degree at Penn in the following year. Despite an announcement at the age of 15 that he had decided "to make a general survey of all that was best in the culture of the world," few people anticipated that he would travel so far, accomplish so much, or influence so many by his personality and activities.

Ezra Pound lived most of his life outside the United States and criticized his native land from afar, yet strongly stated his Americanism until the end of his days; he lived in London for eleven years and, except for a few close friends, heartily disliked the English; he spent four years in Paris, yet abandoned France for Italy in two periods, one of twenty years and another of fourteen, separated by an interval of twelve years in the United States in a hospital for the criminally insane. The asylum was St. Elizabeth's Hospital in Washington, D.C., and Pound's crime was broadcasting over Rome radio during World War II from 1941 through 1943 in support of Mussolini and Hitler. The audacity of his tirades on the air did not destroy the prestige he held as a poet, for on the final year of his confinement he was awarded the $1,000 Bollingen Prize by the Library of Congress for his *Pisan Cantos*. The prize was subsequently withdrawn from the Library and assigned to Yale University, an action that was only one of the general manifestations of disapproval for Pound's attitudes and behavior. Yet his monuments remain and may be briefly traced.

During the English period, from 1908 until 1919, Pound with F. S. Flint, Richard Aldington, Hilda Doolittle, and other poets then in London, founded the Imagist Movement, an effort to break the formalism then holding poetry in a traditional mold. This group stressed visual and sensory impressions above intellectual statements as the essence of poetry. The members stressed freer cadences than the iambic meter which had become a straightjacket for the rhythm of verse. Amy Lowell and John Gould Fletcher joined the Imagist program in the United States. That complete freedom could turn poetic rhythm into prose was a risk the movement seemed willing to take. In the opinion of some critics, many of Ezra Pound's famous *Cantos* (1925-1965) may be classified as poetically conversational prose.

While in Paris from 1920 to 1924, Pound was associated with the great Irish innovator, James Joyce, whose masterpieces, in both prose and verse, Pound brought to public notice. The Italian periods, 1924-1945 and 1958-1972, could be described as both triumph and disaster, for during his first residence at Rapallo, a resort town near Genoa, he was enchanted by the sea, admired by the townspeople, and a focal point for admirers throughout the world. In the second period, following the imprisonment in America, illness and disorientation led to separation from his wife, followed by depression and death.

A final tribute to Pound is the encouragement he gave to younger poets, illustrated by communication with editors of little magazines, both American and European. In the spring of 1930, he contributed a letter to *Morada*, No. 3, published by Norman Macleod, a young poet who was an instructor in English at the University of New Mexico in Albuquerque. The letter replied to an inquiry as to the meaning and use of the word "proletariat." Pound stated that the word originally applied to that part of the population engaged solely in reproducing the human species, but historically it was once limited to the poorest and lowest class in a community or state. However, said Pound, when any individual or group assumed a political role outside its status in a social organism, it ceased to be proletariat but became a reservoir of "undifferentiated energy, without self consciousness and without power of self-direction." He added that, whether in New Mexico or elsewhere, a handful of cliches (abstract ideas) and "notable principles" were no more useful than the results they achieved and no "revolutionary party" would reform "*anything*" until they at least learned what they were setting out to reform. Among the other contributors to *Morada*, No. 3, were George St. Clair, chairman, Department of English, the University of New Mexico, and B. A. Botkin, a distinguished folklorist at the University of Oklahoma.

The reference in *Letter 99* to Nicholas Murray Butler (1862-1947), eminent American educator, president of Columbia University, and also president of the Carnegie Endowment for International Peace, does not render justice to a man who shared the Nobel Peace Prize in 1931 with Jane Addams (1860-1935), the social worker and founder of Hull House in Chicago. Butler, because of his prestige as an educator and statesman, was given to oracular pronouncements, one of which provoked Mary Austin to send a short article to the *Saturday Review of Literature*. Her communication was published on December 21, 1929, and was entitled "On Discovering Greatness." She reports that Bliss Perry, of Harvard University, in a previous issue of the *Saturday Review*, had quoted Butler's statement "that there is today in the world no great poet, no great philosopher, and no great religious leader." As editor of the *Atlantic Monthly*, Perry had published instalments of Austin's *The Land of Little Rain*, but when he agreed with Butler's pronouncement, he led Mary Austin to write that in the course of history such a philosopher as Socrates, such a playwright as Shakespeare, or such a religious leader as Jesus was not recognized as great in his time. She added that schools and colleges usually viewed figures of the past with more respect than those of the present, and seemed to draw up criteria of greatness for dead leaders but were unable to gauge such qualities in living men and women.

Austin offered her opinion that there were great philosophers and great religious teachers at that time who had not been discovered. Furthermore, she named Robinson Jeffers as one poet who should be recognized by the criteria of greatness. When Pound in his letter alludes to "the deadness of the universities," he openly makes the same point as Austin did, whatever his unexpressed opinion may have been about Jeffers as a great poet.

_____ **99**

RAPALLO

VIA MARSALA, 12 INT. 5

13 April 1930

My Dear Mary Austin

I note with pleasure that you have been taking a shot at Nic. M. Butler's pompous facade.

Do you think it wd. be possible for someone like yourself, who has the ear of the public to indicate that there is in America "no college president of any intellectual preeminence," no person in high academic position using that position to stimulate the intellectual life of the country, and that Dr. Butler as head of the Carnegie Peace Foundation has steadily neglected the opportunity of getting that foundation to do any effective work. It is especially noticeable that their research NEVER by any chance focused on the CAUSES of war. Some of these causes are known, I mean in a general way, but exposure of the mechanism in detail wd. be of more use than a study of the "effects of war." (vide their yearly reports).

There are two parts of this indictment. A. the deadness of the universities re/ a mental life.

B. The particular neglect of opportunity in the endowment of which Dr. B. is the figurehead.

Obviously many other big endowments are equally otiose.

yours very truly

Ezra Pound★

★Printed with the permission of New Directions Publishing Corporation, Agent for the Committee for Ezra Pound.

A photograph of Diego Rivera (1885-1957) standing before a mural appears in Mary Austin's *Earth Horizon*. The mural is one of sixteen panels he painted for the Palace of Cortez in Cuernavaca, Mexico. These panels deal with the history of that region, beginning with the conquest by Cortez, the seizure of Cuernavaca, the building of sugar refineries, and the revolt of the peasants, which was led by the Mexican leader Zapata. The panels portray the dictatorial church, the tyranny of the landowners, and the downtrodden peasants who are led to resistance by a brave priest named Miguel Hidalgo, founder of the Republic of Mexico. Standing to the right of Rivera in the photograph is Mary Austin, who had gone to Mexico in July of 1930 to participate in a conference on cultural relations. She reports that she watched Rivera as he painted, describing his attitude while painting as one of "quiet fury" as he used his brush "with justice and understanding." Her statement stresses the charm of this man, but it minimizes the message as Rivera's panels condemn the social structure of capitalism and preach the gospel of communism. His murals were to carry the gospel of communism into the United States two years later as the *Telegram 112* and the *Letters 113* and *114* will show. Mary Austin pays tribute to the Indian blood in Rivera's family heritage.

Letter 100 indicates that Austin met Rivera when she attended this Conference on Cultural Relations held in Mexico City from July 14 to July 31, 1930. The address she gave at the opening of the conference explained the difference between what she called "genuine" and "sophisticated" art. An interview with Austin was reported in translation by the leading newspaper *Excelsior* on July 31, 1930. Her return to Santa Fe was announced by the *New Mexican* on August 1, 1930.

Diego Rivera and his wife Frida were in Detroit early in 1932 when he created murals for the open court of the Institute of the Arts. When completed, the murals filled the entire wall space with twenty-seven panels which displayed machinery in motion, laborers at work, and an automobile assembly plant. But there were also scenes of the geology in the Detroit area, the lake and river location, the wavelike motion in currents of water, electricity, and the continuous development of life. Photographs of these and other murals by Rivera are reproduced in his *Portrait of America* which has an explanatory text by Bertram D. Wolfe (1934). In March of the following year, the Riveras moved from Detroit to New York City where Diego was under contract to decorate a first floor area of Radio City Music Hall in the new R.C.A. Building in Rockefeller Center. This activity will be further discussed in the introduction to the Andrew Dasburg *Telegram 112*, and *Letters 113* and *114*. Despite the cordiality expressed by Rivera in *Letter 100*, there is no evidence that he made a visit to Santa Fe while he was in the United States in 1931 and 1932. Considering the amount of painting he had contracted for in Detroit and New York City, the omission of a trip to Santa Fe is easily understood.

_____ 100

Avenida Londres, 127
Coyoacan, D. F.
October 5, 1930

Dear Mrs. Austin:

It gave me pleasure to receive your letter, and I thank you for having spoken of me to your publishers. It may be that before very long I shall have something to offer them.

I want to express to you again the pleasure in having met you, and I regret that we had so little opportunity for conversation. I hope, however, to be able to visit Santa Fe during my visit in the United States, when I may see you and other friends in Santa Fe.

With cordial greetings from Mrs. Rivera and myself, I am

Very sincerely yours,

Diego Rivera

Mrs. Mary Austin
Santa Fe,
New Mexico

Walter Stanley Campbell (1887-1958) was more widely known as "Stanley Vestal," the name by which he wrote more than twenty books and edited several others. He was the son of Walter Mallory Vestal and Isabella Louise (Wood) Vestal, who moved to the Kansas village of Severy not long before Stanley was born. His father died when the boy was very young, and his mother became a teacher, a profession she followed during most of her life. She remarried, choosing an educator, J. L. Campbell, as Stanley's stepfather. In 1901, J. L. Campbell became the first president of the Southwestern State Normal School at Weatherford, now Southwestern Oklahoma State University. With this academic background, Walter Stanley Campbell won the first Rhodes Scholarship from the state of Oklahoma. After spending four years at Oxford, he earned both the B.A. and the M.A. degrees with Honors in English Language and Literature. Campbell's first professional teaching was in the Male High School at Louisville, Kentucky, from 1911 to 1914. He then became an instructor in English at the University of Oklahoma in 1915, and was promoted through academic ranks to professor and director of professional writing courses in 1939. Eight years later his title became Research Professor at the University, a position he held for many years.

The surprising element in W. S. Campbell's career is that his outlook swept from English language and literature to Western American life and personalities. The families of his father and mother had been from Massachusetts and Virginia. However, his education before going to Oxford had been in Fredonia, Kansas, and in two Oklahoma communities, Guthrie and Weatherford. During this Western boyhood, he became interested in Western history. His stepfather was a reader of the California historian and publisher Hubert Howe Bancroft (1832-1918), whose research in Pacific Coast records was encyclopedic. When Campbell began to write, his mother suggested that he publish under his own name, Stanley Vestal. He adopted her proposal. Vestal's first publication appeared in 1924 when he edited John Homer Seger's *Early Days Among the Cheyenne and Arapaho Indians.* Vestal's better known works are *Kit Carson, The Happy Warrior of the Old West* (1928), *Sitting Bull, Champion of the Old Sioux* (1932), and *Jim Bridger, Mountain Man* (1946).

Campbell was an outdoor man, traveling on horseback and camping over most of the Plains and Rocky Mountain States. During the 1930s, he taught for a number of summer sessions at New Mexico Normal University in Las Vegas, which later became New Mexico Highlands University. On July 7, 1934, he presided over a Round Table on various phases of poetry writing. Participating in the discussion were John Gould Fletcher of Little Rock, Arkansas, Peggy Pond Church of Otowi, and Haniel Long and Alice Corbin Henderson of Santa Fe. At a later hour, Campbell spoke on epic treatments of the West. With his wife, Isabel Jones Campbell, and two daughters, the Campbells made their summer home in Santa Fe for a number of years.

_____ **101**

THE UNIVERSITY OF OKLAHOMA
NORMAN, OKLAHOMA

c/AMERICAN EXPRESS CO.
NICE FRANCE
October 9, 1930

Miss Mary Austin,
Santa Fe, New Mexico.
U.S.A.

Dear Miss Austin:

I wish to thank you most heartily for your great kindness in helping me out with the symbolism of the necklace. It will help me a lot.

We are settled finally in Nice, in large sunny rooms looking out across some gravel, palms, and olives to the blue sea. I find conditions for work very good indeed, and labor most of the day regularly. We have much such an even climate as you do.

Though no Franco-phile, I am enjoying a taste for Burgundy snails and wine which had been interrupted for twenty years. I am afraid the shades of Sitting Bull might be offended to think his life was being written under such circumstances. He was such a strict teetotaller himself.

My regards to the Nordfeldts and any other friends in Santa Fe.

Yours very cordially,
Stanley Vestal

Arthur Davison Ficke (1883-1945), a lyric poet of distinction, visited in Santa Fe after his friend Witter Bynner moved there in 1921. Ficke was two years younger than Bynner. They had become friends at Harvard, where Ficke graduated in 1904, one year before Bynner finished there. The two men had similar interests in art and literature. Ficke made a specialty of Japanese prints, and Bynner gave his special attention to Chinese poetry and painting. Late in 1916, they traveled together in both Japan and China comparing the two major cultural traditions. Each of them served a brief period teaching college English, Ficke in 1906 and 1907 at the State University of Iowa, and Bynner at the Berkeley campus of the University of California, 1918-1919. Ficke then adopted his father's profession and practiced law. He volunteered for the American Army and rose to the rank of lieutenant colonel during World War I. At the conclusion of army service, he gave up his legal practice and became a writer.

Ficke once observed that he became better known for a prank he played in writing poetry than he did for his serious efforts. Witter Bynner came to Ficke's hometown, Davenport, Iowa, early in 1916, and between them they concocted a make-believe school of poetry called "Spectrism" (see introduction to Bynner's *Letter 97*). A number of famous poets and critics were deceived as were the editors of some poetry magazines. Ficke commented that he feared he would never live down his reputation as a clever fraud. Nevertheless, he wrote twelve books of serious verse and was invited on two different occasions to give the annual Phi Beta Kappa poem at his Alma Mater.

In the Preface to his *Selected Poems* (1926), he defined poetry as

those rare moments for a poet when, for good or evil, the consciousness of life sweeps through him like a flame . . . the moments when he becomes passionately aware of the crises of his spirit's secret drama, and sees a pattern taking shape in the void, and words of utterance come singing to his lips.

Ficke was twice married, first in 1907, to Evelyn Bethune Blunt, who bore him a son; the marriage was later dissolved. In 1923, he married Gladys Brown, a painter, who illustrated several of his books. Arthur and Gladys Ficke were photographed with a group of friends in Santa Fe standing before a windowed wall, which may be on the terrace at the side of Mary Austin's house.

Between 1927 and 1934, Ficke sent fifteen letters to Austin, the first addressed to her in May of 1927 from 922 Canyon Road. Others are from Hillsdale in New York state, and the last three in 1933 and 1934 from a Post Office box in Sarasota, Florida. Ficke's letters are the most frank, affectionate, and occasionally dissenting letters in Mary Austin's entire correspondence. In one he praises the poems he has read in *The Children Sing in the Far West* (1928); in another he wishes he could sit down "in the shade of an old apple tree" and discuss her autobiography; a third expresses disappointment with Bynner's play *Cake* and hopes Bynner will never do another like it; and a later letter gives Edna St. Vincent Millay's address as Austerlitz, New York.

Letter 102 is no exception in tone and free expression to the entire group. Austin answered *Letter 102* on March 27, 1930, insisting that she recognized no obligation to present "vast documentation" for her thesis as Ficke requested and that "nobody undertakes" to prove everything. She adds that "being a Harvard man" his classic background probably made him less susceptible to native rhythms and folk materials present in the United States than she herself was. She urges Ficke to hurry out to Santa Fe so that they might be able to "engage with all our forces."

———— 102

ARTHUR DAVISON FICKE
HARDHACK
HILLSDALE, NEW YORK

March 11, 1930

Dear Mary—

Many years ago I found the time had come to explain to my infant son "where babies came from," etc. I did as good a job as I could; and when I was through, I said—"Are there any questions you want to ask me?" "No, Father." "Do you think you have understood what I've tried to explain to you?" "Yes," he replied with perfect calmness and good-temper, "but I don't believe a word of it."

I fear that I am in much the same position as poor Stan, when it comes to your "American Rhythm" which you kindly sent me. I simply "do not believe a word of it." I do not believe that, during the brief period of the occupation of this continent by men of European descent and civilization, the natural forces of the land have influenced their rhythm much more than the stars have. Further, I believe that the rhythm of New Mexico is utterly different from the rhythm of the Berkshires; and there is no one American rhythm in nature but dozens of them. Lastly, I believe that, if nature affects civilized man to anything like the extent you believe, their similar climates will produce similar poetic rhythms all over the world quite irrespective of mere nationality.

Only this much of your thesis seems to me possibly valid:—I will possibly grant that *perhaps*, if white men exterminated the Indians, and lived in New Mexico *as the Indians live*, and completely discarded their own culture,—then perhaps they would develop a "New Mexico Rhythm." But it would be wholly different from the rhythm which their brothers in upper New York State would by that time have developed. Thinking this, as I do, I am absolutely stumped by your calm assumption of the *existence* of a general "American rhythm"—a thing the existence of which you nowhere demonstrate. You do not in the least "bawl me out of court" when you tell me of the "crass and inexcusable ignorance among our intellectuals of these things": I merely reply that your main obligation in the book was to demonstrate to the intellectuals the *existence* of an American rhythm so clearly that all thinking men could follow you,—by means of vast documentation, specific reference and detailed analysis. But you do not deign to do this.

Indeed, even the feeble case you make out for the existence of an American rhythm that is specifically national is sadly damaged when, on page 32, you grant a probable relation between "the rhythms of all deep forested river bottom lands." Does not this take the ground right out from under you?

You do not deal seriously with any one of the three doubts which I have raised in my second paragraph. All these three things would take a great deal of proving: it is hardly fair of you to state them on the sole authority of your own feeling, and expect me, the reader, to take your word. Furthermore, you do not give me, the reader, a very good impression of your credibility as a witness, in other matters: I, the reader, do not doubt your honesty; but I note that you state as facts wholly incredible things *which are susceptible of clear proof by you if true, but which you do not prove.* I refer to your statement that you can see as far into the future as into the past, and that "Time is a dimension accessible from more than one direction." Were this true, I feel confident that you would realize that it was morally necessary that you furnish the world with evidence of it, under such carefully safeguarded test-conditions as would amount to mathematical proof: you would realize that no other work ever done by any human being would surpass in importance the work you would then be doing. Since you do not make this demonstration, I have a right to assume that you cannot make it—just as you would have a right to doubt my statement if I were to tell you that I can, if I care to, write the greatest epic that has ever been written. Now, to go back.—Since in this most vital matter of the nature of Time you have given mistaken testimony, therefore I do not feel like taking your word for the subtle and difficult matters involved in your thesis about rhythm. And I take my stand on the position that, if these things are true, it is your business to put the evidence before me, and not merely to reproach me for not discovering this alleged evidence for myself.

The part of your book which deals with the subject of Amerind verse seems to me interesting and valuable, and many of your poems are admirable. It is only your vast general assumption, expressed in your title, that I object to—with as much ferocity as literary good-manners permits!

As ever yours
Arthur Davison Ficke

Dear Mary—if you want to print this somewhere, and slay me in your reply to my objections, you have my permission. I have not hesitated to write perfectly frankly, for I know that all honest literary controversy interests you.

A. D. F.

The "Americanizing" of Louis Adamic (1899-1951) began when he arrived as an immigrant in New York City in 1913. He was 14 years of age, and had received the equivalent of a high school education at Lublyana, the cultural center and capital of Slovenia in northeastern Yugoslavia. Adamic's parents lived in the village of Blato where he had known the peasant life described in his biographical volume entitled *The Native's Return* (1934). His fanciful novel *Cradle of Life* (1936) dramatizes this background. Adamic worked as a day laborer during the early years of his life in the United States. Reading books about immigrants, and "land of promise," and "the Melting Pot" stirred Adamic to tell his own story. In 1928, when H. L. Mencken accepted two sketches for the *American Mercury*, Adamic began to present the problems of newcomers in the United States, and to analyze them for human interest, history, and sociology.

The books written by Louis Adamic were widely read and, like the works of Upton Sinclair, were viewed as social commentary whether in fictional or factual style. Almost everything Adamic wrote expresses his concern for America. In *The Native's Return*, he states that after nineteen years in America he has become almost fanatically interested in the American scene as he studies the forces operating in his adopted land, the tendencies and personalities of influence in social, economic, and political spheres. One of the influential people he met was Mary Austin, to whom he wrote twenty-one letters between March 27, 1930, and January 19, 1934. *Letter 103* was third in the series. The fifth letter praised descriptive passages in her novel *Starry Adventure.* His letter on November 23, 1932, was written from Dubrovnik, Yugoslavia. He called *Earth Horizon* "a great and beautiful book." The final letter told her that he was sending a copy of *The Native's Return*, which had been selected by the Book of the Month Club as the choice for February 1934. He expressed the hope that he and his wife might visit Santa Fe when they toured the country in the next two years. Austin died in August of the year this letter was written.

Adamic's tribute to Austin in *My America* was heartfelt. He wrote of meeting her on one of her semiannual visits to New York in the 1930s; of helping her to verify data in the New York Public Library when she was writing her autobiography; and of the comments she made about biographical writing in general. He stated that he felt affection and great respect for Mary, calling her a tragic and heroic woman, who became one of the most interesting American woman writers and a force in the awakening culture of the West. Adamic married Stella Sanders, a New York woman whom he met in Los Angeles. They corresponded after she returned to New York and graduated from college. He accords his marriage twenty-three lines in *My America*, and concedes that the chapter is inadequate but the best that he could do. He solves what seems to be a mystery by adding two lines which are: "There is a censor within me. There is another too near me to be disregarded."

Louis Adamic was a member of the Authors League of America, the Civil Liberties Union, the Foreign Policy Association, the American Committee for the Protection of Foreign Born, the Indian League of America, and several Slavic organizations. He was honored by Marshal Tito of Yugoslavia with the Order of National Unity. Adamic's death was reported from Flemington, New Jersey, September 9, 1951, under circumstances that indicated suicide. However, the Associated Press despatch referred to him as a Titoist, and stated that police investigators looked for fingerprints on a .22 caliber rifle, an ax, and several oil cans in the gutted farm house at Milford.

_____ 103

1189 Sheridan Ave., New York
January 10, 1931

Dear Mrs. Austin:

I felt that I couldn't do the Knopf article. I really know so little of Indian affairs, and Mr. Smith, the publicity man, told me that material they would give me was very scanty. And, on second thought, I wouldn't want to pose as an authority on a subject on a basis of second-hand information.

If my personal affairs take a turn for the better, I hope to spend a few months later this year in New Mexico. I suppose you saw Carey McWilliams' chapbook, "The New Regionalism." I like it, especially the last four or five pages.

I'll be happy to see you when you come to New York in February. I hope you can let me know a little ahead of time when you come—unless you intend to stay here several weeks—, as I plan to go to the coal regions of Pennsylvania for a few days to do an article for Harper's on the situation there. A month ago I went to New England and wrote an article on the terrible situation in such towns as Lowell, Lawrence, New Bedford, Fall River, Manchester, etc. This economic depression is upsetting me terribly. It really is fierce out here in the East.

Faithfully yours,
Louis Adamic

Of fifteen books written by Carey McWilliams (1905-   ), six deal with the problems of ethnic and minority groups in the United States. Two of the titles discuss the needs of migratory farm laborers; two other books treat of racial intolerance, and one is an exposé of heresy hunting. If to these publications are added biographies of the social critic Ambrose Bierce and that champion of the immigrants, Louis Adamic, only three volumes remain to present non-controversial themes, and two of these are profiles of California, his home for nearly twenty years. The remaining book is a small essay called *The New Regionalism in American Literature* (1930) which defends little magazines, folklore societies, and regional writers of short stories and novels.

Arizona, New Mexico, Oklahoma, Texas, Iowa, Oregon, Montana, and some of the Southern states were centers for regional writing. McWilliams names magazines and writers that championed local color fiction and local viewpoints for poetry, narratives, and criticism. He summarizes the creed of the regionalists as a romantic view of the past, a glamorous estimate of primitive living, and a preference for rustic and agrarian society. In addition, the regionalists blamed unrest and poverty on the congestion and complexity of industrial and urban settlement. The output of these writers added variety and stimulus to the period between 1920 and 1940. Many small presses were supportedby the regional movement, which also led to the increased number of university presses and encouraged local historical, political, and biographical writing.

In the biography *Louis Adamic and Shadow America* (1935), McWilliams shows how the young Yugoslavian writer began to appraise his adopted land soon after he arrived in it. The two young men became acquainted just after McWilliams graduated from the University of Southern California in 1927 and Adamic was clerk to the pilot of the port of Los Angeles. The two men shared a concern for the "losers" in the social set-up of America. They numbered as friends-in-common, the Robinson Jeffers, the George Sterlings, Upton Sinclair, H. L. Mencken, and Mary Austin.

Letter 104 is one of sixty-six communications sent by McWilliams to Austin between April 25, 1927, and October 3, 1931, covering topics of mutual interest with the underlying theme of social betterment. The article referred to in the first paragraph, was entitled "The Feel of the Purposeful Earth, Mary Austin's Prophecy." The author, Henry Smith, was then a professor of English at Southern Methodist University. He also served as editor of the *Southwest Review*, published at that university in Dallas. This issue of the *New Mexico Quarterly* was Volume I, No. 1. The magazine came from the University of New Mexico Press beginning February 1931, and continuing through Volume XXXVIII, No. 4, Winter-Spring 1969. Smith pays eloquent tribute to Mary Austin's achevement in a series of novels and her naturist books. He writes that she contributed to an understanding of American society in her time through interpreting inherited traditions and the role of women in her writing and the belief expressed that "nature" was not merely an escape from society but a guide to its physical and spiritual future.

The "McLeod" mentioned in paragraph four refers to LeRoy McLeod, who was born on a farm at Anderson, Indiana, in 1893. After finishing college at DePauw University in 1915, he became active in local politics, but in 1921 worked as a journalist in Colorado and California, and from 1922 until 1930, wrote advertising in Los Angeles as an associate in the firm of Waters and McLeod. His literary career began when he left this agency. McLeod was the author of a collection of poems entitled *Driven* (1929), which was published in both England and America. He later wrote two novels, the earliest of which, *Three Steeples* (1931), may have been the book which met with the approval of Mary Austin as stated in *Letter 104*.

After practicing law in Los Angeles from 1927 through 1938, Carey Mc-Williams moved to New York City as contributing editor to *The Nation*, becoming successively associate editor, editorial director, and editor after 1955. His contribution to American thought has been consistently what he stated in *Letter 104*: "a study of American liberalism."

———— 104

CAREY McWILLIAMS
900 Spring Arcade Building
Los Angeles, California

October 3rd, 1931

Dear Mrs. Austin:

I glanced at a most interesting article about your work by Henry Smith in the New Mexico Quarterly at the library last night but did not get a chance to read it. I am writing for a copy.

You are quite right in thinking that my law work will interfere with what writing I do. The clash between the two is becoming very difficult to manage. I fear that I shall soon write like a lawyer and argue like a writer. I'm thinking about giving up my practice, but you know how difficult these things are, particularly when one needs an income.

I'm outlining a book now which, if I can get a contract from a reliable publisher, may be a way out. It is a study of American Liberalism or, more properly, "The American Liberal," a sort of composite case history. I think the typical American liberal rather feeble and propose to find out why this is so,—having, of course, some notions on the subject in advance.

Awfully glad that you liked McLeod's novel.

We spent last week end in Santa Barbara with Edmund Wilson and his wife. He mentioned having called on you while in Santa Fe.

I had read the poem in the Sat. R. before your letter arrived and had meant to write you about it. I liked it, in fact, like all of your verse that I have read. Believe I have written you about some of the individual poems that I liked particularly. One "I Have Known Poets" that appeared a year or so ago was excellent.

With best wishes,

Carey McWilliams

I'm reviewing "Outpost of Empire" by Herbert Bolton for the N. Y. Evening Post, Have you read it? I liked it immensely.

Frederick Webb Hodge (1864-1956) was one of Mary Austin's closest friends. Their acquaintance began in 1899 when she went to teach at the Normal School in Los Angeles. By this time Hodge had established himself as an archeologist in the Bureau of American Ethnology, a branch of the Smithsonian Institution in Washington, D.C. Two years earlier, he had climbed the Enchanted Mesa in New Mexico, a flat tableland thought by the Indians to be the home of the rain gods and other spirits that brought well-being or the opposite to earth people who failed to honor them. In the next decade, Hodge completed research for his *Handbook of American Indians North of Mexico* in two volumes (1907, 1910). He became ethnologist in charge of the Bureau from 1910 until 1918. In that final year he accepted a similar appointment with the Museum of the American Indian, established by the Heye Foundation of New York City. Much of his research at the Zuni Pueblo in New Mexico, between 1896 and 1910, had been published by the Heye Foundation.

In her autobiography, Austin reports that Hodge, whom she calls "the Indian specialist," taught her "the thing she most wanted to know, the way of collecting and recording Indian affairs." "Let be," he said, "the strange and unusual; fix on the usual, the thing that is always done, the way of the tribe; the way of the average; the way and the why of it." Her friendship with Hodge was largely responsible for the welcome she received from officials in the School of American Research when she visited Santa Fe for the first time in 1918. Thirty-four letters from Hodge are in the Mary Austin Collection and the first of them, on September 30, 1928, is written on the stationery of the school. In this letter, Hodge tells her how to find the Zuni pueblo where he had a field camp. The correspondence then skips fourteen years before *Letter 105*, which was written in the year after he left the Museum of the American Indian in order to become director of the Southwest Museum in Los Angeles, a position he held until retirement in 1955.

With the guidance of Hodge and through his contacts, the Southwest Museum became a center for outstanding collections of artifacts and handcrafts representative of Southwestern Indians. He also helped to build an extensive library for research in Western Americana. His personal contribution to this archive included scores of publications ranging from archeology to history and biography. One of his biographies is that devoted to Adolph Francis Alphonse Bandelier, a Swiss anthropologist, and novelist as well, author of *The Delight Makers* (1890) and *The Gilded Man* (1893), fiction based upon archeological and historical backgrounds. Hodge edited and annotated the journals of seventeenth-century Spanish American explorers; held advisory posts for museums and learned societies; and was awarded honorary degrees by Pomona College, the University of New Mexico, and the University of Southern California. After retirement, he lived in Santa Fe where he enjoyed his gardening and the association with long-time friends and fellow scientists. His third wife, Gene Patricia Meany (1898-   ), whom he married in 1936, is the author of books on Indian ceremonials and religious handcraft. Hodge wrote the Foreword for her book *The Kachinas Are Coming* (1936, 1967), which is illustrated with colored reproductions of eagles, corn, snow, and other forms of nature found in Indian legends and ceremonies.

_____ 105

THE SOUTHWEST MUSEUM
Los Angeles, California
Office of the Director

April 4, 1932

Mrs. Mary Austin
Santa Fe, New Mexico

Dear Mary Austin:

It is good to hear from you and to know that should you come this way, which would delight us beyond measure, you will stay with us. You may do as you please—lock yourself up in peace and quiet, or pick flowers in the garden, or go motoring, just as the spirit moves you. Should the lecture engagement, or any thing else, bring you to Los Angeles, you will let us know a little in advance, I am sure, so that we shall be able to meet you.

It is like you to place your treasures where they will do the most good and where they will be preserved for all time. Of course I refer to the San Fernando basket given you years ago by General Edward F. Beale, and the goatskin water bottle which you obtained from one of the sheepherders on the Tejo Ranch. I hope, however, in view of your present intention to give them to the Southwest Museum when you have done with them, that it will be a very long time ere we receive them.

We are very happy here. The Museum is prospering as well as can be expected under present conditions everywhere; that is, we do not have very much money, but there is the finest spirit you ever saw, and that means everything.

We sincerely hope that you have recovered your strength entirely and are now able to buckle down to work with your usual vigor.

Cordially yours,
F. W. Hodge

FWH:BPT

———————— **106**

THE SOUTHWEST MUSEUM
Los Angeles, California
Office of the Director

June 23, 1934

Mrs. Mary Austin
Camino del Monte Sol
Santa Fe, New Mexico

Dear Mary:

As I mentioned to you last Tuesday, I am enclosing the deed of gift, in duplicate, of the camel bell and the San Fernando basket.* Will you kindly sign both on the line indicated, and return them to me in the enclosed stamped envelope?

I had a comfortable trip back, as the desert was pretty well covered with fog, tempering the heat to weary travelers. I do not need to tell you again what a beautiful time I had in Santa Fe and how happy I am at having been able to snatch a few words with you. But you must regain your strength very soon, for you still have much to do for us.

With every good wish, and again our appreciation of your goodness in giving us the specimens, which will forever be kept and cared for, believe me, as ever,

Affectionately yours,
F. W. Hodge
F. W. Hodge
Director

FWH:T

*Also the little dipper

———————————————————————————

When *Earth Horizon* was published, there were different versions in the first printings which told of Mary's meeting with H. G. Wells and the conversation that occurred between them at tea on a Sunday afternoon at the Wells home. The trip in 1907 was Austin's first visit to Europe, and when she arrived in England in mid-December she called upon the Herbert Hoovers and afterward went to meet Mr. and Mrs. Wells. Mary had with her a copy of her new book of short stories, which she entitled *Lost Borders*. She presented a copy of the book to H. G. Wells, and she states in the earliest printing of her autobiography that he read the story called "The Walking Woman." Then she reports that he said to her, "I have just advised my wife that a friend of mine is about to have a child by me." He added that his wife replied, "Well, we must be kind to her." In *Lost Borders*, the Walking Woman wanders the mountain stretches of sheep pastures, lives with a herder for a time, and bears him a child, stressing the essentials of work, loving, and having a child. She fulfills a stark and ultimate destiny by walking away from society and its values. Whatever connection the story had with Wells, the English novelist protested to the publishers that he could not have made the statement because at that time the event described had not occurred nor even been foreseen. Wells insisted upon a reprinting of the pages. Mary Austin, therefore, rewrote the two pages and said that her conversation with Wells was about a recent novel he had written which, though unnamed, she said had shocked the conventional morality of England and alienated many of the author's friends and admirers.

In order to fill in space that had previously been used, Austin described a dinner party given by the Hoovers at which she found the conversation rather boring because the guests were chiefly mining and engineering people. She explained that the Hoovers had few acquaintances among the literary folk of London. By her changes, Austin pacified the irritation of Wells but disparaged the hospitality of the Hoovers. She also presented the public with two passages in a first edition which should make either volume authentic but one less valued than the gossipy first one printed. Wells called the rewritten version acceptably bland.

The introduction to *Letter 45*, written fifteen years earlier than *Letter 107*, makes clear the admiration Mary Austin at first felt for H. G. Wells. In *The World Set Free* (1914), written under the pseudonym of Reginald Bliss, he also paid tribute to her as one of the most intellectual women in England and America. He wrote that her work would live "when many of the more portentous reputations of today may have served their purpose and become no more than fading names." However, Mary Austin was a feminist before all else, and when she made her second trip to London in the summer of 1921, she saw Wells only once. He had just finished his *Outline of History*; to her he seemed to have lost some of his flair. He complained of the work he had been doing and wished for an American secretary. On page 343 of all the printings of *Earth Horizon*, she quotes him as saying: "You really have them, but here, if I get a young man he climbs on me, and a young woman insists on being seduced." Austin wrote that "she felt like suggesting that if he had a different approach to young women, it might turn out better, but refrained from saying it." Wells did not insist upon having this quotation removed, but commented that it would have been stupid for him to make such a statement since it would cast a slur on anyone he afterward employed as a secretary.

Letter 107 is a masterful defense and apology for the strain in their relationship. The second paragraph of the letter is an implied rebuke to an author who had been a stern critic of society but who would not accept criticism of himself in return. Wells wrote seventy-five books that explore almost every facet of human thought and behavior. Mary Austin used what weapons she could find to meet him on his own terms.

_____ 107

November 4, 1932

My dear Mr. Wells:

I am greatly relieved to receive your cable, expressing satisfaction with my suggested alterations in the text of EARTH HORIZON. I have been quite ill with distress about it. I wish that you could realize that to me your frankness seemed only what was to be expected from a man of your calibre, and extraordinarily refreshing to one brought up in the hypocrisies of middle-class life. As I said in the cablegram, it gave me a happy sense of having found someone at last to whom the actualities of conduct were more important than opinions about it, so that it really came to me as a great shock to find that you were offended by it. If there had been so much as a suspicion on my part that you would take offense, I would have referred the matter to you, but actually, our whole American attitude has so changed on these things that if you have been reading American biographies, you will realize that they are making admissions about themselves and saying things about each other, compared to which my comment on you is inconsiderable.

Also, I think it possible you do not realize that you have been a sort of pace-maker to pre-thinking Americans, and that many incidents in your life are perfectly well known to the American public, so that I should greatly have regretted having to call attention to the fact that you objected to plain speaking about it, and that what was so simply and directly told me, without any suggestion of secrecy or over-straining of confidence could be the cause of offense to you. I trust that you will accept my humble apologies and that there need be no diminution of that great respect in which I have always held you.

I enclose a copy of the alterations which I am making in the text in confidence that they will be entirely satisfactory to you. I thought it best not to depart too absolutely from the original text, as I am anxious to avoid any newspaper publicity which could fix attention on the excised copy. So far, you will be glad to hear, not a single reviewer has paid the slightest attention to it.

Sincerely yours,
Mary Austin

H. G. Wells, Esq.
Chiltern Court
Baker Street
London, N. W.
England
MS:N.
M.A.

The publishing market between 1920 and 1930 was dominated by expansive surveys of history, philosophy, and religion. Beginning with Hendrik Willem Van Loon's *The Story of Mankind* (1921) and H. G. Wells' *Outline of History* in the same year, readers during the decade looked into Will Durant's *The Story of Philosophy* and Lewis Browne's *This Believing World* in 1926, followed by Oswald Spengler's *The Decline of the West* and L. Adams Beck's *The Story of Oriental Philosophy* in 1928. Van Loon (1882-1944) supplemented *The Story of Mankind* with *The Story of the Bible* (1923) and *America* (1927). All of his works were very successful and in the following decade he prepared *Van Loon's Geography* (1932), *The Arts of Mankind* (1937) and *The Story of the Pacific* (1940). Each of these books was a broad account of mankind's survival and achievement in a sphere of activity or an area of the terrestrial globe. Van Loon, whose final name was pronounced "lone," came to the United States from Rotterdam in 1903. His schooling in Holland had been so adequate that after a year at Harvard and three years at Cornell, he received the A.B. degree at the latter university in 1905. Six years later he studied at Munich and earned his Ph.D. at the university in that city.

At an early age, Van Loon learned to draw. As a result, he was able to illustrate his books, adding greatly to their value as reading and entertainment. A frontispiece for *The Story of Mankind* has the drawing of a fireplace with a broad hood before flames in a grate. Above the drawing is a quotation from Lewis Carroll's *Alice in Wonderland*: "What's the use of a book without pictures?" The complete quotation adds "or conversations?" Van Loon's last books were autobiographies entitled *Van Loon's Lives* (1943) and *Report to St. Peter* (1947).

Six million copies of Van Loon's books are said to have been sold in numerous printings and a variety of translations. In addition to readers, hundreds of people knew him as a lecturer in colleges and as he reported on radio stations for what he calls his "Air University" in *Letter 108*. He used a Boston radio station to broadcast to Holland during World War I, using the nickname "Uncle Hank" for these personalized communiques. Van Loon was a large man with a cheerful personality. His strong physique carried him through difficult service as a correspondent for the Associated Press at Moscow and Warsaw during the Russian Revolution in 1906 and in Belgium at the outbreak of World War I. The strain of such work probably contributed to the heart attack that killed him at the age of 62.

Four letters and four Christmas cards were sent to Austin by Van Loon between February 2, 1922, and the Christmas of 1932. The cards were his own drawings. The picture in 1923 showed an old man with a stove-pipe hat who is riding a wooden horse numbered "1923." In one hand the man holds a tattered banner labeled "1922." The card for 1932 portrays a clergyman with a large nose which holds spectacles. He stands before a lighted candle and a radio microphone. Van Loon's letter on May 3, 1925, explained that Mary did not understand his point of view in preparing *The Story of the Bible.* He states that he has "written a little philosophy of life to elucidate the more obscure problems of existence" and will send it to her. On November 18, 1932, Van Loon's letter calls "the present war" more merciless than the last one and signed himself "Yours in humble devotion, Hendrik Willem." A note on March 4, 1924, from Van Loon's wife expresses concern for Mary's illness while "fighting the Bugs on Barrow Street," and urges her to come out in the country and escape the "flu germs." The Van Loons lived in Old Greenwich, Connecticut.

Letter 108 is typed on letterhead paper with an oblong drawing by the author. He has sketched a horizon of mountains, fields, and city towers, with a sky full of books flying open, sideways, and upside down. The caption "University of the Air" is illustrated by the scene displayed. The word "Lodfe" describes a pleasurable way of life.

_____ 108

UNIVERSITY OF THE AIR
"THE MAKING OF TOMORROW"
By HENDRIK WILLEM VAN LOON
33 Washington Square West
Nieuw Amsterdam
2 December xxxii

Dear Mary Austin,

The book arrived together with the flu bugs and I have not read a line since then. Tonight I had to get up to keep the home-fires of my fool Air University burning and now I shall go me back to my couch and wait for the dear little creatures to either increase and multiply or depart for Citizens Unexplored. I am going however to take a week's holiday or rather my idea of a holiday . . . do nothing except what you really want to do . . . no dull dinners . . . no dull people who have advertised you to all their neighbors and who use you to pay a year's hospitality to their Lodfe. And I shall read your book and let the world go to the devil. This is my first effort at a letter since many days. The paper just came in and I thought it might amuse you to have the first or dedicatory page. A serious attempt is being made to turn the radio to some good and serious though entertaining use. The big stations tell me it can not be done and it is being done. Without a cent but with a lot of fresh air at our disposal. And now back to bed for wobbly is the word. It was a great and grand and good thing to see you once more. You are after all the best excuse I have found for America in many years of ardent searching.

Jimmie is taking Noodle for his little walk.
Otherwise she would join me in every sort
of affectionate wish
and since this mimeograph paper
will hold no ink I say it
in printing
Hendrik Willem

When Robinson Jeffers (1887-1962) brought his wife to Carmel in 1914, they had been married for just a year. However, the marriage followed a courtship of nearly eight years. Una Call Kuster, who became Mrs. Jeffers, had just obtained a divorce from her lawyer husband. She had met Jeffers when he entered the Graduate School at the University of Southern California, and she lent Robinson a book about Wordsworth, a book that cemented their mutual interest in literature. However, Jeffers changed his concentration upon literature to research in medicine which was the profession of his father, Dr. William Hamilton Jeffers, who had been a Presbyterian minister in Pittsburgh as well as a practicing physician. John Robinson Jeffers, his second son, was born in that stronghold of Presbyterian orthodoxy, and came to Pasadena, California, in 1903 when his father's health demanded a milder climate. Una Jeffers may have met Mary Austin in 1913 when Mary came to Carmel to direct a performance of her play "Fire," which was to be produced by the Forest Theater Society. At the time this play was staged, the George Sterlings were still at Carmel, Van Wyck Brooks had been a recent visitor, Lincoln Steffens and others of literary and stage fame were frequenters of the scenic peninsula. The earliest of the letters from Jeffers to Austin, written on January 14, 1929, stated that her presence was still felt at Carmel, and that his wife remembered meeting Mary there. He thanked Mary for sending him a copy of her book *The Man Jesus*, newly reissued as *A Small Town Man*, and called it an enlightened and beautiful volume. He informed her that he had just finished "a sort of passion-play" about Christ which he planned to call "Dear Judas," adding that his ideas are "farther than yours from common life, but not in the serene direction."

On December 19, 1932, Una Jeffers wrote *Letter 109* from Carmel, telling Austin that Mabel Luhan had been to the colony for a short visit and was trying to find a house for the coming month. Spud Johnson was driving Mabel's car, and upon their return to Taos the Jeffers hoped to join them in order to see the Deer Dance performed by the Taos Indians on January 6 (see Willard Johnson, *Letters 74* and *75*). Una stated that her husband greatly enjoyed Mary's *Earth Horizon*. They both thought it was the finest book Mary had written. In March, Jeffers himself wrote *Letter 110* in which he acknowledged receipt of an autographed copy of the autobiography and promised to send her a book of his own which would be published in the spring of 1934. He declared that he planned to read much of *Earth Horizon* to the twin sons when they were finished with high school for the summer. An undated communication, sent by Una on La Fonda, Santa Fe, stationery, probably in 1930, expressed regret that her family would miss visiting with Mary *en route* to Taos, but she said that Jeffers planned a trip from Taos to see Mary when it was convenient for her.

Letter 109 was handwritten by Una Jeffers on December 19, 1932. She described a visit to Carmel by Mabel and Tony Luhan accompanied by Dorothy Brett. They took a house at the end of the Point, and Brett painted seascapes there while the Luhans visited with friends. Una Jeffers and Mabel Luhan planned a trip to San Francisco. In their absence, Brett was to take care of Jeffers and the boys. Brett had announced that her book about D. H. Lawrence would soon be in print. This reference was to *Lawrence and Brett, A Friendship* (1933).

Four other letters that Mary Austin kept in her Collection have been printed in *The Selected Letters of Robinson Jeffers, 1897-1962*, edited by Ann M. Ridgeway and published in 1968. The December 20, 1929, letter begins with what seems to be a defense by Jeffers of his emphasis upon sex in such narrative poems as *Tamar* (1924) and *Roan Stallion* (1925). He acknowledges that sex as a motive in literature may not be essential, but adds that in practical terms it is a great help when such other driving emotions as fear and hunger may be lacking. Rather than pursue the discussion, Jeffers concludes that any author must probe his own creative sources in seeking motivation for his characters.

No more dissimilar writers than Mary Austin and Robinson Jeffers have appeared in American literature. Their meeting ground, creatively speaking, has been that both could be called naturists, which means that both were absorbed with the dominant influence imposed upon living creatures by the environment. For Jeffers, the rugged seacoast and forest slopes at Carmel provided a background for harsh human entanglement: incest, rape, murder, and arson in *Tamar*; and drunken sex, death under a horse's hooves, and rifle bullets in *Roan Stallion*. The horror is softened in the first poem by the momentary mood of Christmas, and in the second narrative by the ties of family relationship, but the oversight of vengeful forces and fatal destinies turn the endings to tragedy.

In addition, Jeffers introduces supernatural figures, such as ghosts, demons, angels, and other apparitions that rarely bring influences that are soothing or benign. By contrast, what can be called Mary Austin's naturism is a pervasive association of forces in the physical environment such as the climate, land, water, wind, rains, and sun that encompass all objects and creatures, the inanimate as well as the animate. Desert areas and neighboring semiarid slopes hold her attention. Even the stationary objects in the landscape contribute to concepts of earth rhythms and natural energy. The effect of the total environment upon mankind was more directive than destructive, and the compulsion of sex was always secondary as a personal or social need.

Robinson Jeffers was not only a writer of great power, but he was also prolific as a producer of books. There are more than 100 titles of volumes listed as his achievement. They contain not only the long narrative works, but also many poems of personal observations as indicated by such titles as "Summer Holiday," "To My Father," "Apology for Bad Dreams," and "George Sterling's Death" in which appear the lines:

> And now it is hard to believe he will not return
> To be our guest in the house, nor walk beside me

Again by the Carmel river
Or on the Sovranes reef.

_____ 109

Tor House   Carmel   California
December 19, 1932

Dear Mary Austin: Mabel Luhan has been here for a few days to get track of a house for January. Spud was along driving for her. She asked me to send you these enclosures. She has gone back to Taos. It is just possible that we shall go there for a few days over the time of the deer-dance. I think January 6th. I can't seal this letter without telling you how thoroughly Robin and I enjoyed your "Autobiography." I think we like it better than anything you've written—and the reception it is getting everywhere makes one feel very encouraged about the reading public in general! With warm good wishes for this holiday season and all the year to come.

Cordially,
Una Jeffers.

_____ 110

Tor House   Carmel   California
March 1933

Dear Mary Austin:
    Una and I are devotedly grateful to you for "Earth Horizon" with your inscription. We had read it already, of course, with enjoyment and admiration, but it is much to have it from you, and I shall read much of it to our boys this summer, when their high school work ceases to afflict them. It is a beautiful record of a singularly varied and exciting life.
    I am awfully sorry to hear that you have been having difficulty with your health again. I hoped it was stabilized for a long time to come, and still hope it will be. It would be a disappontment to us to find you absent in Mexico, if we should be in New Mexico again this summer, as

seems quite likely, but I know that you love the country southward, and have valuable interests there.

I expect I'll have a book out this spring, and shall claim the honor of sending you a copy, but not as a return for yours.

Sincerely yours,
Robinson Jeffers

_____ 111

Tor Hourse   Carmel   California

February 15, 1933

Dear Mary: I'm sorry I didn't sit down at once to answer your letter. Robin had me lay it aside for him to do, but his flu set him back so badly that he has had to write many more hours a day than usual with him—and never a letter does he achieve.—

Mabel is here as you know just a few seconds away from us. I wonder do you remember Reamer's house way at the end of the Point? Just beside it now is a big house and garden with a magnificent view. The house isn't interesting, but it is comfortable and has plenty of room. One can look out to sea—up the valley, across the Lagoon and river mouth and of course to Pt. Lobos and the Santa Lucia Mts. I think they are happy there. Tony goes and comes and has friends from Pacific Grove to Watsonville. Brett has done several sea pictures—two of them very good. Her book is in the press now. Have you read any of it in ms? It's interesting and her deafness has shut off so many things that what she has heard—and all of what she has seen is done intensely. Brett means to go on to New York about March 10. Mabel and I have great larks—you know what an amusing companion she is—nothing escapes her eye. She and I are going up to San Francisco tomorrow for three days. Brett is to take care of Tony and Robin and the boys.

There is a possibility that we will come to Taos for June or July. Mabel talks of a trip for us to Blue Lake. We hope to see you if we come. Robin would enjoy seeing some of the country you know so well.

I don't suppose you see the Catholic paper "The Commonweal." A friend sends it to me and weeks ago I cut out this clipping to send you.

We have both read your "Earth Horizon"—I think I told you in my last letter, but cannot resist saying "yes" to your kind offer to send us a copy. We have had to cut down on many things we like to buy, this year and read the library copy. Robin will be happy to respond with his new book which will be published next month.

With affectionate greetings from all the Jeffers.

Cordially,

Una Jeffers.

A chapter in Diego Rivera's *My Art and My Life* (1960), an autobiography prepared with the help of Gladys March, is entitled "Holocaust in Rockefeller Center." Rivera (1885-1957) dictated the notes giving the artist's side for one of the most controversial events in modern art history. Since Rivera had formed an acquaintance with Mary Austin (as described in *Letter 100*), the *Telegram 112* and *Letter 113* are not surprising. Andrew Dasburg, a noted artist living in Taos, New Mexico, urged Austin to assist in organizing a protest by artists and writers to the owners of Radio City in Rockefeller Center in New York City, for rejecting a contract they had signed with Rivera in March of 1933. Hugh Robertson, one of the owners of a construction firm providing equipment for painting at the Center, stated in *Letter 113* that a great many people had written or telegraphed either supporting or disapproving the action taken by John D. Rockefeller, Jr. and Nelson Rockefeller. A pro-artist biographer, Bertram D. Wolfe, in *Diego Rivera, His Life and Times* (1943), states that Robertson delivered the order to abandon the painting and handed the artist the final check which was due to him. Robertson's letter seems somewhat apologetic for the decision which was made.

Letter 113 clearly indicates that Austin's voice had been heard, and that she was regarded as a leader among the forces supporting Rivera. A supplementary letter, also in the Austin Collection, was sent by Merle Crowell on Rockefeller Center, Inc., stationery and dated May 25, 1933. He requested that Austin serve as "liaison officer" for the group signing the telegram, adding that if the protesters were made aware of all the details pertaining to the Rivera incident they would recognize the justice of the move by the Rockefellers. The uproar echoed criticism following the dedication of Rivera's murals painted in 1932 for Detroit's Institute of Fine Arts. He was a confirmed revolutionary, and perhaps the owners of Radio City should have been alerted to the probability that his painting would be subject to debate beyond its merit as art. The Detroit murals stressed contributions of labor to industrial achievement. The subject matter was chiefly the component parts of factory interiors. Initially, viewers called the pictures inartistic and symbols of working class struggle. Finally, however, the paintings won approval from laborers, engineers, and discriminating art critics. Rivera made his scenes inventive in both design and execution. This success led to his commission for the murals in New York's Radio City.

In March of 1933, the artist began to fill more than one thousand square feet of wall in the RCA Building with designs based on the following theme: "Man at the Crossroads Looking with Hope and High Vision to the Choosing of a New and Better Future." Such a theme was so broad that no subject matter was excluded, and preliminary sketches were not examined with due concern. In April, a photograph of one fresco received approval from Nelson Rockefeller. However, a reporter for a New York afternoon newspaper announced that the central figure in the mural facing the main entrance of the building was Nikolai Lenin (1870-1924), founder of the Communist Party in Russia. He was an advocate of dictatorship by the proletariat and the elimination of all other political groups in organized society. Lenin was shown in the center of marching and singing workers; next to him and the workers was a stadium filled with happy girls going through exercises; an opposite scene portrayed a night club occupied by the debauched rich, while unemployed workers outside were being clubbed by the police.

Informed of the political context of this mural, Nelson Rockefeller on May 1 suggested a reasonable adjustment, such as substituting a less recognizable face than that of Lenin, and replacing the carousing rich with the figure of Abraham Lincoln freeing the slaves. When Rivera refused to make any change, his supporters arranged to picket the building. Protests like that in *Telegram 112* were sent from outside New York City. The owners of Radio City ordered the unfinished mural to be covered and further work suspended until the entire project was reconsidered.

_____ 112

WESTERN UNION TELEGRAM

Received at 52 Lincoln Avenue (On the Plaza), Santa Fe, N. Mex.

VG 47 43 DL=TDP   BRYNMAWR PENN 10 133p   1933 May 10 PM 12 05

MARY AUSTIN=SANTAFE=NMEX=

PLEASE ORGANIZE PROTEST OF WRITERS AND PAINTERS

TO MR. JOHN D ROCKEFELLER JR AGAINST POSSIBLE
DESTRUCTION OF DIEGO RIVERAS WORK AT RADIO CITY
AND REQUEST THAT HE BE ALLOWED TO FINISH IT IN
ACCORDANCE WITH MR. ROCKEFELLERS PREVIOUS LIBERAL
ATTITUDE TOWARD MODERN PAINTING

ANDREW W. DASBURG

_____ 113

Miss Mary Austin
Santa Fe
New Mexico.

Dear Madam:
   A great many letters and telegrams relating to the Diego Rivera
mural have been forwarded to the managing agents of Rockefeller Center
from the office of Mr. John D. Rockefeller, Jr., and Mr. Nelson Rockefeller. These communications voice both approval and disapproval of
our action in terminating Mr. Rivera's work. We regret that you feel
our decision was ill-advised.
   Newspaper accounts of the factors behind the decision were necessarily incomplete. To avoid stimulating a scattered and confused discussion we have refrained from amplifying our original statement. We
assure you, however, that in the light of all the existing circumstances
our action seemed to us not only logical but inevitable.

Sincerely,
Hugh Robertson

   According to a report in the *New York World Telegram* for
May 12, 1933, the owners of Radio City had pledged not to destroy or mutilate
Rivera's unfinished fresco. A handwritten note in the Mary Austin Collection is
postmarked May 18, 1933, and, in summary, the brief contents congratulate
Austin on the response she provoked in Rivera's defence. The letter also states
that the situation had been very damaging to the artist, causing the General
Motors Company to cancel the commission given to Rivera for a mural at the
World's Fair in Chicago. The card bears a printed heading "Long House

Bryn Mawr P.O. Pennsylvania," and bears the surname of the owners of Radio City, a signature that has not been acknowledged.

On February 9, 1934, the Rivera mural was destroyed. A well-known Spanish artist, Jose Maria Sert (1876-1945) was invited to paint the frescos at Radio City. Rivera remained in New York long enough to contribute twenty-one murals to the New Workers School on West 14th Street, which were later moved to a building on 33rd Street. He provided paintings of such American historical figures as Thomas Paine, Ralph Waldo Emerson, Henry David Thoreau, and Walt Whitman in a series he called "Portrait of America." He also included a caricature of the financier J. Pierpont Morgan as a symbol of the capitalist society in the country where Rivera was a guest. Upon returning to Mexico City, he painted again the mural begun at Radio City, adding one figure to the group in the night club scene: That was a portrait of John D. Rockefeller, Jr., who had been one of his hosts in the Radio City fiasco.

The novels written by Eugene Manlove Rhodes (1869-1934) gave identity to a landscape between two natural phenomena known as the White Sands and the Rio Grande Valley in New Mexico. Rhodes peopled the mountainous country and neighboring communities with fictitious characters as real as the landscape in which they lived, worked, and managed rodeos, bank robberies, jail breaks, baseball, card playing, fist fights, ballad singing, horse play, and family life. He wrote more than eighty stories which appeared in *Out West*, *McClure's*, *Cosmopolitan*, the *Saturday Evening Post*, and other periodicals, some of them serialized into ten full-length novels. He wrote about what he called "his parish," or the cattle kingdom inhabited by ranchers, cowboys, sheriffs, politicians, homesteaders, and of course, animals.

Rhodes was born on a farm in Tecumseh, a village in southeast Nebraska, where his father had moved after service with the Twenty-Eighty Illinois Volunteers in the Civil War. Prairie cyclones and grasshoppers encouraged a move to Cherokee, Kansas, and Colonel Rhodes opened a store there. When his past military career helped to win appointment as Indian Agent for the Mescalero Apaches in 1881, Gene Rhodes was just 13 years old, but he soon found a job on a ranch near the Indian Reservation in Lincoln County, New Mexico. His education both as a cowboy and future writer about cowboys had begun.

Aside from two years, 1889-1890, spent at the University of the Pacific, then located at San Jose, California, Rhodes was self-taught. An omnivorous reader, he absorbed vast amounts of what he read and allusions by characters in such a novel as *The Desire of the Moth* (1916) to Keats, Shelley, and Shakespeare disabuse the reader as to the literacy of the Sheriff John Wesley Pringle and his intimate associates. These Westerners understand metaphors drawn from the Bible and the writings of Oliver Wendell Holmes and Washington Irving. One of the accounts of early reading by ranch hands in the Gene Rhodes circle was that the tobacco they smoked came in two-ounce sacks with a coupon and four-ounce sacks with two coupons. Four coupons bought any paperback title in Munro's Library of Popular Novels, free and postpaid from New York City. The selections ranged from Charles Dickens to Conan Doyle and included Alexandre Dumas, Jules Verne, Robert Louis Stevenson, and others.

Rhodes married May Louise Davison on August 9, 1899. She lived in New York state and had read some of his early writings, especially poetry. They became acquainted through correspondence. He went east with a shipment of cattle from New Mexico. After the wedding he returned to his ranch where she joined him in June of the following year. They lived near Tularosa, New Mexico, until 1906 when they moved to a farm in his wife's former community of Apalachin. Gene raised chickens, but he continued to write. The Rhodes's were in New York from 1906 until 1926, and during that time he published six of his ten novels, including the famous novelette *Paso por Aquí*, a story which is a forerunner of a type of fiction which forty years later became a model for the anti-hero type of Western fiction. The plot dealt with a red-haired cowboy who robs a bank in a small town and plans to flee to Texas. He eludes capture, but is delayed when he stops at a mountain cabin where a Spanish family is suffering from diphtheria. He helps to feed and treat them. He lights a signal fire which brings nurses and the sheriff. Then the lawman learns that the robber did not keep the bank loot, but threw it behind him before escaping. The sheriff rides with the cowboy and sees him off on the train. *Paso por Aquí* in Spanish states "He passed by here." Rhodes believed that the ends of justice are not always served within the law but outside it.

Gene and May Rhodes returned to Santa Fe on October 12, 1926. The *Santa Fe New Mexican* carried a headline on the editorial page which read "Santa Fe is waiting to welcome Eugene Manlove Rhodes." Gene and May Rhodes were greeted at the entrance of their hotel by N. Howard (Jack) Thorp, author and collector of cowboy songs, who wrote "Little Joe, the Wrangler," one of the best known Western ballads. At their home in Tesuque, north of Santa Fe, they were visited by Mary Austin who joined Rhodes in a speechmaking and reception at the Museum of New Mexico in the Palace of the Governors. However, the altitude of the Santa Fe area was high for Rhodes, who had been taking medication for his heart. He and May moved to Alamogordo, which was at a lower altitude and less expensive in which to rent a house. In the summer of 1930, they moved to a still lower altitude in San Diego, California, and in May of 1931, they bought a house with two lots at Pacific Beach between La Jolla and San Diego, where Gene wrote *Letter 114*.

This letter is the second of five mailed by Rhodes to Austin, the first dated September 18, 1933, and the last January 24, 1934. One of the letters has a hand-printed return address as:

Eugene Manlove Rhodes
c/o St. Peter
Paradise
(Please forward)

In the others, Rhodes tells that he has been reading a number of Austin's books; he thanks Mary for some cakes she brought them at Christmas when they were living in Tesuque; and agrees with opinions she has expressed about books by Waldo Frank and Van Wyck Brooks. Despite the amusing camaraderie of *Letter 114*, there is doubt that Eugene Manlove Rhodes would, for any length of time, have been entirely congenial with Mary Austin's dominating personality. It is certain that he was unable to attend her lecture in Los Angeles. Their deaths occurred within seven weeks in 1934: his on June 27 and Mary Austin's on August 13.

—————— 114

Old Loring, Pacific Beach, Calif.
Oct. 12

My dear Mary Austin:

We will be more than delighted if you can come to see us here. And if I am physically able would be almost as delighted—not quite— if I could come up to L. A. to see you—If I may be permitted my natural uncouthness, may I say Golly?—As thus: Golly, I want to talk to you about one of your books "The Flock," I think it was—the hidden, secret people. Because of our own hidden people—the "folk"—the old British blood, Welsh, English, Scotch, Irish and the Scotch-Irish. No one has ever mentioned the free masonry that exists among these people—the yokels, morons, hicks, barbarians, boors of Mr. Mencken and the Menckenoids.—I am one of them. And I know them at the most casual meeting. My people have worked at the map-making trade through seventeen states—from Massachusetts down to North Carolina, then northwest through Tennessee, Kentucky, Indiana, Illinois, Wisconsin— then west to the Pacific. And these quiet people have kept their tradition quite unchanged even during the last thirty years.

Will you let me know, if you will be so kind—when, where and how long? Extremely doubtful, doctor's care, my feeble strict diet—orange juice, lettuce, spinach, celery and co. It's a wise child that knows its own fodder.—But if my crazy body should have a lucid interval, I could hop in to the wheelbarrow and drive in. If not, not.

Anyhow—best wishes and (perhaps) thanks for your incitement of H.M. Co. An autobiography is what I will not perpetrate. Reminiscences, perhaps—expurgated. Roses in December. Moratorium salutamus. We who are about to go broke, salute you.

Yours—

Gene Rhodes

The last letter to be listed here from the Mary Austin Collection was written by John Chipman Farrar (1896-1974), chairman of the firm that published her final book. That was a small volume entitled *Can Prayer Be Answered?* (1934). Farrar wrote *Letter 115* just ten days before Mary Austin died, and although she told him in her letter of July 30 that her health was improving, such was not the case. They were longtime friends. He had edited a book of essays in 1924 called *The Literary Spotlight*, and Mary Austin was one of the prominent authors reviewed in the book. Farrar was New England born, in Burlington, Vermont, and his education in his home state was followed by an A.B. degree from Yale University in 1918. After two years on the staff of the *New York Sunday World*, he became editor of *The Bookman* magazine, a position he held when he found contributors to *The Literary Spotlight*. This book was something of a novelty, for all the essayists were anonymous, an arrangement that made frank criticism possible. Only by an invasion of freedom of the press could any opinion expressed in the book be traced to the reviewer who made the statement.

In his Preface, Farrar admitted that he was one of the critics. He states that among the other reviewers were a famous playwright, a major poet, a popular novelist, an editor of one of the largest magazines, and a publisher. He wrote that half the fun in reading the book consisted in trying to guess who wrote which criticism about which author. Among thirty writers discussed, eleven were Austin's correspondents, plus Austin herself. Nine of the eleven have letters printed for readers of the Mary Austin Collection: Sinclair Lewis, Amy Lowell, H. L. Mencken, Edgar Lee Masters, Sherwood Anderson, Fannie Hurst, and Henry Seidel Canby, in addition to Farrar and Austin. Floyd Dell and Louis Untermeyer were also written about in the book and numbered among Mary Austin's letter writers, but their letters were not selected for inclusion in this book.

While still editor of *The Bookman*, John Farrar also assumed duties as editor for the George H. Doran Company in 1927 and he remained with Doran when the company became Doubleday, Doran. From 1929 until 1933 he became first editor and later chairman of the board with the company he incorporated as Farrar and Rinehart. During these busy years, he also wrote or edited twenty books, seven of which were plays for children. One was an allegorical drama with an American Indian theme. Another was a literary study entitled *The Middle Twenties*, published in the same year as *The Literary Spotlight*.

The anonymous writer in the last-named book points out that Mary Austin's distinctive gift in story-telling and descriptive power was presented most favorably in such works as *The Land of Little Rain, The Flock,* and *Lost Borders,* all three of which deal with the semiarid western United States and the way of life for people conditioned by that environment. He describes her mind as rigorously disciplined, coping with austerity and desolation as well as the perception which sees intimacy and loveliness where they are most subtly concealed. He points to one essential lacking in the fullness of her view: the element of humor. Her monumental integrity displayed in the novels she wrote called for more relief provided by moments of the ridiculous contrasting with the serious and the sublime.

Can Prayer Be Answered?, "the little book" praised in *Letter 115*, describes the universal longing by human beings to reach some power outside themselves. However, instead of examining the outer manifestations of deity, Austin looks within the individual for the resources each one can use to approach the power outside him. She believed in a creative spirit in the universe which is shared by humanity, and that an exchange can occur when a person clears his mind of tensions and then can allow his or her needs to rise slowly to consciousness. The final stage of prayer is when the petition is placed in two or three sentences that can be run off rapidly. Gesture is important in many religions, primitive as well as more advanced, but Austin does not make a clear recommendation in this regard. She concludes that although prayer may not get everything a person desires, praying can bring what the individual needs to face problems that otherwise would bring frustration and despair. She writes interestingly of prayer rituals as she has observed them among Indian, Christian, and non-Christian societies.

_____ **115**

FARRAR & RINEHART
Incorporated
PUBLISHERS
232 Madison Avenue
Cables . . Farrine . . New York

3rd August 1934

Miss Mary Austin,
Santa Fe,
New Mexico.

Dear Mary:
   I have been so distressed about you and was delighted to have your good letter of July 30th and to hear that you are improving.
   While the little book got off to a very small advance sale, it is beginning to attract an enormous amount of interest, and I am certain that we are going to be able to go a long way with it. We have distributed some three hundred free copies, reactions to which have been slow in coming to us as so many of the people are away on their vacations, etc. However, I am enclosing copies of a splendid letter from John Haynes Holmes, one from J. Stanley Durkee which doesn't say very much and one from William Ludlum of _The Challenge._ Reviews have also been slow, but a nice one in the New York _Times_ has brought really amazing results: at least fifty cash orders, for instance, from all parts of the country. I am sending you a copy of the _Times_ review in case you didn't see it and also a copy of the review from the New York _Daily Mirror_ and one from the Beaumont, Texas, _Journal._
   I think that the controversial idea is good, and we will see what can be done about it. I am also writing to Michael Williams at once. Many of your good friends have been sent copies of the book and undoubtedly we will be getting further reactions slowly but steadily. Any suggestions you may have we will, of course, listen to eagerly, and I cannot tell you what an enormous satisfaction it is to all of us to have published this book of yours.

Of course, I am tremendously interested in the possibility of your doing a more extended study of your discoveries about prayer, and I do hope you will feel like going ahead with this. I am certain that CAN PRAYER BE ANSWERED? is going to make many people anxious to hear more from you. If I can be of any help in this connection, let me know.

I am so glad that Mary Hunter is with you. I had a nice letter from her which I am answering right away. We will be keeping constantly in touch with both of you.

My very best wishes to you,

J. F.

JF:MR
Enclosures.

Six days after *Letter 115* was written, Mary Austin suffered a heart attack. It was customary for her to attend "The Poets' Roundup," an event planned by Alice Corbin Henderson, and called a "roundup" because the poets appeared in western garb to add local color to their platform appearance. The performance was to benefit the Southwest Indian Association. Among those invited to read, in addition to Alice Henderson, were the Santa Fe authors, Dorothy Belle Hughes, writer of mystery stories as well as poetry; Langdon Mitchell, poet-dramatist; Haniel Long, poet-essayist; John Gould Fletcher, critic and poet, from Little Rock, Arkansas; and Stanley Vestal, biographer and balladist, from Norman, Oklahoma. No one expected Mary Austin to appear, and there was a little stir when she walked across the lawn of the garden to the platform where the lectern and address system had been placed. Her face was pale, but she read with a strong, vibrant voice from her book *The Children Sing in the Far West*. The selections were four short poems in a group called "Prayers to the Outdoor Saints." These titles appeared as "Santa Doucelina," "whose eyes did see the peach turn rosy on the tree"; "San Ysidro," "the ploughman saint"; "Santa Guadalupana," who made roses bloom "out of bare rock"; and "San Francisco," who "walked in the wilderness with wild creatures." Her faith in prayer could not have been more firmly shown. Her death came on August 13, 1934. Farrar's letter was among those she received in the final week of her life.

The correspondence catalogued in the Mary Austin Collection at the Henry E. Huntington Library, San Marino, California, offers a panorama of the American social as well as literary scene during three decades at the outset of the twentieth century. As a record of people, places, and events, the writers portray their attitudes toward life in the United States and also outside it. Their concern is manifest for the welfare of people as both individuals and as members of a community. Mary Austin is shown as both listener and participant in the exchange of her letters.

BRIEF SKETCHES OF SELECTED LITERARY FIGURES MENTIONED IN THE MARY AUSTIN LETTERS

___APPENDIX___

LOUIS ADAMIC immigrated to the United States from Yugoslavia in 1913, and recorded the early years of his life in this country while writing *The Native's Return* (1934). His viewpoint is that of an outsider who loved America despite its faults.

ANDY ADAMS was a Georgia farm boy, who moved to Texas and grew up on ranches. What he learned about ranching, he put in *The Log of a Cowboy* (1903), a book describing trail drives, roundups, cattle rustlers, and stampedes. The book is a classic from that memorable era of American history. He lived in Colorado Springs until his death in 1935.

ANSEL ADAMS began his professional life as a pianist, but he soon turned to photography and became famous for his combinations of light and shadow as he photographed studies of Death Valley, Yosemite, and the American Southwest. He and his wife make their home in Carmel-by-the-Sea, California.

GEORGE ADE, an Indiana essayist, storyteller, and playwright, wrote *Fables in Slang* (1889), *People You Knew* (1923), and other books which made use of the local idioms and vocabulary characteristic of the region and period in his lifetime.

WINTHROP AMES belonged to a group of patrons and producers who developed new themes and techniques for the American theater. He directed the Castle Square Theater in Boston from 1904 until 1908, and established playhouses in Chicago and New York for the production of experimental dramas.

SHERWOOD ANDERSON was a central figure in what has been called the Midwestern School of Writers, which included such authors as Theodore Dreiser, Carl Sandburg, Edgar Lee Masters, and Sinclair Lewis. Anderson abandoned a successful career as a business man to write *Winesburg, Ohio* (1919), and other masterful works in the craft of storytelling.

SUSAN B. (for BROWNELL) ANTHONY left few literary monuments beside speeches in her biographies and the volumes she contributed to the *History of Woman Suffrage* (1881-1887). However, as leader in the Equal Rights

Movement and the National Woman Suffrage Association, she brought women into the main stream of political life in the United States.

WILLIAM ARCHER was a Scottish playwright and drama critic, whose play *The Green Goddess*, produced in 1921, was enormously successful in both England and America.

GERTRUDE ATHERTON, a foremost novelist, may have left her most lasting achievement in the stories she wrote of California history and Spanish traditions. However, her novels *Resanov* (1906), *Black Oxen* (1923), and a fictional biography, *The Conqueror* (1902), with Alexander Hamilton as its hero, are notable successes and so is her autobiography, *Adventures of a Novelist* (1932).

ADOLPH BANDELIER, early American anthropologist, was born in Switzerland and came to the United States when he was 8 years old. He was both a scholar and writer of fiction. His novel *The Delight Makers* (1890) has its setting in New Mexico; *The Gilded Man* (1893) reports a legend widely known in Peru and throughout South America.

DAVID BELASCO combined the roles of actor, playwright, and producer in a career that covered more than fifty years. He contributed *The Girl of the Golden West* (1905), *The Return of Peter Grimm* (1911), and other plays to the American stage.

STEPHEN VINCENT BENET wrote poetry, novels, and folk operas. Among the most notable were a long verse narrative entitled *John Brown's Body* (1928) and *Western Star* (1943), a partially completed epic, both of which were awarded Pulitzer Prizes for poetry.

AMBROSE BIERCE, an Ohian, earned fame as a journalist in San Francisco where he wrote *Tales of Soldiers and Civilians* (1891), stories combining horror and irony, and *The Devil's Dictionary* (1911), which joined satire with realism.

MAXWELL BODENHEIM, a gifted Bohemian poet, also wrote fiction and plays, both of which were frequently touched with cynicism and satire. The mood of his verse is conveyed by poems in *Against This Age* (1923).

VAN WYCK BROOKS developed his theories as he tested literature for ideology, esthetics, and cultural sources. He wrote twenty-five books, the most famous of which may be *The Ordeal of Mark Twain* (1920), *The Pilgrimage of Henry James* (1925), *The Flowering of New England* (1936), and *An Autobiography* (1965).

HEYWOOD BROUN was both a journalist and social critic, whose outlook was expressed in New York City newsprint and columns of the Scripps-Howard chain of daily newspapers. Broun also wrote books and articles for magazines. *Sitting on the World* (1924) was a collection of journalistic columns.

GELETT F. BURGESS invented the word "goop" to describe an undisciplined but useful child. A series of poems about this specimen made Burgess famous, as did his quatrain about seeing "a purple cow" but not wanting to "be one." He also edited a magazine called *The Lark* (1895-1897) and wrote a novel entitled *The Heart Line* (1907).

JOHN BURROUGHS, though a naturalist with scientific credentials, looked upon nature with philosophical insight, as his books *Accepting the Universe* (1920) and *My Boyhood* (1922) testify. He was a prolific writer on the species of wild life.

WITTER BYNNER, a New Yorker and Harvard graduate, spent the major portion of his life in Santa Fe, New Mexico, where he composed half a dozen books of poetry, translated a Chinese anthology called *The Jade Mountain* (1929) and prepared *Journey with Genius* (1951), his recollections of a trip to Mexico in the company of the English novelist D. H. Lawrence and his wife Frieda. (See "The Spectrist Hoax," under A. D. FICKE.)

JAMES BRANCH CABELL, a native Virginian, authored forty books between the years 1904 and 1962, of which eighteen deal with an imaginary country called Poictesme, peopled during the Middle Ages and at later times with kings, princes, dukes, emperors, popes, demons, centaurs, sleeping beauties, and heroes who develop an imaginary history. The most famous of the volumes was *Jurgen* (1919), which was condemned as pornographic and drew more attention than all the other volumes together.

WALTER S. CAMPBELL, an Oklahoma author-teacher, using the pen-name "Stanley Vestal," wrote histories of frontier fur traders, Texas Rangers, and Indian chieftains. *Sitting Bull* (1932), *Jim Bridger* (1946), and *Dodge City* (1952) are outstanding. He also was author of *The Missouri River* (1945) and *Dodge City, Queen of the Cow Towns* (1952).

HENRY SEIDEL CANBY, as professor of literature at Yale and editor of the *Saturday Review of Literature* (1924-1936), contributed books on numerous authors and aspects of American life. *Family History* (1945) is a survey of his own background.

BLISS CARMAN, Canadian-born, moved to New York City in 1888 and became known as an American poet. His early publication (with Richard Hovey) of *Songs of Vagabondia* (1894) made clear the lyric themes of his verse and his joy in the pleasures of nature and life out-of-doors. His Canadian background justified Canada's claim upon Carman as poet laureate, however unofficial.

WILLA SIBERT CATHER as a child moved with her family from Virginia to Nebraska where her father was a physician in Red Cloud. After earning a degree at the University of Nebraska, Cather drew upon this village background for such novels as *O Pioneers!* (1913), *My Antonia* (1918), and *One of Ours* (1922). The pioneer theme also found expression in her New Mexico novel, *Death Comes for the Archbishop* (1927).

PEGGY POND CHURCH is a versatile poet and interpreter of her native state, New Mexico, having lived in the community of Los Alamos before that location was selected by the Manhattan District of the United States Army for the scientific laboratory to build the atomic bomb. In *The House at Otowi Bridge* (1959), she tells of the scientists in that neighborhood, and in her collection of poems, *Ultimatum for Man* (1946), she views the nuclear age with both detachment and concern.

SAMUEL LANGHORNE CLEMENS, who adopted the pseudonym "Mark Twain" early in his writing career, was popular as a lecturer and eminent as an author. Twain's mood before he died in 1910 was pessimistic as his financial investments had failed. The buoyancy with which he had written *Tom Sawyer* (1876) and *The Adventures of Huckleberry Finn* (1884) changed to frustration. However, during the period traced by *Literary America*, Twain's prestige was established. Both the man and his work were venerated, as they deserved to be.

JOSEPH CONRAD was born in 1857, of Polish parents who lived in Russia. He went to sea on a French ship in 1874; then transferred to an English merchant vessel four years later and became an English subject. Books about the sea made him famous, especially the characters in *Lord Jim* (1900) and *Typhoon* (1903).

INA COOLBRITH became influential not only as a poet, but also as one who helped to plan and administer the Oakland, California, Library. She assisted the short story writer Bret Harte when he was editor of the *Overland Monthly*, and organized in 1915 a World Congress of Authors during the Panama-Pacific Exposition in San Francisco.

COUNTEE CULLEN was a Black poet whose education at New York University and Harvard became the background, but hardly the substance of his early books of poetry which were *Color* (1925), *Copper Sun* (1927), *The Ballad of the Brown Girl* (1927), and *The Black Christ* (1929). Cullen died in 1946, at the age of 43. In *Color*, published when he was 22 years old, he wrote: "black boy and the white

> Locked in arm they cross the way"
> in "the golden splendor of the day
> The sable pride of night."

FLOYD DELL not only wrote novels, but he also wrote criticism of fiction, drama, and other subjects viewed by a journalist in Chicago and New York. His novels receiving widest attention were the semiautobiographical *Moon Calf* (1920) and *Janet March* (1923), a study of revolt against convention.

HILDA DOOLITTLE, a Pennsylvanian, became a follower of the poet Ezra Pound, one of the group that called themselves Imagists. She married the English scholar-poet Richard Aldington in 1913, and thereafter lived in

London. As a professional writer, she used the initials "H.D." to sign the manuscripts for nine books of poetry and several volumes of fiction.

EDWARD DOWDEN, an English professor of literature, became known as an editor of Shakespeare's plays and the author of a discerning volume entitled *Shakespeare, His Mind and Art* (1875). Dowden also wrote biographies of Shelley, Southey, Browning, and Montaigne.

THEODORE DREISER, one of the most influential American novelists, introduced a mood of harsh realism in his novel *Sister Carrie* (1900), which at one time was banned from library shelves. He continued his tragic outlook in *Jennie Gerhardt* (1911), *An American Tragedy* (1925), and more than twenty other books.

MAX EASTMAN, as a critic, was both versatile and diversified. Living in New York, he became editor of several liberal magazines dealing with political and social causes. By contrast, he wrote *The Enjoyment of Poetry* (1913), and collected his own verses in *Poems of Five Decades* (1954). The author of biographies dealing with Eugene V. Debs, Isadora Duncan, Mark Twain, Charles Chaplin, Leon Trotsky, Sigmund Freud, and John Dewey, he expressed broad interest in widely distributed fields of thought and action.

THOMAS STEARNS ELIOT, though American born and a graduate of Harvard in 1910, went to England in 1914 and became a British subject thirteen years later. His influence and achievement were so extraordinary that he was awarded the Nobel Prize for Literature in 1948. The poem called *The Waste Land* (1922) not only signaled what he identified as sterility in Western culture, but it also innovated a new poetic style of imagery and allusion. Eliot's bibliography is extensive.

JOHN CHIPMAN FARRAR served as editor of *The Bookman* from 1921 until 1927; later he held management positions with Doubleday, Doran; Farrar and Rinehart; and Farrar, Straus, and Giroux, publishing companies. He lectured widely and was closely associated with literary activities throughout his lifetime. Farrar wrote half a dozen books for children and several for older readers.

EDNA FERBER was a Midwesterner who wrote novels and plays on location, but preferred New York City as a base of operations. The most famous of her successes in fiction were *So Big* (1924), *Show Boat* (1926), which later became a musical drama, *Cimarron* (1930), and *Giant* (1950). A number of her novels were produced as motion pictures.

ARTHUR DAVISON FICKE, an Iowa poet who wrote both verse and fiction, joined Witter Bynner in 1916 to concoct a satire on the poets who called themselves Imagists. In 1916, under the pseudonyms of Emanuel Morgan and Ann Knish, they claimed to be writing poetry that broke up the beautiful hues of light and reflected the aftercolors of a poet's vision. Bynner confessed the fraud at a college lecture in the spring of 1918. Ficke wrote ten volumes of imaginative romantic poetry between 1907 and 1942. He also wrote a novel, *Mrs. Morton of Mexico,* in 1939.

F. SCOTT FITZGERALD spent his youth in St. Paul, Minnesota, and then entered Princeton in 1913. While serving in the Army during 1917, he wrote a novel that was published in 1920 as *This Side of Paradise.* The subject matter was collegiate life in the "Jazz Age." His novel *The Beautiful and Damned* was printed in 1922, and his best-known work, *The Great Gatsby,* appeared in 1925. Fitzgerald wrote scripts in Hollywood for motion pictures before he suffered a fatal heart attack in 1940.

JOHN GOULD FLETCHER belonged to a long established Little Rock, Arkansas, family, which provided tutoring, private academic schooling, and travel in Europe after he left Harvard in 1907 without earning a degree. He became a leader of the Imagist poetry group in London where he lived from 1909 until 1914. Upon returning to the United States, Fletcher joined another literary group made up of Southerners who called themselves "The Agrarians." Among his books of poetry are *Irradiations* (1915), *XXIV Elegies* (1935), and *Selected Poems* (1938). *Life Is My Song* (1937), Fletcher's autobiography, tells the story of American and British poetry during his lifetime.

F. S. FLINT, an English poetic innovator, who was a lesser member of the original group of Imagist poets in 1915, is given brief biographical notice in John Gould Fletcher's *Life Is My Song.*

GLEN FRANK, associate editor of *The Century* magazine, from 1919 to 1921, and editor-in-chief, from May 1921 to September 1, 1925, became president of the University of Wisconsin after his journalistic career and remained as an educator until 1937. He lectured and wrote about national and world issues, commenting upon them in *An American Looks at His World* (1923).

WALDO FRANK, commentator and author, made his home at Truro, Massachusetts, on the eastern peninsula of Cape Cod, but his publishers were in Boston and New York City. He supplied them with stories, essays, and manuscripts for more than twenty books, plus additional volumes that he coauthored or edited. *Our America* (1919) and *Dawn in Russia* (1932) are among his titles.

HENRY GEORGE, an American economist, was born in Philadelphia, but left high school to work his way on shipboard to India where he noticed the gap between the multitudes in poverty and the few in wealth. Upon his return to the United States, he found work in California as a printer and then became managing editor of the *San Francisco Times.* In this position, he advocated taxing land as a single way to raise the insecurity of the poor at the cost of the well-to-do. He wrote a book called *Progress and Poverty* (1879) setting forth his ideas. Then he moved to New York City in 1889, and ran for mayor twice, being defeated both times. His sixth book, *The Science of Political Economy* (1887), presents a combination of idealism and realism which were characteristic of his life and practice.

ELLEN GLASGOW, among Southern novelists, has probed deeply the human and social consequences of false chivalry and the changing status of women in the Old South. Gifts of satire and irony appear in such stories as *Virginia* (1913), *The Builders* (1919), *Barren Ground* (1925), and *The Romantic Comedians* (1926).

LADY AUGUSTA GREGORY, an Irish playwright, helped to found the Abbey Theatre in Dublin in 1904, and wrote such humorous dramas as "Spreading the News" and "The Rising of the Moon" for production there and published in 1909. Her book, *Our Irish Theatre*, tells of the developing awareness of folklore and folk history in Ireland. Her plays were often produced in the United States.

FRANCIS GRIERSON, who became known as both musician and author, was a member of an English family that came to Illinois and lived in a log cabin not far from Springfield, where the presence of Abraham Lincoln made possible his book, *The Valley of Shadows: Recollections of the Lincoln Country, 1858-63* (1909). He also wrote a personal memoir, *Abraham Lincoln, The Practical Mystic* (1918).

GEORGE BIRD GRINNELL, a naturalist, after finishing a Ph.D. at Yale, accompanied General George Armstrong Custer in 1874 to the country of the Sioux Indians in South Dakota. The expedition resulted in the discovery of gold in the Black Hills. Grinnell explored Yellowstone park in 1875 three years after its opening, and made other expeditions into the West. His books include *The Story of the Indians* (1895) and *The Fighting Cheyennes* (1915).

HUTCHINS HAPGOOD translated his observations as a journalist in Chicago and New York into fiction. His association with radical and bohemian groups furnished subject matter for three of his books: *The Autobiography of a Thief* (1903), *Types from City Streets* (1916), and *The Story of a Lover* (1919).

BRET HARTE, along with Mark Twain, opened a path of literary venturing in the American West as rare as the richness of the gold rush in the nineteenth century. Harte was born in Albany, New York, but after he went to California in 1854 and settled in San Francisco in 1860, his stories in the *Overland Monthly* and the *Atlantic Monthly* led to the writing of ballads and stories for more than forty years. *The Luck of Roaring Camp and Other Sketches* (1870) introduced a pattern of storytelling that survived Harte's death in 1902.

BEN HECHT was a product of the disillusionment following World War I when, as a newspaper reporter in Chicago, he established a little magazine called the *Chicago Literary Times* and wrote *Erik Dorn* (1921). This is a daring novel which combines the emotional entanglements of individuals against a backdrop of radical groups in America and Communist intrigue abroad. Of Hecht's numerous publications, *Tales of Chicago Streets* (1924) and *1001 Afternoons in New York* (1941) are pseudodocumentary and intriguing chronicles of his time. *Letters from Bohemia* (1964) is a book recalling such friends as Sherwood Anderson, Maxwell Bodenheim, H. L. Mencken, and others.

ALICE CORBIN HENDERSON published her first book of poems in Chicago when she was 18 years old. The title was *Linnet Songs* (1898), and the poems were conventional in thought and theme. This collection, however, was not prophetic of the future. In 1912, she became assistant to Harriet Monroe, editor of *Poetry, A Magazine of Verse*, and moved into the line of fire directed at the "new poets" who planned to free poetry from the shackles of the nineteenth century. Henderson joined Monroe in editing an anthology called *The New Poetry* (1917), which became a monument to the progressive modern movement. Henderson moved to Santa Fe, New Mexico, in the previous year and wrote *Red Earth* (1920) and *The Sun Turns West* (1933) in the new poetic idiom. She also wrote *Brothers of Light* (1937), a study of the Penitente religious organization in the Southwest.

JOSEPH HERGESHEIMER contributed to a trend of writing fiction which examined the plots for narratives in terms of regional chacteristics in the United States. *The Lay Anthony* (1914) and *Mountain Blood* (1915) were romantic novels with plots contrasting life styles in seacoast Virginia and the upland inlanders. *The Three Black Pennys* (1917) contains studies of Pennsylvania characters, and *Java Head* (1919) turns to New England not just for a change of scenery but for sociological conflict as well. Some of his later novels emphasize action and setting in Cuba and Mexico rather than stressing character.

EMERSON HOUGH, after earning a law degree from the University of Iowa, sought legal and territorial excitement in White Oaks, New Mexico, where he became an early reporter of both romantic and humorous episodes in the frontier West. *Heart's Desire* (1905) is still a refreshing experience for a reader, with accounts of the introduction of croquet to the cowboys and of an osteopath who treats a cross-eyed horse. Hough's *Story of the Cowboy* (1897) has been widely read, and *The Covered Wagon* (1922) was not only read but viewed by moviegoers as well.

DOROTHY B. HUGHES, writer of mysteries, spent her first year after college assisting the editor of the women's page on a Kansas City newspaper. But the road led to New York City, later to Santa Fe, Los Angeles, and Santa Fe again. Of her fourteen "whodunnits," *Ride the Pink Horse* (1946), *Fallen Sparrow* (1942), and *In a Lonely Place* (1947) were made into motion pictures, the last starring Humphrey Bogart. Hughes also writes poetry, winning the Poetry Prize in 1931 for her entry in the Yale Series of Younger Poets.

FANNIE HURST taught school for awhile after graduating from Washington University in St. Louis, but she went on to take graduate courses at Columbia University while working as a waitress at Childs' and as a salesgirl in Macy's. Her life experience provided material for short stories and books, and by 1914 she was one of the nation's most popular storytellers. She wrote eight volumes of short stories of which *Humoresque* (1919) is best known. Of her fifteen novels, *Lummox* (1923), about an immigrant servant girl, and *Great Laughter* (1936), which has a matriarch for the central figure, are outstanding.

ROBINSON JEFFERS, a California poet, wrote many lyrics which appeared in volumes bearing the titles of his narrative poems, but the plots of the longer poems, with dramatic passages in the scripts, were the lure for readers when poetry was not their primary concern. In his academic career, Jeffers was a pre-medical student and he never entirely abandoned the objective view of nature and man fundamental to medicine. *Tamar and Other Poems* (1924), *The Women at Point Sur* (1927), and *Give Your Heart to the Hawks and Other Poems* (1933) are among the most exciting of his eighteen books. *Dear Judas and Other Poems* (1929) may offer the most evidence he found redemptive for mankind. Jeffers and his family lived at Carmel-by-the-Sea, a place providing seascape and landscape for his view of the world.

DAVID HERBERT LAWRENCE came from England to Taos, New Mexico, in the fall of 1922. He wrote that he seemed to be falling on the moon where people were speaking English. He qualified the statement by referring to Pueblo Indian and Spanish dialects that he heard later on. Lawrence was 37 years old and the author of short stories, novels, and poetry. In a poem called "O! Americans!," he states that "the old countries have a past to be faithful to; America has still an unrevealed future." He wrote a few articles and several stories, began a novel in Mexico, and returned to England in 1925. The Mexican novel was *The Plumed Serpent* (1926).

SINCLAIR LEWIS became a journalist upon graduation from Yale in 1907, and contributed reports to newspapers in New Haven and San Francisco and to a newspaper syndicate. Although he wrote five novels between 1914 and 1920, he was not entirely free to write until the success of *Main Street* (1920). Novels followed every year or two after that, the most successful being *Babbit* (1922), *Arrowsmith* (1925), and *Dodsworth* (1929). In 1930, Lewis was the first American to be awarded the Nobel Prize for Literature.

LUDWIG LEWISOHN, as a child, came to the United States from Germany, and like the children of other immigrants had to adjust to a foreign country, difference in language and social customs. These problems are examined in several of his many books, especially the autobiographical *Up Stream* (1922) and *Mid-Channel* (1929). *Expression in America* (1932) is a challenging analysis of traditional roots with the overlay of later cultural settlements.

VACHEL LINDSAY's themes and measures in poetry are strikingly American. Walking in 1912 across the United States from his home town, Springfield, Illinois, he gave away *Rhymes to Be Traded for Bread*, and with the publication of *The Congo and Other Poems* (1914) his rhythms danced their way with rhyming lines long and short into his own poetic medium. He lectured throughout the land, chanting his verses and his visionary love for democracy. Some of these books are *The Chinese Nightingale and Other Poems* (1917) and *Johnny Appleseed* (1928).

JACK LONDON grew up along the waterfront in Oakland, California, a period of his life that he fictionizes in his novel *Martin Eden* (1909). After a sealing cruise to Japan, he went to Alaska in 1897 and returned home to write of his experiences. *The Call of the Wild* (1903) and *White Fang* (1906) were two of the early novels that made him famous. London is said to have written fifty books in sixteen years. He read widely and translated philosophical and social ideas into his stories of action.

HANIEL LONG, who taught at Carnegie Institute of Technology from 1910 to 1929, brought a missionary zeal into the keen esthetic values of his gift for writing essays and poetry. Beneath the lyric beauty of verses in his *Atlantides* (1933) and *The Grist Mill* (1945) was a search for the purpose in human life, more fully expressed in the prose sketches of *Pittsburgh Memoranda* (1935) and *Interlinear to Cabeza de Vaca* (1936). After he resigned at Carnegie Tech, Long and his family moved to Santa Fe, New Mexico, where he participated in a cooperative publishing enterprise called Writers' Editions.

AMY LOWELL broke with tradition when she rebelled against the verse patterns employed by a famous relative, James Russell Lowell, and furthered her rebellion against the formalities of her time by smoking cigars on public occasions, a practice reserved exclusively for men in her day. The innovations in verse were manifest in her first book, *A Dome of Many-Colored Glass* (1912). Cadenced lines replaced metrical patterns, and forms that neglected rhyme were more prominent than those that observed it. In addition to eight volumes of poetry which she wrote between 1912 and 1925, the year of her death, she completed in that year her impressive biographical study, *John Keats*. Her volume published in 1917 was entitled *Tendencies in Modern American Poetry*. In this book, she analyzed the technical aspects of her own poetry as well as the practices of other contemporary poets.

MABEL DODGE LUHAN became famous as a patroness of literature and art in both Europe and America. She describes numerous artists, writers, and social reformers in her four-volume autobiography, *Intimate Memories* (1933-1937), which covers her youth and early marriage in Buffalo, New York; life with her second husband in an Italian villa near Florence; the return to America where she established a salon on Fifth Avenue in New York City; and the final period when she moved to the artist colony in Taos, New Mexico. Many of her former friends visited there, among them the English novelist D. H. Lawrence and his wife Frieda. Details of this visit, for some months of each year, 1922-25, are fully presented in Luhan's book, *Lorenzo in Taos* (1932).

CHARLES FLETCHER LUMMIS became historian, archeologist, folklorist, ethnologist, balladist, and librarian after leaving his Ohio home and arriving in Los Angeles in 1885. His arrival was phenomenal, because he had walked 3,507 miles to get there from Cincinnati through seven states and two territories, facing hazards of weather, animals, and terrain. All of this he describes in *A Tramp Across the Continent* (1892). As city editor for the *Los Angeles Times*, he became acquainted with the community, and served it in many ways, including the founding of the Sequoya League and the Southwest Museum, which he served as secretary from 1913 until 1915. At his death in 1928, he left a bibliography of seventeen books and scores of articles, stories, and ballads.

PERCY MacKAYE, although city-born and urban-educated in New York and Boston, is associated with literature and pageantry portraying rural life. As a dramatist he wrote two plays, *The Canterbury Pilgrims* (1903) and *The Scarecrow* (1908), which draw both their plots and characters chiefly from the countryside. In 1921, he visited the Kentucky mountains and learned traditions and tales that resulted in folk plays and stories for theater viewers and readers everywhere. MacKaye's range of subject matter, however, included verse plays about Joan of Arc and characters in Shakespeare's plays.

CAREY Mc WILLIAMS, like Edgar Lee Masters, abandoned a legal career for writing. Social change drew McWilliams to research the background for *Factories in the Field* (1939) and *Ill Fares the Land* (1942), both of which discuss the problems of migratory labor. *North from Mexico* (1949) and *Witchhunt* (1950) were written before McWilliams moved from California to New York where he became editor of *The Nation* in 1955.

EDWIN MARKHAM rose to fame from a schoolroom in Oakland, California. It was here that he wrote "The Man with the Hoe," a poem that dramatized a famous painting by the French artist Millet. After his poem was published in a San Francisco newspaper, the title was used for Markham's first book of verse in 1899. Later books of poetry included *Lincoln and Other Poems* (1901), *Gates of Paradise* (1920), and *Ballad of the Gallows Bird* (1926). He moved to New York City, where he became one of the founders of the American Poetry Society and its honorary president.

EDGAR LEE MASTERS wrote poetry while he was still a member of a law firm in Chicago. In his autobiography, *Across Spoon River* (1936), he states that his interest in people led both to success as a lawyer and to success as a poet. Nothing he wrote before his *Spoon River Anthology* (1915) aroused as much interest as this collection of imaginary epitaphs in free verse, spoken as monologues in a cemetery. There were 244 such personal narratives, all of them confessional in type giving insight to private lives. Masters wrote sixty books, including a narrative poem, *The New World* (1937). and such biographical studies as *Lincoln, The Man* (1931) and *Vachel Lindsay* (1935).

H. L. MENCKEN, a Baltimore journalist and linguist, was a milder man than his caustic attacks upon bigotry, social hypocrisy, and intolerance led many readers to believe. His series of volumes called *Prejudices* (1919-1927) gave him free rein to curb excesses in morality, ignorance in religion, foolishness in education, and obscurities in science. His epochal achievement in recording the varieties of regional English speech in *The American Language* (1919, with revisions and supplements until 1948) became more than a scholarly pastime. Twenty different titles contain his comments on literary figures, politics, history, and his sphere of journalism.

JOAQUIN MILLER chose to reject two given names, "Cincinnatus and Heiner," for the more romantic nickname of "Joaquin," which identified a noted bandit in the California mountains during the period of the gold rush. Miller's background is vague, except that his birthplace was Indiana and he followed the trail to Oregon in 1854, if not before. He went to San Francisco when his first book of poems, *Specimens*, appeared in 1868; a year later his second book appeared, *Joaquin et al.* Miller's best known poem, "Columbus," with the repeated stanzaic endings—"Sail on! sail on! and on!"—was at one time in most elementary school readers.

HARRIET MONROE, a Chicago poet, had published a book of her poetry and some plays before she founded *Poetry, A Magazine of Verse* in 1912. The significance of this entry into the literary world cannot be overestimated, because the periodical became the voice of the experimental group which became the leaders in American verse writing. Monroe's later books include *Poets and Their Art* (1926; revised 1932) and her autobiography, *A Poet's Life* (1937). (*See also*, ALICE CORBIN HENDERSON.)

MARIANNE MOORE, after graduation from Bryn Mawr College, chose to live in New York City, where she became associated with *The Dial Magazine*, a review that offered its pages to many of the avant-garde writers and artists of this period. She became its editor from 1925 until 1929. Moore wrote sparingly, adopting a cross-referenced type of imagery, which was at once imaginative and intellectual. The poet-critic, T. S. Eliot, wrote the Introduction to her *Selected Poems* (1935), calling her work "part of the small body of durable poetry written in our time." She won the Bollingen Prize, the National Book Award, and in 1953 the Pulitzer Prize.

FRANK NORRIS lived as exciting a life as did some of the heroes in his early novels. After writing *McTeague* (1899), an action novel of San Francisco that involved characters in deception and murder, the author enlisted in the Boer War, was imprisoned and released only to go to Cuba as a war correspondent in 1899 and to return to plot an epic story dealing with wheat ranchers and speculation in grain. *The Octopus* (1901) and *The Pit* (1903) were widely acclaimed, but Norris died midway between the publication of these two books. He had planned a third book to be called *The Wolf*, but it was left uncompleted.

EUGENE O'NEILL, after an apprenticeship in his father's company of actors, and life as a sailor, wrote his first play, *The Web* (1914), and then entered the playwriting workshop of George Pierce Baker at Harvard University. He joined the Provincetown Players, a group that produced many of his early plays. As a founder of the Theater Guild, he developed such notable tragic plays as *Beyond the Horizon* (1920), *The Emperor Jones* (1920), *Anna Christie* (1921), *Desire Under the Elms* (1924) and *Ah, Wilderness!* (1933), a folk comedy. *Long Day's Journey into Night* (1956) is an autobiographical drama written at an earlier time and produced after O'Neill's death in 1953.

EUGENE MANLOVE RHODES, author of eleven books containing more than eighty stories about cowboys and ranch life, was called "the novelist of the cattle kingdom" by the critic Bernard De Voto, who wrote an Introduction to *The Hired Man on Horseback* (1938), a biography written by Rhodes's wife. Rhodes deserved both titles. His stories, many of them short novels, were written between 1902 and 1934. They presented both serious and humorous views of the native Spanish-Americans and the transplanted Anglo-Americans whose adjustments to the territory Rhodes knew at first hand.

LOLA RIDGE became known as a poet when her long poem called "The Ghetto" first appeared in the *New Republic* during the year 1918. The subject matter described the pushcart workers, factory laborers, men in mills, foundries, and mines. In 1922-1923, she edited *Broom, An International Magazine of the Arts*, in New York City, where she was known for her fiery spirit in the cause of the downtrodden.

JAMES WHITCOMB RILEY moved from journalism to the writing of verse in the Indiana folk speech. *The Old Swimmin' Hole and 'Leven More Poems* (1883) was succeeded by *Rhymes of Childhood* (1890), containing such familiar poems as "Little Orphant Annie," "Knee Deep in June," and "The Raggedy

Man." Riley gave readings of his poems until 1916, many of which were familiar to listeners before he read them.

CARL SANDBURG found poetry a means to lift the everyday and commonplace event to a position of appreciation and even beauty. He was first recognized as a poet when *Poetry, A Magazine of Verse* in 1916 published "Chicago," a rough-hewn statement cataloging the city's stockyards, freight handling, lusts, and pleasures in vivid, eloquently cadenced lines. *Smoke and Steel* (1920) and *Slabs of the Sunburnt West* (1922) further captured the democratic freedom in imagery and speech which made Sandburg's poetry distinctive. He compiled ballads and folksongs, wrote stories for children, and produced a monumental biography, *Abraham Lincoln*, in six volumes (1926-1939). He won the Pulitzer Prize for his *Complete Poems* (1950) and the Lincoln volumes in 1939.

LEW SARETT not only produced poems about natural beauty in the fields and forests, but he lived with the people and wildlife in largely uninhabited areas, especially with the American Indians. He was a woodsman and a forest ranger, taking time from teaching at the University of Illinois and Northwestern University, and from the writing of books to learn from nature and the wilderness. Such titles as *Slow Smoke* (1925), *Wings Against the Moon* (1931), and *Covenant with Earth* (1956) point to an outlook of a man under the sky.

ERNEST THOMPSON SETON, Scotchman, Canadian, and American, became known to readers throughout the United States and elsewhere when he wrote *Wild Animals I Have Known* (1898), and he became known to thousands of youths later when he founded the Woodcraft League in 1902. After a period in Connecticut and California, he moved to land on a Spanish grant east of Santa Fe, New Mexico, where he wrote many books and founded Seton Village for meetings of young and old who were interested in natural history. The story of his life is told in the autobiography, *Trail of an Artist-Naturalist* (1940).

UPTON SINCLAIR was born with an instinct for letters. As a youth, he began to write dime novels, a popular art between 1860 and 1895 after expansion began into Indian Territory and the "wild West." However, his early novels, published between 1901 and 1904, were written while he was a graduate student at Columbia University. He came to broader notice when he wrote *The Jungle* (1906), about corruption in the operation of the Chicago stockyards. Sinclair's pattern of attacking the abuses of power led to exposés of social malfeasance in mining, industry, and politics, resulting in more than 100 titles for pamphlets, books of nonfiction, and novels. *King Coal* (1917); *The Brass Check* (1919), a story of journalism; *The Goose-Step* (1923), dealing with education; and *I, Candidate for Governor* (1935) are selected readings. Sinclair's *Autobiography* (1962) surveys the course of his life with conviction.

LINCOLN STEFFENS was a constructive force in literature and politics from the time he graduated at the University of California. At first, he chose journalism in New York City, where he managed *McClure's Magazine*, 1902-1906, and published *The Shame of the Cities* (1904) which exposed corruption in municipal government. His *Autobiography* (1931) written at Carmel, California, is a thoughtful discussion of reform movements in American society.

MARK TWAIN. *See* SAMUEL LANGHORNE CLEMENS.

LOUIS UNTERMEYER, himself a poet, was better known as a critic of the work of other poets. His earliest edition of *Modern American and British Poetry* (1922) is kept by collectors as the forerunner of frequent revisions. He was a New Yorker, whose own volumes—poetry in *Burning Bush* (1928) and *The Wonderful Adventures of Paul Bunyan* (1945); prose narratives in *Moses* (1928) and *Lives of the Poets* (1960); and two autobiographies, *From Another World* (1939) and *Bygones* (1965), earned the respect of his contemporaries.

CARL VAN DOREN, as college professor and literary editor, wrote studies of contemporary novelists, histories of American literature, and biographies of significant figures, past and present. He also edited the contemporary literary scene for *The Nation* (1919-1922) and *The Century* (1922-1925). Selected titles of his books are *The American Novel* (1921, with revision in 1940), *Sinclair Lewis* (1933), and *Benjamin Franklin*, for which he won the Pulitzer Prize in 1938.

MARK VAN DOREN, like his brother Carl, lived in New York, taught English in a university where he wrote ten volumes of poetry, one of which, *Collected Poems* (1939), was a Pulitzer Prize winner. He turned to the novel in *The Transients* (1935), and wrote biographical studies entitled *Thoreau* (1916), *Dryden* (1920), *Shakespeare* (1939), and *Hawthorne* (1949). He succeeded his brother, Carl, as literary editor of *The Nation* (1924-1928).

HENDRIK WILLEM VAN LOON, a native of Holland, studied at Cornell, Harvard, and Munich. Consequently, he was able to use his European background for such books as *The Fall of the Dutch Republic* (1913), *The Rise of the Dutch Kingdom* (1915), and *The Golden Book of Dutch Navigators* (1916). He was an Associated Press correspondent in Russia during the revolutionary outbreak in 1906, and also in Belgium at the beginning of World War I. Van Loon's depth of knowledge resulted in popular surveys of various fields, such as *The Story of Mankind* (1921) and *The Story of the Bible* (1923). He wrote a number of biographies, and called his own autobiography *Report to St. Peter* (1947).

CARL VAN VECHTEN brought wit and urbanity to an era distinguished by realism and flawed by social and personal errors. Born in the Midwest, Van Vechten became music and drama critic for New York newspapers, and turned his sophisticated touch to fiction dealing with the arts and the social refinements. He took himself as the model for *Peter Whiffle* (1922) and found models in his circle for the dialogue and activities in *Firecrackers* (1925) and *Parties* (1930). His *Spider Boy* (1928) is a satire on the motion picture industry. Van Vechten was literary executor for Gertrude Stein, whose manuscripts he edited for posthumous publication.

STANLEY VESTAL. *See* WALTER S. CAMPBELL.

H. G. WELLS, English novelist and historian, exercised a pervasive influence upon many American writers. After a period of teaching school, his writing liberated Wells for a career in literature. His first two books were *The Time Machine* and *The Wonderful Visit*, both in 1895. He was 29 years old and carried on with pseudoscientific best sellers such as *The War of the Worlds* (1898) and *The First Men on the Moon* (1901). A flood of engrossing novels stimulated writers in the United States for theorizing and social experimentation: a few titles were *Kipps* (1905), *Ann Veronica* (1909), *Tono Bungay* (1909), and *Mr. Britling Sees It Through* (1916). *The Outline of History* (1920) was a monumental survey of the advancement of mankind.

EDITH WHARTON, one of the most skillful and refined practitioners of the art of fiction, stands apart from the dominant streams of the novel in her time. Her stories plead no social, economic, or political reforms, but shape individual characters who live for readers as memorable for their occupational and ethical choices. Of her nearly forty titles, perhaps *Ethan Frome* (1911) is best known. The novel tells the struggle of a man and two women to escape from their emotional involvement on a bleak New England homestead. *The Old Maid* (1924), a short novel with a setting in New York City, treats the anguish of jealousy between two cousins over a child who misunderstands the relationships among the three of them.

STEWART EDWARD WHITE, a Michigan author whose writing career was chiefly in California, sought material throughout the American West, and Alaska and Africa as well. He turned personal experiences among lumberjacks, miners, and big-game hunters into such novels as *The Blazed Trail* (1902), *Gold* (1913), and *African Campfires* (1913). The nonfiction titles *Dog Days* (1930) and *Speaking for Myself* (1943) are autobiographical.

WILLIAM ALLEN WHITE combined literature with politics because, as a newspaperman, his talents were devoted to both callings. He was editor of the Emporia, Kansas, *Gazette*, from 1895 to 1944, and was aroused by social injustice, as his most famous novel, *A Certain Rich Man* (1909), reveals. The subject matter centers about monopolies in railroad management and flour mill centers in the Midwest. Another successful novel, *In the Heart of a Fool* (1918), he called "a hell-raising book" because it took the side of labor against industrial power and depicted the judicial system as partial to industry. White's editorials were published as *The Editor and His People* (1924) along with other books of both fiction and nonfiction. His *Autobiography* (1946) documents acquaintance with five presidents of the United States: William McKinley, Theodore Roosevelt, Woodrow Wilson, Calvin Coolidge, and Herbert Hoover.

KATE DOUGLAS WIGGIN, as the author of *Rebecca of Sunnybrook Farm* (1903), became known to the majority of the literate children in the United States when the book was first published. The fictional Rebecca was resourceful and exemplary as she helped her widowed mother and family through days of hardship on their farm. Following a popular motion picture, a Shirley Temple Edition was published in 1959. *Mother Carey's Chickens* (1911) was another widely read title among the dozen books she prepared for young readers. Her autobiography, *My Garden of Memory* (1923), tells of her travels and the organizing of free kindergartens for poor children on the Pacific Coast.

HARRY LEON WILSON combined an interest in history with a strong sense of humor, succeeding in both as a writer of fiction. His father published a newspaper in a small town west of Chicago, and perhaps the suggestion of printing began in his youth. A sketch he sent to *Puck*, the humorous weekly, was accepted in 1887, and in 1892 he joined the staff, becoming editor in 1896. Wilson's first serious novel was *The Lions of the Lord* (1903), a story of the Mormon overland migration to Utah. In 1915, *Ruggles of Red Gap*, the story of a British butler in a Western environment, provided humor for American readers. It was followed in 1922 by *Merton of the Movies*, a story about Hollywood. In 1912, Wilson and his second wife moved to Carmel, California, where he made his home until the time of his death in 1939.

OWEN WISTER's collected works fill eleven volumes with fiction, poetry, and nonfiction, but his fame rests chiefly upon his novel, *The Virginian* (1902), which was based upon his observations when ill health sent him from Philadelphia to a Wyoming ranch in 1885. One sentence from that novel passed into American lingo: "When you call me that, smile!" He wrote *When West Was West* (1928) and a biography of Theodore Roosevelt, entitled *Roosevelt, The Story of a Friendship, 1880-1919* (1930).

GENERAL SUBJECT INDEX

ABOUT THE EDITOR

T. M. Pearce is professor emeritus of English at the University of New Mexico in Albuquerque. A personal acquaintance of Mary Austin's, he is the author of many books, including *Lane of the Llano, Southwest Heritage, Mary Austin,* and *Spoon River on Campus.*

Contributions in Women's Studies

The Chains of Protection: The Judicial Response to Women's Labor Legislation
Judith A. Baer

Women's Studies: An Interdisciplinary Collection
Kathleen O'Conner Blumhagen and Walter D. Johnson, editors

Latin American Women: Historical Perspectives
Asunción Lavrin, editor

Beyond Her Sphere: Women and the Professions in American History
Barbara J. Harris